BLAND COUNTY VIRGINIA

COURT ORDER BOOK

1872-1877

Compiled
by
Parke Coleman Bogle

Heritage Books
2024

HERITAGE BOOKS

AN IMPRINT OF HERITAGE BOOKS, INC.

Books, CDs, and more—Worldwide

For our listing of thousands of titles see our website
at
www.HeritageBooks.com

A Facsimile Reprint
Published 2024 by
HERITAGE BOOKS, INC.
Publishing Division
5810 Ruatan Street
Berwyn Heights, MD 20740

Originally published 1998

International Standard Book Number
Paperbound: 978-0-7884-7771-3

INTRODUCTION

The following condensed material represents six years of the court records of Bland County Virginia. I have entered the proceedings of every court day only removing the legal phraseology and putting it into layman's language.

Since death records were not mandatory in these years, the probate proceedings and guardianships provide much genealogical information.

The locations of the roads in those early days were constantly changing and each change was noted in the Court Order records. Land owners were held responsible for the upkeep of the roads and often this did not suit the land owner.

Overseers of the Poor held responsible positions and sometimes abused the privileges.

Courts dockets were full in those days as they are today and many, many cases were continued from term to term. The revenue laws were broken then as they are today. These misdemeanors were punished very slightly.

Between the terms of court, many deeds were recorded in the Clerk's Office. These are recorded in these records and often the Deed Book and page number is given. In all cases the date is given and one need only go to the court house and look up the deed to learn the particulars of the land deal.

One may find names in these old records that were never mentioned before in any publication.

I owe a debt of gratitude to Ronald Hall, Clerk of the Bland Court for making these records available to me for copying. He has gone beyond the duties of his office to be helpful to me.

Parke C. Bogle
1117 High Street
Pulaski, VA 24301
Email- <parkebog@swva.net>

- The first 14 pages are blank.
- Page 15, Wednesday February 7th 1872.- Ordered that the rule entered on yesterday against H.R. Mustard, J.W. Kitts and John A. Bennett for failing to attend the court as petit jurors be and the same is hereby discharged.
- Isaac Swindle, plaintiff against R.L. Newberry, defendant. Ruled in favor of the defendant, he to recoup costs.
- John R. Bird, against John C. Crockett- Parties compromise and adjust their differences. Defendant denies that he ever uttered words he is accused of. Admits Plaintiff is an honest man. Signed by both John R. Bird and John C. Crockett.
- Overseers of the poor, against John W. Harman- Case dismissed

Page 16- February 7, 1872- William M. Bird VS Geo. W. Suiter, a case of debt. Case continued at cost of defendant.
- William P. Bogle VS Hugh C. Fanning. Case continued with exceptions from both parties.
- Commonwealth VS James Preston. Preston fined $5.00.
- Compton & McGinnis & Co. VS Henry Dowling. Jurors were, J.C. Painter, E.G.Thompson, A.F. Miller, Elias Blankenship, Wm. P. Hornberger, Uriah Bane, H.A. Neel, Robt. C. Green, Geo. W. Stowers, Isam Bi???, J.D. Thom. and John Havens. Adjourned until tomorrow.

Page 17- February 8, 1872- Compton McGinnis & Co. VS William P. Bogle. Jurors could not agree. By consent of parties one juror withdrawn and others dismissed. Case continued.
- Cynthia Grayson VS John R. Compton, John W. McGinnis, H.H. McGinnis, constituting the firm of Compton McGinnis & Company and L.H. McGinnis. A case of debt. Plaintiff to recover from defendants $200.00 in gold with interest from 23rd of February till paid plus costs. Credit given for $20.00.
- Randolph Grayson VS same defendants as above, debt of $517.69. Plaintiff to recover from defendant $517.69 and also $400.00 in gold with interest till paid.

Page 18- February 8, 1872- On motion of Uriah Bean, ordered that Felix Buck, commissioner for Sharon Township examine the route and make report on establishing a roan leading from house of Uriah Bean (Bane) through the lands of Frank Groseclose to a point on the Rich Valley Turnpike.
- A.A. Chapmen VS Austin French, suit of ejectment. Case continued.
- St. Clair French VS John R. Compton. Case continued.
- On motion of Robt. S. Hoge, John H. Hoge, is appointed special commissioner to settle accounts of Robt. S. Hoge, attornty for A.C. Waggoner, late sheriff of Bland County.
- Henry Davidson VS G.W. Brown et al case of debt. Case continued

Page 19- February 8, 1872- William H. Howe VS Gordon C. Thorn. No verdict given
- Peter C. Honaker VS G.W. Brown et al. Case continued by consent.
- John C. Davis VS William T. Tolbert. Defendant says he was in the heat of passion when he

said what he said and that he meant the plaintiff no harm when he accused him of falsly swearing perjury. Case dismissed at cost to the defendant. Signed by both Davis and Tolbert.
- Jerry D. Thorn VS A.T. Suiter, on warrant. Continued to March 1st.
- Wm. P. Cecil VS Austin French, debt. Case continued.

Page 20- February 8, 1872- John Williams, Exor of James P. Holmes, decd. VS John Mustard. Mustard to recover from Williams .73 cents and costs.
- James Robinett VS Elias Harman, debt. Verdict in favor of defendant. Robinett to pay Harman $5.00 damages and costs.
- William P. Haller VS Elizabeth Wohlford's administration. Continued
- Robt. C. Green VS William Stuart, continued at defendant's cost.
- Samuel H. Newberry VS Barther?- Case continued.
- D.A. Snow?? VS S.J. Crump, debt. (Something about lost papers. S.J. Crump having intermarried with J.C. Crockett) Verdict illegible.

Page 21- February 8, 1872- J.B. Miller VS John R. Compton, assessor, for a correction of his land holdings. He was assessed in 1871 for 700 acres valued at $1.00 per acre. He says correct acerage is 500 acres valued at .25 cents per acre. Ordered that correction be certified.
- Hopkins Harper & Kemp VS Wm. N. Harman. Plaintiffs to collect from defendant the sum of $165.07 with interest and costs. Credit given for $120.00 made on March 6, 1871.
- Court is adjourned until tomorrow.

Page 22- February 9, 1872- P.W. Strother, presiding
- Commonwealth VS Ray Kitts, misdemeanor, jurors were, A.A. Muirhead, A.J. Keeling, A.G. Updike, D.L. Tickle, John F. Umbarger, Granville Waddle, JOhn Kyle, C.F. Snead, Gordon Sanders, Wm. M. Bird, Hiram A. Pauley and J.D. Thorn. Verdict, defendant not guilty.
- John N.? Havens VS N.B. Dotson et al in debt. Case dismissed.
- P.C. Honaker VS Compton McGinnis & Co. in debt. Case dismissed at cost of defendants.

Page 23- February 9, 1872- John W. Johnston VS Elias Harman & Wm. N. Harman, verdict for plaintiff. Defendant asks for stay of execution for 60 days to allow him to get a writ of error. Allowed by court.
- Commonwealth VS Ray Kitts, carrying a concealed weapon- Not guilty.

Page 24- February 9, 1872- Commonwealth VS HenryThompson, on a misdemeanor. Not guilty
- Commonwealth VS Geo. Lindamood, indictment. Defendant acquitted.
- Commonwealth VS Isaac Kegley, misdemeanor.- Not Guilty.

Page 25- February 9, 1872- William C. Williams VS Henry Newberry. Case dismissed with each party paying his own costs.
- Wm. P. Mustard VS Joseph Fanning's administration. Jury waived. Mustard to recover from Fanning's admr. $6.50. Plaintiff took exception to ruling. Exception noted and ordered recorded.

- John Mustard VS Joseph Fanning's admr. Defendant to recover against the plaintiff his costs for his defense. Plaintiff makes exceptions which are made part of this record.

Page 26- February 9, 1872- Acles Fanning, VS Compton McGinnis & Co.- Plaintif to recover from the defendants $32.14. Each party to pay for own costs.

Page 27- February 9, 1872- Charlotte Richardson, administratrix for Wm. J. Richardson, decd. VS Eli F. Groseclose. Defendant says he has payed debt in full. Verdict is illegible.
- Elias Harman VS Hiram Muncy in debt. Muncy claims to have paid his debt. Verdict is unreadable.
- Elias Blankenship VS J.W. Finley. Continued at cost of plaintiff.

Page 28- February 9, 1872- Commonwealth VS Wm. P. Bogle, motion for state revenue.
- Commonwealth VS Wm. P. Bogle, motion for county levy.
- Commonwealth VS Wm. P. Bogle, motion for school funds.
- Commonwealth VS John C. Stowers et al, motion for county levy.
- Commonwealth VS John C. Stowers, motion for school funds.
- Commonwealth VS Geo. Lindamood, indictment, misdemeanor.
- Commonwealth VS Rufus French. A&B
- Commonwealth VS Albert French, A&B
- Commonwealth VS ??? Harman, trespass.
- Commonwealth VS Joseph Thomas, A&B
- Commonwealth VS Giles Thomas et al, public riot.
- Commonwealth VS Wm. Burnett, violation of revenue law.
- Commonwealth VS Henry Lambert, violation of revenue law.
- Commonwealth VS William Lovel, violation of revenue law.
- Commonwealth VS William Burnett, violation of revenue law.
- Ordered that these cases be continued.

- Following are the names of petit jurors and amounts paid to them:
J.C. Painter, $4.00; E.G. Thompson, $4.00; A.F. Miller, $4.00; Wm. P. Hornberger, $4.00; Uriah Bane, $4.00; H.A. Neel, $4.00; Robt. C. Green, $4.00; Isom Birdett, $4.00; Jo?,Jr. Thorn, $3.00; John Havens, $4.00; J.W. Compton, $4.00; A.A. Muirhead, $4.00; A.J. Keling, $4.00; A.G. Updike, $4.00; D.L. Tickle, $4.00; John F. Umberger, $4.00; Granville Waddle, $4.00; John Kyle, $4.00; Gordon Saunders, $4.00; Wm. M. Bird, $4.00; Hiram A. Pauley, $4.00; J.D. Thorn, $4.00; H.R. Mustard, $3.00; John A. Burnett, $2.00; Mitchell Kegley, $2.00. The same to be certified to board of supervisors.
- Ordered that the following be allowed the sum of $1.00 each for their services as petit jurors at this term of court on the trial of misdemeanors: J.C. Painter, A.F. Miller, Elias Blankenship, Wm. P. Hornberger, Uriah Bane, Robt. C. Green, Geo. W. Stowers, J.D.Thorn, John Havens, A. Fannon, Peter Kitts, John R. Compton, A.A. Muirhead, A.J. Keeling; A.G. Updike; D.L. Tickle, John F. Umbarger, Granville Waddle, John Kyle, C.L. Leval, ??? Saunders, Wm. M. Bird, Hiram A. Pauley, and Lorenza Thorn. Ordered to be certified to the auditor of public accounts for payment..

Page 29- February 9, 1872- A claim by Samuel W. Williams, prosecuting attorney for County, for $20.00, which claim was allowed and sent to auditor of public accounts for payment.
- On motion of Elias Blankenship that the road commissioners view road in Mechanicsburg as to the expediency of changing same.
- B.H. Penley VS Wm. P. Mustard. Penley to recover against Mustard in the amount of $154.10. Credit of $29.00 allowed.
- John Williams for benefit of John Wiley, VS G.W. Morgan. Plaintiff to recover against defendant the sum of $75.00. J.M. Hamilton, D.C.

Page 30- March 4, 1872- present P.W. Strother, Judge.
- Following is a list of deeds presented in the Clerks office and with certificate of acknowledgement and relinquishment of dower & being stamped, admitted to record, viz-
- James Thompson to Henry Newberry, Deed conveying real estate.
- Uriah Bean Deed of homestead.
- Alexander F.Suiter & wife to Henry Newberry. Conveying real estate.
- Wm. Hedrick & wife to James H. Neel. Conveying real estate.
- James M. Kidd & wife to Geo. ? Martin. Conveying real estate.
- John F. Locke, trustee, to Harman Newberry. Conveying real estate.
- Bery Blankenship & wife to Wm. Ramsey. Conveying real estate.
- Jerry D. Thorn VS A.T. Suiter. By consent of parties, Thorn to have judgement for $25.00. Parties to divide costs. No execution, as the debt is paid.
- E.R.G. Hager VS Wm. P. French, warrant. Court sustains motion by defendant to quash the proceeding.

Page 31-March 4, 1872- On motion of Elias Blankenship & William N. Harman, ordered that the Commissioner of roads for Mechanicsburg Township go upon said road and report on the expediency of changing the road from Geo. W. Fannings to Elias Blankenships. Mentions "Hectors Road", "Slaty Bank" "Old Pauley Cabin".
- On motion of Wm. P. Bogle, collector for Mechanicsburg Township, George Bogle is permitted to qualify as his deputy.
- A.H. Bradham VS D.J. Bradham, case of debt. Calvin Crockett paid to A.H. Bradham $210.00. Compromise between parties. Case dismissed and stricken from the docket.
(Continued on page 32}

Page 32- Frank S. Blair, attorney forCalvin Crockett, S.H. Bradham agent for D.J. Bradham and Wm. N. Harman, attorney for A.H. Bradham.
- Ordered that Court adjourn until next regular term.

Page 33-April 1, 1872- Quarterly Term of Court, April 1, 1872.
- Following is a list of deeds presented at the Clerks office and with certificate of acknowledgement and relinquishment of dower are admitted to record viz-
- H.C. Fanning, Homestead deed. Book #2, page 276.
- M.A. Francis & wife to George W. Fanning. Book # 2, page 276.
- M.A. Francis & wife to George W. Fanning. Book #2, page 277.
- F.G. Helvey & wife to B.H. Oxley. Book # 2, page 278.

- Commonwealth VS Lee A. Kitts. A&B Kitts confesses his guilt and is fined $5.00 plus costs.
- Commonwealth VS Wm. A. Bennett. A&B- Bennett confesses guilt, fined $5.00 plus costs.
- James M. Fanning, admr of Joseph Fanning, decd., VS Wm. N.& Elias Harman. motion on a bond taken for the forthcoming property at the day of sale. Case continued until tomorrow.

Page 34- April 1, 1872 - Ordered that M.J. Robinett; Stephen Fox; Wm. S. Kidd; Jas. N. Justice; Elias Foglesong, foreman; Henry Groseclose; Archibald Thompson; James M. Stowers, Jr.; Hiram Hounshell; Paul James; Daniel Tickle; Newton Shufflebarger; Harvey Gross; John R. Bird; Allen Mustard; George Wohlford; C.M. Rudder; Gordon Sanders; Wm. M. Bird; Chas. Grayson and John H. Hoilman, sworn a grand jury of inquest in and for the County of Bland having recieved their charge were sent out of the Court, to consider of their presentments and after some time returned into court having found the following indictsments:
- Commonwealth VS John M. French, felony, endorsed a true bill.
- Commonwealth VS John M. French, felony, endorsed a true bill.
- Commonwealth VS Stephen Ory, misdemeanor, endorsed a true bill.
- Commonwealth VS John M. French, misdemeanor, endorsed a true bill.
- Grand jury adjourned until tomorrow at 9 o'clock.
- Appointment of judges of election for their respective Township voting places in the county, to wit:
For Sharon voting place, Isaac Hudson, John Deavor & Elias Foglesong.
For Rocky Gap voting place, Newton Shufflebarger, John A. Davidson and W.W. Compton.
For Mechanicsburg voting place, Wm. E. Hoge, George Wohlford and Hiram Rider.
For Seddon voting place, Henry Newberry, Franklin Grayson, and William Hedrick.
For Cameron's precinct in Rocky Gap, Duncan Cameron, John A. Smith and James T. Myers. - -
- Ordered that Henry Newberry, Isaac Hudson, John A. Davidson, Wm. E. Hoge and John A. Smith designated as commissioners to meet at the Clerk's office on the second after the election to canvass the votes and perform all other duties required of them as such commissioners.

Page 35- April 1, 1872- Commonwealth VS Rufus French. A&B (Assault & battery) Jurors, James A. Dillow, Peter Kitts, H.W. Steel, H.F.Bruce, I.K. Price, B.H. Oxley, E.G. Thompson, A.W. Kidd, Miller B. Allen, D.L. Tickle, Sanuel Bradham and A.F. Miller, returned verdict "We the jury find the defendant guilty and fine him $10.00. Defendant by his attorney moved the court to set aside the verdict, which motion the court took time to consider.
- Commonwealth VS Newton Compton, felony. Verdict, not guilty of the felony charged but guilty of assault and battery and asks his fine to be $75.00 and costs.

Page 36- April 1, 1872- Wm. H. Hale VS Wm. N. and Elias Harman. Plaintiff to recover from defendants, $217. 18, but this judgement is to be discharged by the payment of $108.59 with legal interest from July 26, 1870 til paid and costs.
- McCajah Saunders, for benefit of S.C. Gleaves VS J.W. & T.N. Finley, plaintiff to recover from the defendant, $32.87 and costs.
- Wm. Crawford VS Wm.P. & H.R. Mustard, continued until tomorrow.
- R.C. James VS A.B. Brown, case dismissed by consent of parties.

Page 37- April 1, 1872- J.M. McCaul, admr. of Harvey George, decd. VS James R.Witten,

admr. of James C. Davidson- judgement for $191.12 and other amounts. Plaintiff to recover from the defendant plus costs.
- R.C. James VS Wm. Stowers- on suggestion.
- Compton McGinnis & Co. VS Peter Kitts- on suggestion.
- J.W. McGinnis VS Peter Kitts- on suggestion.
- Wm. N. Harman VS H.C. Fanning- on suggestion.
{ These last four cases docketed and continued until tomorrwo.}
- Overseers of Poor VS George W. Suiter- warrant # 1.
- Overseers of Poor VS George W. Suiter- warrant # 2.
- Overseers of Poor VS George W. Suiter- warrant # 3.
{ These last three cases continued until next May Term.}
- Ordered that the following persons be appointed as special police for Bland County with all powers conferred by law to arrest any parties of said county. Colby Stowers, Captain; Stephen Robinett, Sargeant; Daniel Robinett; Harvy Stowers; John W. M??; Charles Walker; Peter R. Stowers; Isaac Stowers; Lee Stimpson; Joseph Thomas; George Stowers and John Suiter, privates.
- Court adjourned untill tomorrow.

Page 38- Tuesday April 2, 1872- present, P.W. Strother, Judge.
-Joseph Fanning, admr. VS Wm. N. & Elias Harman concerning notes due. Ordered that there be court supervision of execution for 60 days.

Page 39- April 2, 1872- Commonwealth VS Rufus French. A&B Defendant fined $10.00
 [A&B = Assault and Battery]
- Commonwealth VS Richard Martin, A&B- Defendant fined $5.00 & costs.

Page 40- April 2, 1872- Commonwealth VS Robert Robinett- misdemeanor- defendant confesses and is fined $5.00 and costs.
- Commonwealth VS Grimes Harman- trespass- indictment quashed.
- Commonwealth VS Wm. Bennett- violation of revenue and debt- defendant is acquitted.
- Commonwealth VS Henry Lambert- violation of revenue- defendant found guilty and fined $30.00. Jurors were- Wm. Kitts, Wm. A. Bennett, B.F. Petrie, A.J. Kitts, H.A. Pauley, J.D. Thorn, Lorenza Thorn, Wm. M. Bird, A.W. Kidd, J.C. Painter, Jno. Havens and John W. Harman.

Page 41- April 2, 1872- Commonwealth VS George Painter- indictment for riot- found guilty and fined $2.75 and costs. Jurors were- E.G. Thompson, B.H. Oxley, Z.T. Weaver, H.F. Bruce, Joseph Cameron, L.J. Ashworth, James A. Dillow, Elias Blankenship, James Crabtree, Jacob Kitts, Peter Kitts and H.W. Steel.
Commonwealth VS William Bennett- debt for violation of revenue law- defendant confesses his guilt and is fined $30.00 and costs.

Page 42- April 2, 1872- Commonwealth VS K.C. Thornton, indictment for trespass. Defendant acquitted.

- Commonwealth VS John Marcus, misdemeanor. Defendant guilty, fined $8.50 and costs.- The following were jurors- E.G. Thompson, B.H. Oxley, Z.T. Weaver, H.F. Bruce, Joseph Cameron, L.J. Ashworth, James A. Dillow, Elias Blankenship, James Crabtree, Jacob Kitts, Peter Kitts and H.W. Steel.
- Commonwealth VS Hugh Davidson- misdemeanor. Guilty, fined $5.00.

Page 43- April 2, 1872- Commonwealth VS Geo. Lindamood, Z. Wilkenson, Ray Kitts and John Pauley, on an instrument of riot. John Pauley,   George Lindamood and Zachariah Wilkenson fined $5.00 each and costs and be confined to jail for 24 hours. Ray Kitts, acquitted.
- Commonwealth VS Albert French- (A&B)
- Commonwealth VS Joseph Thomas- misdemeanor.
- Commonwealth VS Giles Thomas- Indictment fro riot.
- { These last three cases be continued.}

Page 44- April 2, 1872- Commonwealth VS Fulton French,- retailing spirits. French acquitted and discharged.
- Commonwealth VS L--- Caldwell- Indictment for felony. Defendant did not appear in court. Capias for his arrest ordered.
- Robt. C. Green VS Wm. Stuart- Defendant has leave to file account of off sets.
- Alexander F. Miller, resigns as Overseer of the Poor for Mechanicsburg Township. Resignation accepted. (excepted)
- John Deavor appointed as registrar for Sharon Township.
- Felix Buck, road commissioner for Sharon district, to view the road from Uriah Banes house through the lands of Frank Groseclose. To show cause if any that road should be changed.

Page 45-April 3, 1872- William Crawford VS Wm. P. & H.R. Mustard, motion on bond for property at day of sale. Defendants failed to appear in court. Judgement in amount of $445.30 with offset of &222.65 plus interest.
- Compton McGinnis & CO. VS Peter Kitts, on suggestion. R.K Kelley says he is indebted to defendant for $25.00. Peter Kitts having filed a homestead deed. Ordered that A.J. Grayson, T.N. Finley and John F. Locke, do appraise the defendant's property and report to the next term of court.

Page 46- April 2, 1872- Cynthia Grayson VS Compton McGinnis & Co. in debt. Defendants agree and judgment against them is ordered for the sum of $200.00 in gold, with interest from Feb. 23, 1869 and costs. A credit of $20.00 allowed.
- R. Grayson VS Compton McGinnis & Co. in debt. Judgement against defendants for $917.69 with interest and costs.
- Wm. N. Harman VS H.C. Fanning- on suggestion- case dismissed and defendant to recover his costs for his defense.
- Commonwealth VS Wm. Lovell, violation of revenue laws. Case continued until next term of court.

Page 47- April 2, 1872- D.W. Dunn, Treasurer, in the name of the Commonwealth, VS Wm. P. Bogle, Collector for Mechanicsburg Township and Elias Harman and F.G. Helvey, his securities and official bond- motion for judgement for State Revenue. It appearing that the defendants have had legal notice of this motion. They still failing to appear. Plaintiff to recover against the defendants the sum of $207.58 and interest at 10% per month until paid plus costs. Subject to a credit of $207.58 paid on April 2, 1872.

- Commonwealth for benefit of Bland County, VS Wm. P. Bogle, collector; Elias Harman and F.G. Helvey- motion for judgement for county levy. Plaintiff to recover the sum of $611.13 with interest. Credit given for $179.53 and $22.50.

- Commonwealth for benefit of School district # 1, Mechanicsburg Township VS (continued on page 48)

Page 48, April 2, 1872- Wm. P. Bogle, collector, Elias Harman and F.G. Helvey- Motion for judgement for school funds. Plaintiffs to recover from defendants $547.66 and interest at 10% plus costs.

- Mechanicsburg Township VS Wm. P. Bogle, collector, Elias Harman and F.G. Helvey. Motion for judgement for Township levy. Plaintiffs to recover from defendants the sum of $395.25 and interest at 10% plus the legal costs for this motion.

- Commonwealth for benefit of Bland County VS John C. Stowers, collector for Sharon Township; A.J. Grayson, George Robinett and W.H. Groseclose,his bond security. Judgement for the plaintiffs.

Page 49- April 2, 1872- Commonwealth for benefit of Sharon School District # 3 VS John C. Stowers, collector for Sharon; and A.J. Grayson, George Robinett and Wm. H. Groseclose, his securities. Motion for judgement for school fund. Judgement for plaintiff in the amount of $191.55 plus intertest and costs.

- John H. Hoge VS Elias Harman- In debt. Defendant to recover against the plaintiff his cost of this suit.

Page 50-April2, 1872- James Robinett VS Elias Harman. In debt. Plaintiff to recover from defendant the sum of $597.57 with interest and costs.

- R.M. Williams VS H.C. Groseclose. In debt. Defendant to recover against the plaintiff his costs for his defense.

- Wm. N. Harman VS Hoge & Ewald. In debt. Case continued.

Page 51- April 2, 1872- Eli F. Groseclose VS Wm. L. ??? et al. In debt. Plaintiff to recover from defendant the sum of $236.85.

- Eli F. Groseclose VS A.C. Waggoner. In debt. Judgement set aside and case continued.

Page 52- April 2, 1872- Ordered that the following jurors be paid $1.00 each for their services in the trial of Nuton Compton, charged with a felony and tried at this term of court. Viz- Miller B. Allen, Calvin G. Crockett, Jas. A. Repass, R.K. Kelly, James M. Stowers, D.W. Dunn, S. Robinett, Isaac Hudson, Samuel Bradham, Henry Newberry, James H. Munsey and Z.L. Weaver.

- Petit jurors and amounts paid to them viz: A.W. Kidd, $3.00; Jas. A. Dillow, $3.00; Peter Kitts, $3.00; H.W. Steel, $3.00; H.F. Bruce, $3.00; I.K. Price, $3.00; E.G. Thompson, $3.00; D.L. Tickle, $3.00; Miller B. Allen, $2.00; B.H. Oxley, $3.00; Samuel Bradham, $3.00; A.F. Miller, $2.00; Jas. Crabtree, $3.00; L.J. Ashworth, $3.00; Z.L. Weaver, $3.00; Joseph Cameron, $3.00;

Jacob Kitts, $3.00; Elias Blan- kenship, $3.00; J.D. Thorn, $1.00; B.F. Petrie, $1.00; Wm. Kitts, $1.00; Wm. A. Burnett, $1.00; A.J. Kitts, $1.00; H.A. Pauley, $1.00; Wm. Hedrick, $1.00; Lorenzo Thorn, $1.00; Wm. M. Bird, $1.00; J.C. Painter, $1.00; John Havens, $1.00 and John W. Harman, $1.00.
- The grand jury adjourned on yesterday returned today and rendered the following indictments-
Commonwealth VS Sebastian and Parris Pauley, for felony, a true bill.
Commonwealth VS Harvey G. Thompson, misdemeanor, true bill.
Commonwealth VS William McHaffey, indictment for trespass.

Page 53- April 10, 1872- Samuel W. Williams allowed $50.00 for services as prosecuting attorney.
- William T. Hamilton, Clerk of Court allowed $2.50 for services in the Nuton Compton case.
- George W. Brown made application to have tax cost per acre changed on 369 acres on Wolf Creek formerly owned by Jeremiah Lambert. Rate changed from $15.00 per acre to $10.00 per acre.
- Ordered that all cases not properly disposed of be continued until next term of court.
- Ordered that Court be adjourned until the next term. P.W. Strother

Page 54- OFFICE JUDGEMENTS- Wm. Crawford VS Wm. N. Harman and John Bogle. In debt. The judgement obtained in this office having been set aside and the plaintiffs being entitled to a final judgement. Plaintiff to recover from defendant the sum of $130.00 and interest from April 18, 1871. Offset by a credit of $6.25 paid Sept. 5, 1871.
{ There was no date on the above item. It was surely entered before April of 1872. John Bogle died in April of 1872. Notice that the verdict says "defendant" and not "defendants". }
- Hezekiah Harman VS L.D. Bogle. In debt. Harman to recover from Bogle $87.82 with interest and costs.
- In the Clerk's office, April 26, 1872- Hiram Peery, assignee of Thomas Cook VS Compton McGinnis $ Co.- In debt. Plaintiffs to recover from defendants the sum of $100.00 with interest from November 7, 1871 and costs. Wm. T. Hamilton, Clerk.

Pages 55 and 56 have been torn from this book.

Page 57- In the County Court of Bland County, "On vacation May 10, 1872" Pursuant to an act of The General Assembly of Virginia entitled, " An act for the government of towns with less than five thousand inhabitants " approved November 5th 1870 and in compliance of Section 1, chapter 282, Acts of 1871-72 entitled "An act to incorporate the Town of Seddon in the County of Bland" I hereby appoint W.W. Hicks, registrar of the said town to continue in office until January Court of said county, 1874. I do also appoint John F. Locke, E.A. Mills and Lewis Hall judges of election for said town of Seddon, to continue as such for the period of one year. To the Clerk of Bland County. Signed, P.W. Strother.

Page 58- Monday June 3rd 1872.- Present, P.W. Strother, Judge.
- The following list of deeds presented in Clerk's office since last term of court and with certificate of acknowledgement and relinquishment of dower and being duly stamped admitted to record.
viz: F.B. McGruder to Geo. P. Price. Conveying real estate.

Warden Stowers to Rufus Stowers. Conveying real estate.

James M. Stowers to Henry Newberry. Conveying real estate.

Rufus Stowers to H.P. Pruett. Conveying real estate.

John Kinsel & wife to Agnes Crabtree. Conveying real estate.

Wm. P. Hornbarger & wife to Paul James. Conveying real estate.

Wm. Hedrick to A.J. Grayson. Trustee, deed of trust.

Elias Harman to D.O. McNiel. Conveying real estate.

Franklin Grayson to H.C. Newberry. Conveying real estate.

Samuel Steel to Ephraim Waddle. Conveying real estate.

F.S. Blair, comm. to G.H. Morgan. Conveying real estate.

Jonas Umbarger to T.P. Umbarger, Conveying real estate.

Richard Moore & wife to Isaac J. Davis. Conveying real estate.

Madison Allen to James R. Miller. Trustee, church property.

- The following reports of settlement made by the administraters & with J.H. Hoge, deputy
Commissioner of accounts were this day filed by leave of the court for exceptions. Viz:
Settlement of Adam Waggoner, guardian of Marietta E. Waggoner, infant of F.P Waggoner,
deceased.

Page 59- June 3, 1872
- Report of Adam Waggoner, guardian of Margaret and Foster Waggoner.
- Report of settlement of James H. Munsey, guardian of Wm. S. Hearn and Lucinda Hearn.
- Report of settlement with A.T. Suiter, guardian of the heirs of James T. Gills, decd.
- Report of settlement of Wm. E. Hoge, executor of B. Helvey, decd.
- Report of settlement of Samuel H. Newberry, administrator of Thomas Wilkenson, decd.
- Report of settlement of A.C. Waggoner, guardian of Marietta E. Waggoner, infant of F.P.
Waggoner, decd.
- This day, Meek Hoge who was elected Justice of the Peace, for Mechanicsburg District, May
23, 1872, for a term of three years, qualified and took oath as prescribed by law.
- G.M. Tibbs took oath as prescribed by law after having been elected as Assessor for Sharon
District. Posts bond in amount of $2,000.00, with Samuel H. Newberry as his security..
- P.H.M. Bird, elected assessor for Seddon Township, Bland County
(Continued on page 60)

Page 60, June 3, 1872- ------- to serve a term of one year, took oath of office as prescribed
by law with A.J. Grayson and Wm. M. Bird, his security posts bond of $2,000.00.
- Z.L. Weaver, elected assessor for Mechanicsburg Township for a term of one year, takes oath
prescribed by law and with J.J. Mustard and I.K. Price, his security, posts bond of $2,000.00.
- A.R. Bogle, elected assessor of Rocky Gap Township for term of one year, takes oath
prescribed by law and with Sam'l. H. Newberry, Joseph Waddle and A.J Honaker, his security
posts bond for $2,000.00.

Page 61- June 3, 1872- P.W. Strother, Judge.
- John C. Stowers, elected Collector for Sharon Township for term of one year, posts bond of
$5,000.00 with Elias Foglesong and Jacob Waggoner his securities. Takes oath as prescribed by
law.

- H.? A.? Chandler, elected Collector for Seddon Township, posted bond for $5,000.00 with A.J. Ingram and J.M. Stowers his securities. Took oath as prescribed by law.
- George Wohlford, elected Collector for Mechanicsburg Township, posts bond for $10,000.00 with J.H. Mustard, John R. Compton and Gordon Wohlford his securities. Took oath prescribed by law. {I wonder why his bond was so much higher than the other collectors. Probably an extra zero added by mistake.}
- James A. Repass, elected Supervisor for Sharon Township, for term of one year. Posts bond of $1,000.00 with Alex. Suiter and A.J. Grayson, his security. Took oath as prescribed by law.

Page 62- June 3, 1872- James M. Stowers, elected Supervisor for Seddon Township, posts bond for $1,000.00 with A.J. Grayson and F.I. Suiter, hs securities. Took oath prescribed by law.
- I.K. Price elected Supervisor for Mechanicsburg Township, posts bond for $!,000.00 with H.C. Fanning and G.C. Thorn, his securities.
Took oath as prescribed by law.
- Thomas H. Kinser, elected Supervisor of Rocky Gap Township, posts bond for $1,000.00 with J.N. Justice abd Wm. Hedrick, his securities. Took oath as prescribed by law.
- Reece Crabtree elected Road Commissioner for Sharon Township, posted bond for $1,000.00 with Felix Buch his security. Took oath.

Page 63- June 3, 1872- H.C. Newberry, elected Road Commissioner for Seddon Township, posted bond for $1,000.00 with Eli Groseclose, his security. Took oath as prescribed by law.
- H.C. Fanning, elected Road Commisioner for Mechanicsburg Township, posts bond for $1,000.00 with Geo. Wohlford, his security.
- Thompson E. Gregory elected Road Commissioner for Rocky Gap Township, posts bond for $1,000.00 with T.N. Finley, his security.
- Wm. L. Yost elected Clerk for Sharon Township for term of one year, posts bond for $2,000.00 with Samuel H. Newberry, his security.

Page 64- June 3, 1872- Present, P.W. Strother, Judge.
- J.W. Compton elected Clerk for RockyGap Twonship, posts bond for $2,000.00 with Thos. H. Kinser and J.R. Johnston his surety.
Takes oath prescribed by law.
- Elias Foglesong elected Overseer Of The Poor, for Sharon Township. Posts bond for $500.00 with John C. Stowers, his security.
- H.G. Davis, is granted leave to perform the rites of matrimony, and posts bond for $1,500.00 with Wm. E. Hoge, his security.
- John H. Hoge, appointed administrator of the estate of John Bogle, deceased. Posted bond for $1,000.00 with G.C. Thorn his security. Allen Sublett, James Stafford, Timothy Hamilton and Ballard P. Stafford are appointed to appraise the personal estate of John Bogle, deceased, in current money and report their proceedings to The Commissioner Of Accounts.

Page 65- June 3, 1872- Present, P.W. Strother, Judge.
- K.C. Thornton, jailer presents a claim for $20.35, against the Commonwealth which was allowed and certified to the auditor.

- Felix Buck, Road Commissioner for Sharon Township presents claim against the county for $12.00. Claim is allowed.
- F.I. Suiter, deputy for Eli F. Groasclose makes claim for $3.00, which is allowed and certified to the auditor of public accounts.
- John K. Helvey made claim for services as a viewer on roads for $5.00, which amount is allowed.
- D.F. Muirhead makes claim as Commissioner of Roads in Mechanicsburg, for $3.00, which was allowed.
- B.F. Petrie makes claim for services rendered as Commissioner of Roads in Mechanicsburg Township, for $10.00, which is allowed.
- James Sheppard VS Compton McGinnis & Co. Defendants had not appeared in court. Verdict for the plaintiff in amount of $204.06, the amount of bond. Judgement to be discharged with payment of $102.03 and interest and costs.

Page 66- June 3, 1872- Acles Fannon applies for permission to keep an ordinary at his residence in the town of Seddon. He is granted permission to keep ordinary at his home in said town.
- Elias Harman VS James Robinett, on motion. Plaintif notice on grounds that judgement of complainant was lawfully rendered upon the overruling at April term of court. Plaintiff excepts and asks the record show such exceptions.
-Compton McGinnis & Co VS Peter Kitts, on suggestion.
-J.W. McGinnis VS Peter Kitts, on suggestion. A.J. Grayson, T.N. Finley and John Locke, who were appointed at last term of court to appraise the real estate and personal property of Peter Kitts, the defendant in the two foregoing cases, having failed to return a report of their proceedings, it is ordered that they be summoned to appear at the next term of court and show cause why they sgould not be fined for failing to make said report.

Page 67- June 3, 1872- Catherine J? {Y.}Thompson et al VS Adam Waggoner et al on a notice. Notice docketed and continued.
- Jas. A. Repass, Justice of The Peace for Sharon Township tenders his resignation. It is accepted by the court.
- John H. Lindamood, appointed Justice Of the Peace for Sharon Township to fill the unexpired term of James A. Repass.
- Hiram Rider elected May 23, 1872 as Justice of The Peace for Mechanicsburg Township for a term of two years, this day appeared in court and qualified as such by taking the oath prescribed by law.
- Mathias A. Fox elected Justice of the Peace for Rocky Gap Township to serve a term of three years, came today and qualified by taking the oath prescribed by law.
- John H. Lindamood, elected Justice of The Peace to serve a term of 3 years, came today and qualified by taking oath prescribed by law.
- Crockett & Blair for J.F. Scot. on debt. (Continued on page 68)

Page 68- June 3, 1872.
-- --- Defendant confesses judgement for judgement of $120.00 Plaintiff to recover from the defendant plus interest and costs.
- Wm. N. Harman Vs Wm. Crawford, on a notice to quash. Overruled

- T.N. Finley, a licensed grocery merchant at Seddon, Bland County, obtains license to sell wine, ardent spirits, malt liquors, cider and mixtures thereof. To be drank elsewhere. License in addition to one to sell groceries.
- J.M. Hicks & Bro., licensed dry goods and grocery merchant at Sharon, Bland County is licensed to sell spirits to be drank elsewhere.

Page 69- June 3, 1872- B.F. Petrie, road commissioner, to view and report on a road from mouth of Kimberling Creek up Walkers Creek to nearest point east of James Stafford's house. Motion filed and road to be established as a public highway, according to commissioners report.
- Z.L. Weaver VS J.E. McDonald, attatchment. Defendant is not a resident of this state. Judgement was taken on a horse. Plaintiff to recover from defendant.

Page 70, June 3, 1872- Concerning order for a road leading from Uriah Bean's house through lands of Frank Groseclose who claimed damages. George Hudson, Elias Repass and John Repass, to go on ground and ascertain damages to Groseclose and report same at the August term of Court. (Seddon Township)
- B.F. Petrie to view and report on the propriety of changing the road from G.W. Fannings to Elias Blankenships.
- Felix Buck, road commissioner for Sharon Township, reported on the road leading from the Black Lick and Plaster Bank road to Doak's Chapel over the lands of S.T.? Patterson, Elias Repass & Robert Doak. Ordered that same be established as a public highway.

Page 71- June 3, 1872- H.C. Newberry, road commissioner for Seddon Township, to superintend the erection of a new bridge over Walkers Creek on Holston Turnpike, near Isaac Kegleys, and report to court.
- George W. Fanning, aggrieved that Wm. P. Bogle, assessor, has erroneously charged him with taxes on 183 acres of land he does not own. Fanning exonerated from paying said taxes.

Page 72- June 3, 1872- Elias Harman VS Wm. P. Bogle, notice to defendant to appear at next term of court.
- Joseph Ewald & Bro. VS Geo. ? Deavers- J.N. Fanning, an infant, by his father and best friend, A. Fannon. Ordered that the cause be put on the docket for next term of court. (Almost illegible)
- J. Henderaon Bruce elected as Justice of The Peace for Seddon Township, for a term of three years. Bruce takes oath of office.
- Overseers Of The Poor VS Geo. W. Suiter, warrant # 2.
- Overseers Of The Poor VS Geo. W. Suiter, warrant # 3.
(Continued on page 73)

Page 73, June 3, 1872- D.O. McNiel and J.H. Bruce, Justices of Bland County, on the complaint of Sarah James, a single woman, charging Geo. W. Suiter with being the father of her bastard children. Ordered that Geo. W. Suiter be charged with the annual payment of $15.00 for each child, payable to the superintendant of the poor for Bland County, from the 20th day of March 1872 until each child reaches the age of 7 years. First child born Feb. 8, 1868 and second child born, March 3, 1871. Suiter posts bond of $500.00 with Acles Fannon and Hiram A. Pauley as his security.

- More than three months having elapsed since the death of Samuel Munsey, decd. and no one having applied for letters of administration on said estate, itis ordered that the same be committed to the sheriff of Bland County.
- Ordered that the court stand adjourned until next term of Court. Signed, P.W. Strother.

Page 74- Court in vacation, June 1872- This day Isaac J. Davis, who was elected Township Clerk for Mechanicsburg Township for a period of one year from July 1, 1872. Qualified and took oath of office and with John R. Compton, his security posted bond for $2,000.00.

Page 75- July 1, 1872- Present, Hon, P.W. Strother, Judge.
- Following is a list of deeds presented in the Clerk's office since the last term of court and with certificates of acknowledgement and relinquishments of dowers, being duly stamped are admitted to record.
F.G. Helvey & wife to Wm. E. Hoge. Real estate.
John W. Havens & wife to I.? G. Pauley. Real estate
James Umbarger & wife to John F. Umbarger. Real estate.
R.C. Kent, commissioner, to Harman Newberry. Real estate.
Wm. Kitts & wife to Wm. T. Hamilton, trustee. Deed of trust
Wm. H. Howe & wife to D.W. Dunn. Real estate.
A.J. Grayson to F. H. Albert. Article of agreement.
Robt. L. Newberry & wife to B.F. White. Real estate.
Randolph Grayson & wife to F. P.? Suiter. Real estate.
- Settlements of estates by the administrators with J.H. Hoge, commissioner of accounts, having been filed at last term of court and filed for exceptions-
‾Settlement of A.C. Waggoner, guardian of M.E. Waggoner.
Settlement of Adam Waggoner, guardian of Margaret & Foster Waggoner.
Settlement of James H. Munsey, guardian of Wm. S. and Lucinda Hearn.
Settlement of A.T. Suiter, guardian of heirs of James T. Gills, decd.
Settlement of Wm. E. Hoge, executor of B. Helvey, decd.
Settlement of Sam'l. H. Newberry, admr. of Thos. Wilkenson, decd.
Settlement of A.C. Waggoner, Marietta E. Waggoner, infant of F.P. Waggoner, deceased.

Page 76, July 1, 1872- This day was presented a report of the settlement of the estate of Wm. Deaver, decd. by his administrator, John Deaver, with J.H. Hoge, deputy commissioner of accounts which was filed for exceptions.
- John C. Crockett appointed administrator of estate of Robert R. Crockett, decd. Allowed to qualify without bond.
- Compton McGinnis & Co. VS Peter Kitts- on suggestion.- R.K. Kelly admits owing Peter Kitts, $25.00. Peter Kitts having took advantage of the Homestead Act, the court finds that the plaintiff have judgement against Kelly for $13.01 on their execution against Kitts.
- Rufus Britton VS A.C. Waggoner- Case continued.
- Ordered that the rule against Peter Kitts for failing to appear in court as a witness in behalf of William Hedrick, at the suit of P.G. Repass, is hereby discharged.

Page 77- July 1, 1872- C.J. Thompson VS Adam Waggoner et al- case continued.

- Franklin G. Helvey, this day appointed Overseer of The Poor for Mechanicsburg Township, with Hugh C. Fanning, his security, posts bond for $500.00.
- B.H. Penley, this day appointed Overseer Of The Poor for Seddon, Township, with R.S. Hoge, his security, posts bond for $500.00.
- Louretta Neal, asks the court to appoint Thos. P. Umbarger as her guardian. No bond required.
- Jacob Kitts makes motion that H.C. Newberry, Road Commissioner for Sedon Township, report on the expediency of a road to be built from Wilkenson's Mill down Walkers Creek to Andrew Kitts' house.
- J.W. McGinnis VS Peter Kitts- Summons on suggestion. R.K. Kelley admitted that he was indebted to the defendant for $25.00. Ordered that Kelly pay McGinnis $11.99.

Page 78- July 1, 1872- James Deavors, having died intestate more that three months ago, and no one having applied for administration of his goods and chattels, and that Eli F. Groseclose, sheriff take same and administer it. Thos. P. Umbarger, Jacob Waggoner and S.J. Patterson to appraise same.
- Wythe G. Waddle, makes motion that the Road Commissioners for Seddon Township view road and report on expediency of establishing a road beginning at Henry Newberry's to Randolph Grayson's gate to a point on Walkers Creek and Holston Turnpike opposite Dr. Stephen Repasses house.
- L.J Miller makes motion that the Road Commissioners for Mechanicsburg Township, view the ground and report on the expediency of building a wagon road from the west end of H.C. Fanning's land and over the Kimberling Springs road near A.W. Millers.

Page 79- July 1, 1872- E.G. Boothe VS A.J. Grayson, assistant assessor of Bland County.- Motion to correct assessment of land. Docketed and continued.
- Geo. W. Kinser makes claim of $8.00 against County. Allowed and certified, to Sharon Board.
- Geo. W. Groseclose, Sharon Township, claims $8.00, allowed.
- Wm. P. Bailes claims $3.00, Sharon Township, allowed.
- R.C. James VS Wm. Stowers, on suggestion. Continued.
- Warden Stowers VS Henry Burton, debt. Continued.
- G.H. Morgan VS Ida Neidermiah, assumption. Continued.
- Wm. H. Howe, VS G.C. Thorn, assumption. Continued.
- E. Blankenship VS J.W. Finley, assumption. Continued.

Page 80- July 1, 1782- H.C & J?? Groseclose, aggrieved at an entry made by R. Compton, assessor of Bland County. A matter of being over taxed. Erroneously tax amount to be refunded.
- H.C. & J.A.T. Groseclose, same as above.

Page 81, July 1, 1872- Ida Neidermier, applies for permission to keep an ordinary at her residence at Booths Springs. Permission granted.
- The Court certifies that R.B. Wyrick lost an arm in the Military Service of this state during the late war. He has never received an artificial limb from any source and that the said Wyrick is so disabled that an artificial arm cannot be worn or used by him.

Page 82- July 1, 1872- Z.T. Weaver VS J.E. McDonald, attachment. Case continued until next term of Court.
- Ordered that the order made in the May term 1871, designating February and July Terms of this court for the trial of Common Law issues and December and April terms for the trial of Chancery Causes. Pleas filed at said April & December terms upon setting aside Office Judgements and for trial of misdemeanors., be and the same rescinded.

Page 83- July 2, 1872- Crockett & Blair VS George W. Suiter, Debt. Plaintiff to recover from the defendant, $35.00 and costs.
- Wm. H. Howe VS Ida Neidermier, admr. for estate of A. Wessendonck, decd. Plaintiff to recover from defendant $50.00, Credit given for $50.00 already paid on August 26, 1871.
- D.A. Snow for James Clark VS S.J. Crump et al. Dismissed.
- The following persons to be allowed the sum of $1.0 for their services as Petit Jurors VIZ:
Jacob F. Kitts, James D. Honaker, J.W. Finley, Thompson Gregory, A.J. Keeling, Jas. S. Robinett, John M. Neel, James H. Mustard, Geo. W. Stowers, Henry P. Mustard, Wm. W. Fanning,Jr., D.W. Dunn, Jacob Sands, James Doke, Sanders M. Hamilton, and Wm. P. Mustard.

Page 84- Tuesday July 2, 1872- Ordered that the Court be adjourned until tomorrow morning at 10 o'clock. Signed by P.W. Strother, Judge.

Page 84- Wednesday July 3, 1871- Allen Mustard VS William N. Harman, Harman asks leave to file his account of payments. Case continued.
- Carroll, Adams & Neer, VS Morgan Wright. Case continued.

Page 85- July 3, 1872- Rufus Stowers VS S.T. Gibson. Case continued.
- William Stowers VS S.T. Gibson. Case continued.
- Wm. B. Brooks, (illegible) of Howard Cole, VS Compton McGinnis & Co. Case continued.

Page 86- Office Judgements- Eli F. Groseclose VS Wm. H. Groseclose, a suit of debt. The whole entry has been marked through, possibly to expunge it from the record.

Page 87- Monday August 3, 1872- Present Hon. P.W. Strother, Judge.
- Following are a list of deeds recorded in the courthouse since the last term of court. VIZ:
James Umbarger to Eliza Kinder, Conveying real estate.
Robert Doak to John S. Wilson. Conveying real estate.
Daniel Perky to Angeline V. Harman. Conveying real estate.
Daniel O. McNiel to Wm. N. Harman. Conveying real estate.
B.S. Walker to J.W. Compton. Deed of trust.
Polly Parson to J.S. Harmon. Power of Attorney to sell real estate.
Frank S. Blair to Wm. E. Hoge. Conveying real estate.
Elias Harman to Wm. E. Hoge. Conveying real estate.
John H. Hoilman to James Trucks. Deed of trust.
- Improper assessment of 40,000 acres of land taxed in Giles County. 20,000 acres had been sold off and was now in Bland County. The heirs of D.G. French, decd, and A.A. Chapman seek

recourse to same. Court relieves them of all liability due to improper assessment. (Part of this item continued on to page 88)

Page 88, August 3, 1872- Joseph P. Stras and David S.? Price are licensed to practice law in this County. They took the several oaths as is prescribed by law.
- Last will and Testamant of Madison Allen, deceased, presented in court and proven by oaths of James B. Miller and Samuel P. Mustard the subscribing wittnesses, is admitted to record. Emily S. Allen, executrix and JOhn P. Allen executor qualify and make bond for $5,000.00 with James B. Miller, Miller S.? Allen, John C.? Crockett and J.C. Carpenter, their securities. John Compton, George Fanning and George Wohlford to apprasie the personal estate of Madison Allen.
- Joseph Wohlford & Bro. for John Williams VS Wm. N. Harman and Elias Harman. Defendants did not appear in court. Plaintiff to have judgement against defendants for $438.38 but judgement to be discharged by payment of $319.00 plus interest and costs.
[Part of this entry was continued onto page 89]

Page 89- August 3, 1872- Franklin Garyson, J.H. Hoilman, Allen Mustard, P.H.M. Bird, Reese? Crabtree, Elias Foglesong, Peter R. Stowers and Thomas Franklin, were sworn a Grand Jury of inquest. They returned to court and having found no indictments, and were discharged.
- R.L. Newberry granted leave to sell religious books in the county and obtain license for same and to pay a tax of $2.50.
- John F. Locke, exor. for benefit of Rachael Harman VS James Robinett et als- Defendant to recover his costs from Plaintff.
- E.G. Booth concerning improper assessment of taxes on his 1,000 acres of land. (Writing is so bad it cannot be deciphered. - P. Bogle)

Page 90- Geo. W. Brown, claims overtaxation on 369+- acres of land on Wolf Creek. Brown , exonerated from paying excess tax. (A.J. Grayson, assessor)

Page 91- August 3, 1872- Road Commissioner of Sharon Township to go on and view road from Uriah Beans through lands of Frank Groseclose and make report. The same is set aside.
- A.C. Waggoner VS Rufus Britton- Injunction. Continued.
- R.C. James VS Wm. Stowers- Suggestion. Continued.
- C.J. Thompson et als VS Adam Waggoner, injunction. Continued.
- Colby Stowers, Capt. of Police, presented claim for $68.00. Allowed - Ordered that the Grand Jury Members be allowed sum of $1.00 each.
- Walter R. Staples VS Elias Harman, in debt. Plaintiff to recover from defendant the sum of $30.00 plus interest and costs.
- Thomas Henegar VS John R. Compton, in debt. Plaintiff to recover $16.00 fro defendant plus interest and costs.

Page 92, August 3, 1872- George Gose VS John R. Compton, in debt. Gose to recover from Compton, $200.00 plus interest & costs.
- Wilson Burnes et als VS Compton McGinnis & Co- In assumption.
Burnes to recover from defendants $378.13 plus interest and costs.
- H.C. Newberry, Road Commissioner for Seddon, makes claim for $6.00 which

was examined and allowed.
- Commonwealth VS Cebastian Pauley and Parris Pauley. Felony. True Bill. Ordered a capias
for arrest of Cebastian and Parris Pauley.
-Ordered that the Court adjourn until next term.

Page 93- September2, 1872- Following, a list of deeds presented in the Clerk's Office since
last term of Court:
- Francis Groseclose to Wm. H. Groseclose. Admitted to record.
- Daniel Perkey to Wm. A. Perkey. Admitted to record.
- Following settlements made with J.H. Hoge, commissioner of accounts
- Report of L.D. Bogle, admr. of estste of Robert J. Rains, deceased.
- Report of B.P. Stafford, admr. estate of John Henderson, deceased.
- Report made by F.G. Helvey, admr. estate of H.W. Helvey, deceased.
- Report of Joel H. Spangler, guardian of M.J. Hudson.
- Rufus Britton VS A.C. Waggoner. Notice. Case continued
- R.C. James VS Wm. Stowers. Suggestion. Case continued.
- Catherine J. (Y?) Thompson et al. VS Adam Waggoner. Case dismissed at cost of plaintiffs.
Adam Waggoner resigns his guardianship of Marietta E. Waggoner, infant child of F.P.
Waggoner. David F. Thompson appeared in court and assumes guardianship of Marietta E.
Waggoner. Posts bond in sum of $1900.00 with James Thompson and Jas. H. Munsey his surities.

Page 94- September 2, 1872- R.C. James VS Wm. Stowers. By mutual consent, case dismissed.
- Samuel E. Stimpson, Clerk of Rocky Gap and Treasurer VS John R. Johnston, Collector of
Rocky Gap Township. On motion for Township Levy. By consent of parties, case dismissed.
- Preston French VS Robt. C. James. On notice to quash execution. Defendant to recover from
the plaintiff his cost. Notice quashed.
- B. Dodd granted license to run an ordinary from his house.

Page 95- September 3, 1872- On motion of H.H. Tilson, Sharon Road commissioners to go on
road and report expediency of a road from Groseclose and Tilson's Mill to the Smythe County
line, passing through the lands of H.H. Tilson. To report back to the Court.
- On motion of D.O. McNiel, Mechanicsburg Road Commissioners to go on and view the road
and report on the expediency of a new road from D.O. McNiels Mill to the house of George
Bogle. Report back to court.
- On motion of Wm. P. Bruce and Ralph Wyrick, Seddon Road Commissioners to view and
report the expediency of a road from the mill of William Wilkenson down Walkers Creek to
Andrew Kitts house.
- Joseph Ewald & Bro. VS J.N. Fannon et al, on attachment. Dismissed.

Page 96- September 3, 1872- R.K. Kelley tenders his resignation as Justice of the Peace in
Seddon Township. It is accepted and Kelly is released.
- Robt. C. James VS Jacob J. Hager. Andrew J. Honaker says he is indebted to the defendant and
will pay to James the sum of $8.00. Plaintiff to recover his costs from defendant.
- On motion of Francis Groseclose, one of the sureites for H.C. Groseclose, guardian of Wm. R.
Tilson, wants release from said surety bond. H.C. Groseclose to appear in court and show

cause why he should not give a new bond.

- H.C. Newberry, Road Commissioner for Seddon Township, to report on the expediency of building a new road from Wilkenson's Mill down Walkers Creek to Andrew Kitts house. Report was made and the court ordered that the landowners, John Wilkenson, Harman Newberry, Jacob Munsey, Wm. Wilkenson, Jas. H. Burton, Jas. T. Burton, R.B. Wyrick, Asa Wyrick and Andrw Kitts be summonsed to October term of court to show cause if any why road should not be built.

Page 97- September 2, 1872- H.C. Newberry, Road Commissioner for Seddon Township, returned his report on building a road from A.J. Grayson's Mill, down Walkers Creek to the Mill of Wm. Wilkenson.The Court approved. Land owners summonsed were, J.M. French, Isaac Bruce, Henderson Bruce and John Wilkenson to show cause, if any, why road should not be built.
- This day Colby Stowers presented a claim against the County for $76.00 which was approved and sent to Board of Supervisors.
- Ordered that the Court stand adjourned until the next term. Signes by Judge P.W. Strother.

Page 98- Monday October 7, 1872- Present, Hon. P.W. Strother, Judge.
- List of deeds presented in the Clerk's Office since last term of court and with certificate of acknowledgement and relinquishment of dower are admitted to record
- Jonas Umbarger & others to Mollie Harner.
- Peter Spangler to School Trustees.
- John Wilkenson to Wm. L. Huddle.
- James Hoge to Wm. E. Hoge.
- James Hoge to A.F. Harman.
- Jas. Robinett to H.R. Mustard, exor. to Wm. Crawford.
- This day reports of settlements made by several admrs. exors. etc. with J.H. Hoge, Deputy Commissioner of Accounts and filed for exceptions, Viz:
- Settlement by Andrew J. Munsey, admr. of Wm. Hearn, decd.
- Settlement by Moses Akers, surviving admr. of A. Bralley, decd.
- Settlement by James M. Fanning admr. for Joseph Fanning, decd.
- Settlement by Isaiah & Josiah Bruce, exors. for Joshua Bruce, decd.
- Settlement by Adam Waggoner, guardian for Marietta E. Waggoner.
- Settlement by D.W. Dunn, guardian of infant heirs of Joseph Dunn.

Page 100- October 7, 1872- Rufus Britten VS A.C. Waggoner. On notice. Case continued at cost of defendant.
- H. Simmerman VS S.J.(I?) Patterson. James Lambert because of a lien, has liability to pay the debt due the plaintiff. Lambert admits debt to the defendant and is ordered to pay same to the plaintiff.
- On motion of Elizabeth Bussey, it is ordered that John Stinson appear in next term of court and probate the will of James Bogle, decd. and order Hiram Rider, Justice Of The Peace to take the deposition of Ralph A. Stafford who is unable to come to the courthouse. A copy of said will to be appended to the said Commission as directed by code of 1860 in regard to probate of wills.
- H.C. Fanning, Road Commissioner to view the road from D.O. McNiels Mill up Walkers Creek to George Bogle's house. Land owners through which new road will pass are: Adam Waggoner in his own right and as admr. for George E. Waggoner, decd., Joseph Hutzell, George Bogle,

19

D.O. McNiel and James H. Munsey, land owners, to appear in court ans show cause if any why road should not be built.

Page 101- October 7, 1872- Ida Neidemier applied in June to have a house of entertainment in her home at Booths Springs. It appearing that a mistake was made on order to run an ordinary. Ordered that Neidermier be released from paying tax on ordinary and that she pay license for a house of public entertainment instead.
- H.C. Newberry, Road Commissioner, having been designated to contact and receive proposals to build a new bridge near Isaac Kegleys, house and ordered that he advertise for new proposals and report same to this court.
- Settlement by F.G. Helvey, admr. for estate of H.W. Helvey, decd.. There were no exceptions. Ordered to be recorded.
- Settlement by B.P Stafford, admr. for estate to John Henderson, decd. No exceptions filed. Ordered to be recorded.
- Settlement by Joel H. Spangler, guardain of M.J. Hudson. Recorded
- H.C. Groseclose, guardian for Wm. R. Tilson, orphan of G.D. Tilson, decd. summonsed to give new bond, since his surety has been removed.
‾Court adjourned until in the morning.

Page 102- Tuesday October 8, 1872- Present, P.W. Strother, Judge.
- Eli F. Groseclose, road commissioner for Sharon Township, to view ground for new road from Groseclose and Tilson'a Mill, tnear the house of Andrew Hanshew.
- The resignation of D.O. McNiel, Justice of Peace for Seddon Township is accepted.
- B.Dodd, granted license to sell alcholic beveridges. Off premises.
- Uriah Bean VS Francis Groseclose. Groseclose to appear and show cause why road should not go through his property.

Page 103- Tuesday October 8, 1872-
- H.C. Fanning, Road Commissioner for Mechanicsburg Township, reports that A.W. Miller and Hiram Muncy owners of the lands which new road from H.C. Fannings to cross the mountain to near A.W. Millers on Kimberling, will appear in court and show cause why road should or should not be built.
- H.C. Newberry, Road Commissioner, made report on expediency of building a new road from A.J. Graysons Mill to William Wilkensons.
- On motion of Geo. W. Easly, agent for the owners of lands assessed in the name of Guy D. French and A.A. Chapman who are aggrieved by an entry in the land book by Wm. P. Bogle, assessor for Mechanicsburg Township, for the year 1871. (Part was on page 104)

Page 104- Tuesday October 8, 1872-
- French and Chapman ask to be exonerated from the erroneously levied tax. Request granted.
- Wm. N. Harman, attorney for Phineas Thruston, who says he was charged, erroneously, by Wm. P. Bogle, assessor, askes to be exonerated from paying said taxes. Request granted.
- W.W. Hicks, appointed Clerk for Seddon Township, to serve as such- Continued on page 105)

Page 105- Tuesday October 8, 1872-   ---until the next general election, together with H.C.

Newberry, his security posted bond for

$1,000.00, and took the oath as prescribed.
- The road from Wm. Wilkenson's Mill to near Andrew Kitts house, ordered to be built. Report made by H.C. Newberry, Road Commissioner.
- Elias Harman VS D.W. Dunn, Treasurer. Papers were submitted and the Court took time to consider same.
- Court adjourned until first day of next term of Court.

Page 106- Monday November 4,1872- Present, Philip W. Strother, Judge.
- Following, a list of deeds presented in the Clerk's office since the last term of court and are ordered to be recorded.
- James Hoge to Wm.E. Hoge.   Deed Book 2, page 332.
- James Hoge to A.F. Harman.   Deed Book 2, page 333.
- Sam'l. Wohlford, admr. for Wm. Crawford. Deed Book 2, page 334.
- R.C. King, trustee for Elias Foglesong. Deed Book 2, page 335.
- James Hoge et al to John H. Hoge.   Deed Book 2, page 336.
- James C. Brown etal to Peter Litz.   Deed Book 2, page 339.
- D.O. McNiel et al to Wm. T. Hamilton.   Deed Book 2, page 340.
- St. Clair French to John H. Hoge, trustee. Deed book 2, page 342.
- Adam Waggoner & wife to D.F. Thompson.   Deed Book 2, page 343.
- Adam Waggoner & wife to M.E. Waggoner.   Deed Book 2, page 344.
- B.H. Penley? to John C. Crockett.   Deed Book 2, page 345.
- John W. Stallard, Esq. to John Havens, assig." Book 2 page 346.
- H.G. Gibbons to Joshua Pruett.   Deed Book 2, page 348.
- Nancy Thompson to R.B. Wyrick.   Deed Book 2, page 349.
- R. Grayson & wife to Margaret J. Mills.   Deed Book 2, page 350.
- B.F. White & wife to Robt. L. Newberry.   Deed Book 2, page 351.
- R.C. Kent, trustee to Samuel Steel.   Deed Book 2, page 352.
Page 106, continued-
- Settlement by D.W. Dunn, guardian of the heirs of Joseph Dunn, dec.
- Settlement by A.J. Munsey, admr. of Wm. Hearn, decd.
- Settlement by Adam Waggoner, guardian of Marietta E. Waggoner.
- Settlement by Isaiah ans Josiah Bruce, exrs. of Joshua Bruce, decd.

Page 107- Monday November 4, 1872-
- Settlement by James M. Fanning, admr. of Joseph Fanning, decd.
- Report of settlement of Moses Acers, surviving admr. of Ansalem Bralley, decd. Ordered to be recorded.
- Rufus Britten VS A.C. Waggoner. Notice. Case continued at cost of the defenndant.
- John Fanning VS Wm. N. & Elias Harman. Verdict for Fanning.

Page 108- Cloyd Adkins VS D.M. McNeel. Case to be reinstated.
- H.C. Newberry to view and report on building a road from Uriah Bane's house through lands of Frank Groseclose.

21

- H.C. Fanning reports on expediency of building a road from his lands across Brushy Mountain near lands of A.W. Miller.
- B.F. Petrie reports on expediency of building a new road from Point Pleasant Academy to Gordon Saunders' house. Ordered, road be built.

Page 109- Road Commissioners find no objection to a road to be built from D.O. McNiel's Mill near George Bogle's house.
- More than 3 monhs have passed since the death of John W. Suiter and no one has applied for letters of administration. On the motion of   J. Mosby Davis, surviving administrator of P.H. Dills, decd., the sheriff shall administer the estate according to law.

Page 110- Blank.

Page 111- Monday January 6, 1873. - P.W. Strother, Judge.
- A list of deeds presented at the Clerk's office, since the November term of court and ordered to be recorded-
- John W. Stallard, Registrar, to John Walsh, assignee in Bank surety of William Stuart. Deed Book 2, page 353.
- John W. Stallard Register to John Walsh, assignee in Bank surety of George Dillman. Deed Book 2, page, 354.
- Phineas Thurston to John R. Bird. Book 2, page 354.
- H. Haupt to E.G. Booth. Book 2, page 356.
- James Bogle to George W. Fanning. Book 2, page 365
- J.W. Finley et als to J.M. Hicks. Book 2, 357.
- Thos. F. Walker to John T. Lambert. Book 2, page 360.
- A.J. Grayson to James Bruce. Book 2, page 368.
- John T. Lambert & wife to Wm. A. Hill & H.C. Dalton. Book 2 page 361.
- James Bruce to A.J. Grayson. Book 2, page 369.
- Moses Acers & wife to Bland County School Board. Book 2, 362.
- A.J. Grayson, admr. to Joseph & Gregory Ewald. Book 2, page 370.
- H.R. Mustard & B.P. Stafford to School Trustees. Book 2, page 363.
- Calvin G. Crockett to Thomas Wohlford. Book 2, page 371.
- A.J. Grayson, commr. to Wm. E. Hoge et al, trustees. Book 2, page 364.
- George W. Brown complains over erroneous tax charges. Refunded.

Page 112- January 6, 1873-
- Henry Kitts complains over erroneous tax on land he does not own. Tax is refunded.

Page 113- R.A. Hutzell, a licensed minister of the Methodist Church, this day appointed by the Court to celebrate the rites of matrimony. Posts bond for $1,500.00, with J.M. French and R.L. Newberry, his securities.
- Asa Wyrick appointed guardian of Joseph and Ella Hearn, infant children under the age of 14, of Harvey C. Hearn, deceased. Posts bond of $60.00 with George Suiter his security.
- Land owner, Frank Groseclose, ordered to appear and show cause if any why road should not be built from Uriah Banes through Groseclose's lands.

- Thompson E. Gregory appointed to view road from Franklin's Store across the mountain to near Jesse Justices. Land owners summonsed to appear at next term of court.

Page 114- Allen Mustard(foreman), A.W. Miller, George Wohlford, Charles M. Rudder, Paul James, John Deavor and Archibald Thompson, sworn as a grand jury returned the following verdicts on indictments-
- Commonwealth VS Thomas Woods, misdemeanor, true bill.
- Commonwealth VS Sallie and Ellen Jones, misdemeanor, true bill.
- Commonwealth VS Emeline Repass, misdemeanor, true bill.
- Commonwealth VS Thomas N. Finley, misdemeanor, true bill.
- Commonwealth VS B. Dodd, misdemeanor, true bill.
- (All indictment verdicts signed by Allen Mustard, foreman)
- James M. Fanning, admr for Joseph Fanning, decd., VS Wm. N. & Elias Harman. Motion on bond. Fanning recovers from Harmans.

Page 115- William Crawford VS Wm. N. & Elias Harman. Motion on bond.
- Reuben Hughes VS Wm. N. & Elias Harman. Motion on bond.
- H.P. Wheeler for bebefit of A.G. Updyke VS Elias and Berry Blankenship and George W. Suiter. Notice of motion for judgement on a receipt given as constable. Plaintiffs to recover from the defendants the sum of $12.61 with interest.

Page 116- dated Jan. 6, 1873.
- Young & Higgenbotham for benefit of Eli F. Repass VS H.G. Thompsom, Sam'l. Newberry, A.N. Thompson and J.B. Thompson. Motion on receipt given as constable. Plaintiff to recover from defendants, with interest due from Dec. 6, 1872 until paid. (Dated Jan. 6, 1873)
- Eli F. Groseclose VS H.G. Thompson, Sam'l. Newberry, A.N. Thompson and J.B. Thompson. Motion on receipt given as constable.
Plaintiff to recover from defendants, with interest from Dec. 6, 1872 until paid.
- A.G. Updyke VS James McCulley. Case continued.
- Z.T. Weaver aggrieved that he is overtaxed for year 1872. Refund due to Weaver if tax is already paid.

Page 117- William T. Hamilton appointed Commissioner in Chancery of this Court in the place of F.F. Repass who is hereby removed. Hamilton took the oath as prescribed by law.
- Rufus Britton VS A.C. Waggoner. Waggoner demanded a jury to try the case to which Britton objected. Court sustained objection. Ordered that Waggoner recover form Britton. Case dismissed.

Page 118- Reese Crabtree, Road Commissioner reports on road from Groseclose & Tilson's Mill to the nearest & best route to Walkers Creek and Holsten Turnpike. Ordered that H.H. Tilson, Gorden Havens, John Kinder & Andrew Hanshew, owners of the land through which the road will pass, to appear on March 1, to show cause why road should or should not be built.
- Cloyd Adkins VS D.M. Neel. Ordered case continued.
- Commonwealth VS Jacob Clark. Ordered that Jacob Clark, colored, be subpoenaed to answer a petition concerning assessment of taxes.

- Court is adjourned until tomorrow.

Page 119- Tuesday Jan. 7, 1873- Robert Crockett VS J.W. Finley. In debt. Crockett to recover against Finley, $60.00 plus interest.
- W.D. Stockdale, B.F. Smith, W.A. Hannaway, and W.P. Clotountry, merchants and partners under firm & style of Stockdale-Smith & Co. VS Gilbert H. Morgan & L.C. Wright, late merchants & partners under firm of "Morgan & Wright. Plaintiffs to recover from defendants. Jan. 8, 1873- A.P. Brown & John L. Alexander (A.P Brown & Co) VS W. C. Williams. Plaintiffs to recover from defendant.

Page 120- Monday February 3, 1873. - Hon. P.W. Strother, Judge.
- List of deeds presented at Clerks office since last term of court-
- Uriah Bean to A.J. Grayson, trustee. Book 2, pg. 372.
- B.D. Graves with H.H. Repass.   Book 2, pg. 373.
- Jas. D. Johnston, comm. to Thos. F. Walker. Book 2, pg. 374.
- J.W. Finley & others to B. Dodd, trustee. Book 2, pg. 375.
- George to D.L. Tickle. Book 2, pg. 377.
- A.J. Grayson, Comm. to Locke & Thompson. Book 2, 378.
- Edwin L. Carpenter & others to James S. Wilson. Book 3, pg. 29.
- Commonwealth VS George Lindamood. Misdemeanor. Lindamood fined $5.
- Commonwealt VS Albert French. Assault & Battery. Fined $5.00.

Page 121- February 3, 1873- Commonwealth VS R.G. Thomas, Assault & Battery. Defendant fined $5.00 and costs.
- Commonwealth VS Giles Thomas, indicted for riot. Fined $5. & costs.
- Commonwealth VS William Livell, violation of revenue law. Fined $5.
- Commonwealth VS Lendo Caldwell, felony. Acquitted.

Page 122- Commonwealth VS John Marcus, misdemeaner. Fined $8.50.
- Commonwealth VS H.A. Chandler, Assault & Battery. Jury consisting of, A.B. Brown, A.R. Bogle, Jas. E. Maxwell, John Kyle, Thos. F. Walker, F.G. Helvey, J.C. Painter, David H. Harman, D.L. Muirhead, Jno. R. Compton, L.D. Bogle and H.A. Pauley, could not agree on a verdict and were discharged.
- Commonwealth VS M.D. Robinett, misdemeanor. Failure to appear in court. Case continued until next term of court.
- Commonwealth VS Paris Pauley, felony. Acquitted.

Page 123- Commonwealth VS John W. French, felony. Acquitted.
- Commonwealth VS John W. French, felony #2. Acquitted.
- Commonwealth VS John W. French, misdemeanor #3. Acquitted.
- Commonwealth VS William McHaffey, misdemeanor. The death of this defendant being suggested, he is acquitted.
- Commonwealth VS Stephen Ory, misdemeanor. Fined $5.00and costs.

Page 124- Commonwealth VS Eli Repass, violation of revenue law. A jury consisting of, B.D. Graves, Rufus Clark, Edward Bruce, B.H. Penley, J.C. Painter, Wm. M. Bird, E.G. Thompson, H.F. Harman, Wm. Kitts, Wm. P. Hornbarger, James Clark and J.L. French, found Repass guilty and fined him $30.00 and costs.
- Commonwealth VS H.G. Thompson, misdemeanor. Acquitted.
- Commonwealth VS James Tolbert, violation of revenue law. Continued.
- Commonwealth VS Fulton French, violation of revenue law. Continued.
- Commonwealth VS Sallie & Ellen Jones, misdemeanor. Continued.

Page 125- Commonwealth VS Thomas Woods, misdemeanor.
- Commonwealth VS Emeline Repass, misdemeanor. (Summons not having been executed the foregoing two causes, it is ordered that a summons be awarded against the defendants directed to the Sheriffs of Bland and Smythe Counties. Returnable first day of next April Term.
- Overseers of The Poor, VS Daniel A. Miller, bastardy. Continued.
- Commonwealth VS Jacob Clark, petition. Clark had failed to pay correct tax. Fined double amount of tax.
- Cloyd Adkins VS Miles Roland & others, unlawful detainer. Case continued at cost of defendant.

Page 126- A.G. Updyke VS James McCulley, case continued.
- H.C. & A.F. Groseclose, exors. of Wm. Groseclose, decd., VS H.G. Thompson & others. Notice. Ordered continued.
- G.J. Holbrook, a gentleman who has been licensed to practice Law in The Commonwealth, has leave to prsctice in Bland County. Holbrook took the Oath as required by law.
- A.A. Chapman & others VS Austin French & others. Ejectment.
-Ordered that case be removed to Circuit Court of Bland County.
- John C. Crockett, aggrieved that he is over-taxed on his lands. Ordered that if already paid, to be refunded. (Part on page 127)

Page 127- Elias Harman VS Hiram Muncy. In debt. Dismissed with plaintiff paying costs.
- John H. Hoge VS Elias Harman. Case dismissed.

Page 128- February 1, 1873- James Tolbert makes motion to court to obtain a license to operate an ordinary from his home.
- Commonwealth VS B. Dodd. Violation of election laws. Court took time to consider.
- Andrew Thompson VS Roland Fletcher's admr.. Plaintiff to recover from Robert W. Harman, admr. of Roland Fletcher's estate, $75.00.
-- Court adjourned until tomorruw at 9:AM. P.W. Strother, Judge.

Page 129- Tuesday morning, February 11, 1873.- P.W. Strother, Judge.
- Court assigns Isaac M. Shrader as guardien of Victoria J. Lambert, infant of John W. Lambert, decd. under the age of 14. Isaac posts bond of $200.00 with John Shrader, his security.
- Commonwealth VS B. Dodd. Violation of election laws. Dismissed.
- Commonwealth VS T.N. Finley. Violation of election laws. Acquitted.
- Court is satisfied that James Tolberts application to operate an ordinary in his home at

Mechanicsburg, was not to keep and entertain travelers but to afford him greater facilities to for selling of the liquors he has manufactured as a distiller which were not given by the distillery license. Tolbert is refused the certificate and the application is dismissed.

-Aaren Criss & Son VS Wm. N. Harman. Judgement for Criss in the amount of $110.23 andf costs. Subject to credit of $50.00 & interest.

Page 130- P.G. Repass VS Wm. Hedrick. Defendant gave notice of his intentions to file additional pleas. Case continued.

- Joseph T. Cooley's admr. VS S.J.(I?) Patterson. Debt. Continued.

- T.E. Mitchell VS Wm. G. Mustard, admr. Continued.

- Warden Stowers VS Henry Burton. Debt. The defendant by his attorney suggested the Bankruptcy of the Plaintiff. It appearing that Warden Stowers is not a resident of this Commonwealth. Case to be dismissed at next term of court unless security for costs and damages etc. be given to the Clerk within 60 days.

- Staples & Caldwell VS Davis King & others (Solomon King). Debt. Case continued until next term of Court.

Page 131- Samuel Newberry, Sheriff and admr. of estate of Thomas Wilkenson, deceased, petitions the Court for instructions as to the paymentof $53.23 left in his hands. Appearing tha Wilkenson owed Henry Zimmerman $62.38. and John Wilkenson (Coobliger) is insolvent. It is ordered that the admr. pay off debt of T.E. Austin now owned by Henry Zimmerman. (Wording not clear in this item)

- Peter Kinder VS Joseph L. Cooley's Admr. Continued.

- Samuel H. Newberry VS E.G. Booth. Case continued.

Page 132- G.H. Morgan VS A. Wesendonck. Case dismissed at cost of Morgan but without prejudice.

- Wm. P. Cecil VS Austin French. In debt. Cecil to recover from French $40.00. Cecil relinquishes the interest.

- A.B. Dodson VS John W. Havens. On warrant. Havens to recover from Dodson $5.00 damages and his costs in defending himself. The case is dismissed.

- Wm.H. Howe VS G.C. Thorn. Howe to take nothing and Thorn to recover from Howe $5.00 damages and costs.

Page 133- Wm. M. Bird VS George W. Suiter. Debt. Jury could not agree on a verdict. Continued until tomorrow at 9:AM.

- St. Clair French VS John R. Compton. By consent, case dismissed.

- Wm. P. Haller VS Elizabeth Wohlford's admr. Haller to recover from Eli F. Groseclose, admr for Elizabeth Wohlford's estate, $114.50, the amount of the debt owed, plus interest and costs.

Page 134- Rufus Britton VS A.C. Waggoner, Adam Waggoner, Henry P. Wheeler, F.M. Harman, Jacob Groseclose, Jacob Waggoner, A.W. Shewey and Elias Repass. Britton to recover from the defendants the sum of $64.32 plus interest and costs.

- Crockett & Blair for benefit of Eli F. Groseclose VS Jacob Waggoner. Plaintiffs to recover from Waggoner, $30.00, with interest and costs.

- R.P. Bailey & Co. VS G.H. Morgan. By consent, case dismissed.
- Wm. P. Cole & Co. VS Wm. N. Harman. Cole to recover from Harman $40.88, with interest and costs.

Page 135- Andrew Spangler VS Jacob Waggoner. Waggoner had refused to pay for 40 1\2 bushels of oats bought at Andrew Spangler's sale. Spangler to recover from Waggoner $21.20 with interest and costs.
- Samuel W. Williams presents claim against The Commonwealth for $70.00 which was ordered to be certified and sent to Auditor.
- Court adjourned until tomorrow at 9:AM.

Page 136- Wednesday Morning February 5, 1873- P.W. Strother, Judge.
- Wm. M. Bird VS George W. Suiter. Debt. Bird to recover from Suiter the sum of $72.65 plus interest. Suiter and his attorney moved that the Court set aside the verdict. The Court took time to consider.
- Wm.P. Bogle VS Hugh C. Fanning. Verdict for Bogle who is to recover damages of $75.00. Fanning moved the court to set aside the verdict. Court took time to consider.
- (This item is totally illegible) Last one on page.

Page 137- Commonwealth VS Elias Repass. Violation of revenue laws. A new trial granted to the defendant.
- Adam Waggoner, personal represenative of George Waggoner, deceased, alleges that he is aggrieved by entry made by A.A. Ashworth, assessor for Mechanicsburg Township. Waggoner asks the Court to exonerate him from paying $11.64 in taxes erroneously charged to him. Exonerated.

Page 138- Thursday February 6, 1873. P.W. Strother, Judge.
- John F. Locke appointed as a Justice for the Seddon Township, in room of D.O. McNiel, resigned. Locke took oath of office.
- Compton McGinnis & Co. VS Henry Dowling. Court granted Dowling permission to file additional lists. Case continued.
- Robt. C. Green VS William Stuart. Attorney for Stuart suggested Bankruptcy for the defendant.

Page 139- Wm. M. Bird VS George W. Suiter. Bird withdrew his motion made yesterday and by consent Bird to recover form Suiter the sum of $80.00 with interest thereon.
- John W. Johnston VS Andrew J. Honaker. Case continued.
- Peter Honaker VS George W. Brown. Case continued.
- Henry Davidson, Com. for benefit of P.C. Honaker VS George W. Brown and A.B. Brown. In debt. Plaintiff to recover from Browns, $75.00 plus interest and costs.

Page 140- February 1873 -
- Carroll, Adams & Neer VS G.H. Morgan. Plaintiff to recover from Morgan he sum of $99.65 plus interest and costs.

- Carroll, Adams & Neer VS G.H. MOrgan & L.C. Wright. Plaintiffs to recover from defendants the sum of $145.02 plus interest and costs.
- Wm. J. Richardson, admr. VS Eli F. Groseclose. On motion of defendant, a rule is awarded him against Jezreal Thompson a witness for failing to appear in Court. . Case continued at defendant's cost.

Page 141- February 1873.
- Wm. M. Bishop VS Wm. P. Slade & others. Case continued.
- Eli F. Groseclose VS Jacob Waggoner. In debt. Ordered that Plaintiff recover from Morgan the sum of $80.75 plus interest and costs. Credits noted.
- R.M. Williams and Rufus M. Williams VS H.C. Groseclose. Ordered that the two cases be consolidated. Groseclose has leave to file his plea.
- Wm. P. Bogle VS Wm. Deavor & others. Case continued.

Page 142- Feburary 1873-
- H.C. & A.T. Groseclose, Executors for William Groseclose, deceased, VS H.G. Thompson, Samuel Newberry and A.N. Thompson. Plaintiffs to recover from defendants the sum of $30.54 and costs.
- Same plaintffs as above VS same defendants. H.G. Thompson is liable as constable. Plaintiffs to recover from defendants the sum of $266.37 plus interest and costs.
- Court adjourned until tomorrow at 9:AM.

Page 143- Friday February 7, 1873. Hon. P.W. Strother, Judge.
- Commonwealth VS A.C. Waggoner & sureties. In debt.
- Z.T. Weaver VS I.E. McDonald & others. An attachment. Motion to set aside a verdict rendered in the June term of Court. Judgement is erroneous and is therefore quashed. The said Isaac McDonald to recover from Weaver his costs. Also ruled that the judgement against John C. Crockett be dismissed at plaintiff's cost.
- Barcraft & Co. VS John R. Compton & John W. McGinnis, partners of the firm of Compton McGinnis & Co. Plaintiffs to recover from defendants the sum of $515.55 plus interest and costs.

Page 144- February 1873-
- Allen Mustard VS Wm. N. Harman. On motion of Harman a rule was awarded him against L.C. Wright & Isaac Swindle, witnesses for the defendant who failed to appear in court.
- Eli F. Groseclose VS Wm. H. Groseclose. In debt. Plaintiff to recover from the defendant the sum of $300.00 with interest and costs. Several credits noted.
- Guggenheimer, Cone & Co. VS Ida Neidermaier. Defendant did not appear. Plaintiff to recover from defendant $127.99.
-

Page 145- February 1873-
- Wm. N. Harman VS Hoge & Ewald. In debt. Case dismissed at cost of the Plaintiff.
- Smith & Harvey VS Ida Neidermaier, admr. for August Wessendonck. Defendant says she did not assume any debts of the deceased Wessendonck who died intestate. Case continued.
- J.J Harner, admr. VS John H. Bennett. Defendant has leave to file a special plea. Case continued.

- Wm. Groseclose, Exor. VS Groseclose & Hanshew. Case continued.

Page 146- February 1873-
- J. Mosby Davis, Admr. VS John R. Compton. Defendant files list of offsets as does the plaintiff. Case continued.
- Kimberley & Morehead VS Compton McGinnis & Co. In debt. Continued.
- Wm. E. Hoge VS John R. Compton, John W. McGinnis and H.H. McGinnis, late merchants and partners. In debt. Ordered that the plaintiff recover from the defendants the sum of $532.79. Credits noted.

Page 147- February 1873-
- W.J. Shufflebarger VS James Clark. In debt. Case continued.
- R.M. Williams, benefit of Justice Hubble VS H.C. Groseclose. Debt.
- Rufus M. Williams for Justice Hubble VS H.C. Groseclose. In debt.
[Part of the following has been penciled out but is still legible. " This day came the parties by their Attornys.--- Amount of debt is $588.18. Plaintiffs to recover from defendants.]

Page 148- February 1873-
- John C. Crockett VS John R. Bird. Ejectment. Ordered tha Geo. W. Kinser, surveyor, go
 on lands in question and with the sheriff, make survey. Move fences if it is required.
- The following persons to be paid $1.00 for their services as petit jurors, viz- B.D. Graves, R.W. Clark, Edward Bruce, B.H. Penley, J.C. Painter, Wm. M. Bird, E.G. Thompson, A.F. Harman, Wm. Kitts, W. P. Hornbarger, James Clark, J.S. French, A.B. Brown, A.R. Bogle, James E. Maxwell, John Kyle, Thos. F. Walker, F.G. Helvey, Davis H. Harman, D.F. Muirhead, John R. Compton, L.D. Bogle and H.A. Pauley.
- The following persons to be allowed the amount next to their names for services on petit jury, viz- A.B. Brown, $3.00; A.R. Bogle, $4.00; James E. Maxwell, $4.00; John Kyle, $4.00; Thos. F. Walker, $3.00; F.G. Helvey, $2.00; J.C. Carpenter, Jr. $2.00; Davis H. Harman, $4.00; D.F. Muirhead, $3.00; John R. Compton, $3.00; L.D. Bogle, $2.00; J.S. French, $4.00; Hiram Hall, $2.00; A.G. Thompson, $3.00; R.W. Clark, $2.00; James Corner, $1.00; James Clark, H.G. Pauley, $4.00; H.B. Pauley, $1.00; John R. Bird, $1.00 and James Corner, $1.00..
_ Court adjourned until tomorrow.

Page 149- Saturday Morning February 8th, 1873. Hon. P.W. Strother, Judge.
- Wm.P. Bogle VS Hugh C. Fanning. Court over rules motion to set aside Jan. verdict.
 Bogle to recover from Fanning, $75.00 plus interest and costs. Exceptions by Fanning, noted.
- Rufus Stowers and William Stowers VS S.T. Gibson. In debt. (2 cases) Plaintiffs not resdents of Virginia. Cases to be dismissed at next term of court unless costs be paid in 60 days to Clerk of the Court.
- John F. Locke VS Hiram Munsey. In debt. Case continued.

Page 150- John R. Compton VS John R. Bird. In debt. Case continued.
- R.M. Williams VS H.C. Groseclose. In debt. Continued. (2 cases)
- Overseers of The Poor VS George W. Suiter. Case of Bastardy. These causes intended to be stricken from docket in 1872, being renewed again. Dismissed at cost of defendant.

- Commonwealth at relation of Eli F. Groseclose VS A.C. Waggoner & Suiter. Plaintiff asks permission to amend his declaration. Granted.

Page 151- February 1873.-
- Elias Blankenship VS J.W. Finley. Finley to recover from Blankenship, $70.00 plus interest and costs. Credits noted.
- Thos. J. Doyle VS Jacob Munsey. Doyle to recover from Munsey, $23.00 plus interest and Costs.
- Elias Harman VS D.W. Dunn, treasurer. Notice. Case continued.
- Elias Harman VS D.W. Dunn, treasurer. Notice. Case continued.

Page 152- February 1873-
- Wm. B. Brooks, assignee, VS Compton McGinnis & Co. Case continued.
- All cases not otherwise disposed of are continued.

Page 153- OFFICE JUDGEMENTS-
- James Robinett and H.R. Mustard, executors of will of Samuel Wohlford, VS Hiram A. Pauley and John Havens. Pauley and Havens failed to appear in court. Plaintiffs to recover from defendants the sum of $55.27 with interest and costs.
- Crockett & Blair for benefit of Wm. L. Huddle VS Wm. N. Harman. In debt. Harman did not appear in court. Plaintiffs to recover from defendant $100.00 plus interest and costs. Credits noted.
- James W. Stuart VS Jacob Waggoner. In debt. Waggoner did not appear in court. Plaintiff to recover from defendant, $35.47 plus interest and costs.

Page 154- February 1873-
- Jacob Waggoner for benefit of Eli F. Groseclose VS James M.C. Wilson. In debt. Wilson did not appear in court. Waggoner to recover from Wilson, $37.35 plus interest and costs. Credit noted.
- N.B. Stimpson VS Peter Housman and G.H. Morgan, late partners under firm name " Houseman & Morgan." In debt. Morgan did not appear in court. Morgan did not appear in court. Stimpson to recover from defendants, $84.07 with interest and costs. Credits noted.
- Anderson Shumate VS Thomas Cook. In debt. Cook did not appear in court. Shumate to recover from Cook, $45.79. Credits noted.

Page 155- February 1873-
- J. Mosby Davis, surveyor, partner with E.H. Harman, decd.- VS Eli F. Groseclose, sheriff, admr. of John W.Suiter, decd. In debt. Groseclose did not appear in court. Davis to recover from Groseclose, $35.00 plus interest and costs. Credit noted.
- Henry Ellis VS Samuel C. Davis. In debt. Davis did not appear in court. Ellis to recover from Davis $51.30 plus interest and costs.
- James M. French VS N.B. Dotson. In debt. Dotson did not appear in court. French to recover from Dotson, $20.00 plus interest & costs.

Page 156- February 1873- - James M. French VS Lee A. and Polly Kitts. In debt.

Lee & Polly Kitts failed to appear in court. French to recover from the Kitts' $50.00 plus interest & costs.

- James M. French VS Ellen J. Suiter, William F. Cecil and Joshua Cecil. In debt. Defendants failed to appear in court. French to recover from defendants $50.00 plus interest & costs.

- Roland J. Tracy, for benefit of Harrison W. and Charles D. Straley, VS John R. Compton. In debt. Compton failed to appear in court. Plaintiffs to recover from Compton $350.00 plus interest & costs.

Page 157- February 1873-
- Holbrook & Spence for benefit of Martin Steffey, admr. of estate of Michael Foglesong, deceased, VS James M.C. Wilson. In debt. Wilson did not appear in court. Plaintif to recover from Wilson $78.20 plus interest & costs.

IN CLERKS OFFICE, February 8, 1873-
- J.H. Doughty (Dougherty?) VS Wm. P. Mustard. In debt. Mustard admits debt. Plaintiff recovers from him $17.00 & interest.

IN CLERKS OFFICE, February 21, 1873-
- Jas. H. Harman for John R. Thompson VS H.G. Thompson. In debt. Defendantadmits debt of $25.00. (Interest & costs added)

Page 158- March 1, 1873- Hon. P.W. Strother, Judge.
- Deeds presented in Clerk's office since last term of Court:
- Jas. B. Miller & others to J.M. and I.F. Pruett.
- Isaac Kegley & wife to J.G. Kegley, trustee for Jane Dowling.
- Isaac Kegley & wife to J.G. Kegley, trustee for Nancy Graves.
- Elias Harman to J.M. Hoge, trustee.
- Geo. W. Suiter to A.T. Suiter, trustee.
- Zachariah Cook, trustee to William O. Yost.
- Jos. A. Fanning to ?. W. Miller.
- Harry James, deed of Homestead.
- Jos. A. Fanning & wife to A.W. Miller. (May be G.W. Miller)
- Prudence Robinett to P.C. Honaker.
- A.J. Grayson, Comr. to D.W. Dunn.
- G.J. Holbrook to Warden Stowers.
- H.B. Estie, licensed to practice Law in Balnd County.
- Elias Harman brings 2 suits against D.W. Dunn. Cases continued.
- Clay Adkins VS D.M. Neel. Case continued.
- Wm. P. Bogle VS F.F. Repass. Case continued.

Page 159- March 1873-
- Overseers of the poor VS Daniel A. Miller. On Bastardy warrant. Ordered that warrant be dismissed.
- Cloyd Adkins VS Miles Roland & Barbara Neel. Unlawful detainer. On motion by defendants by their attorneys, case is dismissed.
- Thompson E. Gregory, road comissioner for Rocky Gap, to view & report on expediency of building a new road from Franklin's Store across the mountain to Jesse Justice's.

- H.C. Newberry to view road from Uriah Beans through lands of Frank Groseclose to the Rich Valley Turnpike.

Page 160- March Term of Court, 1873. -
- John W. Harman is exonerated from paying taxes unlawfully entered against him by A.A. Ashworth, county assessor.

Page 161- March 1873-
- Eli F. Groseclose VS Andrew Hanshew. On road establishment. Ordered that Commissioner Crabtree return and report more fully on the road leading from Groseclose & Tilson's Mill to Walkers Creek and Holston Turnpike.
- Wm. L. Huddle, admr. for James R. Crabtree, decd. makes motion to turn estate over to the sheriff to administer it.
- B.F. Petrie, returned his report on the expediency of building a new road leading from the Walkers Creek and Holston Turnpike at Harvey Nicewanders across the mountain to the Tazewell line. Same to be established according to the changes set forth.
- H.C. Newberry to view and report on building a new road from Raleigh & Grayson Turnpike down Walkers Little Creek to Wytheville & Mechanicsburg road.
- Jacob H. Sands & others ask for a change in the location of the Tazewell & Peppers Ferry Road near Wm. N. Harmans. H.C. Newberry to view and make report on same.

Page 162- - Court adjourned until first day of next term.

Page 163- Monday April 7, 1873. - Hon. James P. Kelley, Judge.
- Following, a list of deeds presented at teh Clerk's office since the last term of Court. Annexed and admitted to record.
- J.M. French, comm. & others to William L. Huddle. Book 3, pg. 47.
- F.S. Blaair, comm., to James Jones.   Book 3, pg. 48
- Joseph Ewald & wife to G.A. Ewald.   Book 3, pg. 49.
- R.C. Kent, trustee, to Rees Crabtree.   Book 3, pg. 50.
- Geo. N. Pegram & wife to Elizabeth Bussey.   Book 3, pg. 52.
- John Gullion & wife to Hiram Hounshell.   Book 3, pg. 53.
- John Williams & wife to Nancy Niswander.   Book 3, pg. 54.
- Wilson A. Parker to Zachariah Cook, trustee.   Book 3, pg. 55.
- B.D. Graves to H.A. Chandler.   Book 3, pg. 56.
- Henry Goar, atty in fact, to J.G. French.   Book 3, pg. 57.
- John T. Lambert agreement with J.G. French.   Book 3, pg. 58.
- Wm. H. Howe, comr. to Elias Harman.   Book 3, pg. 59.
- Clement C. Banks to Don P. Halsey. Bill of sale. Book 3, pg. 60.
- John C. Crockett & wife to William B. Crumpt.   Book 3, pg. 61.
- Report of settlement of William Kitts, guardian for Florence R.   Bogle, infant child of L.D. Bogle, filed for exceptions.
- Report of settlement by Elias Harman and Richard ?? admrs. of ®)3®)1¯Samuel McGuire, decd. Presented and filed for exceptions.
- Report of settlement by H.C. Groseclose, guardian of Wm. R. Tilson, presented and filed for

exceptions. (In margin, withdrwan and void.)
- The following persons appointed Judges of Election at the various precincts. (Continued on page 164)

Page 164- ---- for Sharon precinct, Isaac Hudson, John Deaver (Devor), and Elias Foglesong. For Rocky Gap- Newton Shufflebarger, John A. Davidson and W.W. Compton. For Cameron's precinct- Duncan Cameron, John A. Smith and James T. Moyers. For Mechanicsburg- Wm. E. Hoge, George Wohlford and Hiram Rider. For Seddon- Henry Newberry, Franklin Grayson and William Hederick.
- Commonwealth VS H.A. Chandler. Assault & Battery. Defendant found not guilty and he was acquitted.
- Commonwealth VS Eli Repass. In debt for violation of revenue laws. Defendant is acquitted.
- Commonwealth VS James Tolbert. Violation of revenue laws. Continued

Page 165- April 1873-
- Commonwealth VS Fulton French. Violation of revenue laws.
- Commonwealth VS Sallie & Ellen Jones. Misdemeanor. Case continued.
- Commonwealth VS M.D. Robinett & others. Misdemeanor. Case continued
- Commonwealth VS Emeline Repass. Misdemeanor. Case continued.

Page 166- April 1873-
- Staples & Caldwell VS David King, Jeremiah Baynes and Solomon King. In debt. Plaintiffs to recover from defendant the sum of $50.00 plus interest and costs.
- Commonwealth VS Thomas Woods. Misdemeanor. Jurors were, Elias Repass, A.D. Groseclose, John S.C. Bean, Thomas Haton, Robt. L. Newberry, Geo. Lindamood, John W. Harmen, Wm. Kitts, Jas. M. Corner, J.C. Painter, Joseph Waddle and Samuel Dilman. Defendant found not guilty and was acquitted.
- Commonwealth VS John Johnston. Petit larceny. Summins not having been executed, capias be awarded against the defendant, returnable here July term of court.

Page 167- April 1873-
- Compton, McGinnis & Company VS Henry Dowling. Continued.
- Samuel H. Newberry VS E.G. Booth. Case continued.
- Peter Kinder VS Joseph T. Cooley's admr. Both parties by their attorneys suggested the bankruptcy of Peter Kinder.
- Court adjourned until tomorrow at 9:AM.

Page 168- Tuesday April 8, 1873- Hon. James P. Kelley, Judge.
- Timothy E. Mitchell for benefit of Joseph Wohlford VS R.A. Morton's admr. Plaintiff to recover from defendant $100.00 plus interest and costs. Credits noted.
- Wm. J. Richardson's admrx. VS Eli F. Groseclose. Groseclose says he has paid his debt in full. Case continued.
- On motion of Jezreal Thompson, that the rule against him for failing to appear in the February term of court as a witness for Eli Groseclose, be and is hereby discharged.

33

Page 169- April 1873-
- Margaret Wessendonck has leave of the court to bind her son Charles Wessendonck, aged
11 years to Ida Niedermair until said minor shall have attained the age of 21.
- James Surrett has leave of the court to bind his son Franklin Surrett to Dr. J.M. Lovell until said
minor shall have attained the age of 21.
- Two cases- R.M. Williams for benefit of Justice Hubble VS H.C. Groseclose. In debt. Jurors
were, Elias Repass, J.J. Hager, John S.C. Bean, Thomas Haton, Robt. L. Newberry, Geo.
Lindamood, John W. Harman, Wm. Kitts, Jas. M. Corner, J.C. Painter, Joseph Waddle and
Samuel Dilman. Jury found for the plaintiff the sum of $588.08. Defendant moved to set aside
verdict The court considered.
- Allen Mustard VS Wm. N. Harman. Case continued at cost of Harman.

Page 170- April 1873-
- Verdict is discharged against L.C. Wright for failing to appear in court as witness for
Wm. N. Harman.
- Wm. B. Brooks, assignee of Howard Cole, VS Compton, McGinnis & Co.- H.H. McGinnis has
died. Case continued.
- Kimberly & Morehead VS Compton, McGinnis & Co. In debt. McGinnis is dead. Suit to
proceed against remaining members. Case continued.
- Wm. M. Bishop VS E.F. Harman and Wm. P. Slade. Bishop to recover from Harman & Slade
the sum of $439.00 plus interest & costs.

Page 171- April 1873-
- Cloyd Atkins VS Miles Roland & Raeburn Neel. Unlawful detention. Case continued.
- Rufus Stowers VS S.T. Gibson. Dismissed
- William Stowers VS S.T. Gibson. Dismissed.
- Wm. Groseclose's executors, VS Groseclose & Hanshew. Dismissed.
- Warden Stowers VS Henry Burton. Case dismissed.
- Smith & Harby? VS A. Wessendonck's administrator. Plaintiff to recover from defendant
$20.00, plus interest, but without costs.

Page 172- April 1873-
- J. MOsby Davis, admr. VS John R. Compton. In debt.
- On motion of Compton, Wm. G. Mustard summonsed to appear as witness for Compton, why
he should not be fined for failure to appear.
- Joseph L. Cooley's admr. VS S.I. Patterson. In debt
- Robert C. Green VS William Stuart.
- P.C. Honaker VS G.W. & J.M. Brown.
- John C. Crockett VS John R. Bird. An ejectment.
- Catherine Waddle VS Thos. Shannon & others.
- J.J. Harner's admr. VS John A. Bennett.
- W.J. Shufflebarger VS James Clark. In debt.
- John F. Locke VS Hiram Munsey & others. In debt.
- Isaac P. Lambert, Jr. & others VS Mary Coopers, exor. & others.
{ The forgoing nine cases to be continued. }

- Morgan Wynn VS Compton-McGinnis & Co. Wynn to recover from the defendants the sum of $68.65 plus interest & costs. Credits noted.

Page 173- April 1873-
- C.H. McCormick & bro. VS Wm. N. Harman & J.W. Finley. Void.
- Commonwealth VS Sebastian Pauley. Felony. Pauley acquitted.
- Robert Crockett VS Isaac Kegley. In debt. Noted by court the Isaac Kegley has filed for bankruptcy in the Federal Court. Case continued.
- Marion Robinett VS Isaac Kegley. In debt. Same verdict as above.
- Michael Waddle VS Isaac Kegley. In debt. Same verdict as above.

Page 174-April 1873-
- Michael Waddle VS Isaac Kegley & George Robinett. Case continued.
- J.M. French VS I.K. Price. In debt. Case continued.
- A.C. Waggoner VS F.M. Harman. In debt. Case continued.
- F.M. Brandon VS Melvina Cubine. In debt.

Page 175- April 1873-
- Elias Harman VS John Myers & Wm. N. Harman. Case continued.
- J.H. & J.M. French for benefit of Locke & Thompson, VS Ballard P. Stafford. In debt. Stafford to recover from plaintiffs, the sum of $5.00 plus his costs.
- The following are allowed $1.00 for service as petit jurors: Elias Repass, A.D. Groseclose, John C. Bean, Robert L. Newberry, Thomas Haten, Geo. Lindamood, Samuel Dilman, F.M. Harman, J.C. Painter, Joseph Waddle and John W. Harman.
- Names of same jurors as above with amount paid to them.

Page 176- April 1873-
- Elias Harman VS Treasurer of Bland County. (2 cases)
- A.J. Wyrick VS James McCulley.
- Wm. P. Bogle VS Wm. Devor & others.
- Cloyd Atkins VS D.M. Neel.
- Elias Blankenship VS H.P. Wheeler.
- Wm. B. Foster VS John Wilkenson.
- Elizabeth G. Gibboney, executrix, VS Eli F. Groseclose.
        { The above 7 cases continued.}
- P.G. Repass by his next friend, Joel Repass VS William Hederick. Case dismissed by consent.
- Rees Crabtree, road commissioner for Sharon District, to view route for a new road from Groseclose & Tilson's mill to Walkers Creek & Holston Turnpike. H.H. Tilson, Gordon Havens, John Kinder, and Andrew Hanshew, owners of land through which road will pass.
- Court adjourned till tomorrow morning at 9:O'clock.

Page 177- Wednesday Morning, April 9, 1873. - James P. Kelley, Judge.
- John W. Johnston VS Andrew J. Honaker. In debt. Honaker to recover from Johnston. Case dismissed.
- F.M. Branden VS Melvina Cubine. In debt. Case continued.

35

- Elizabeth G. Gibboney, extrix. of Robt. Gibboney, decd. VS Eli F. Groseclose. Groseclose to recover his costs from Gibboney. Quashed.
- J. Mosby Davis, admr. VS James L. Day & others. In debt.

Page 178-
- Report of settlement of S.H. Newberry, admr. of Thomas Wilkenson, decd. with J.H. Hoge. Filed for exceptions.
- Wm. J. Shufflebarger VS James Clark. In debt. Each party to pay his own costs. Shufflebarger withdraws papers filed.
- Acles Fannon VS H.S. McPherson. Case dismissed. Each party paying own costs.
- F.M. Branden VS Malvina Cubine. In debt. Branden not an inhabitant of this state. Case dismissed until Branden can post bond with the Clerk of this Court.

Page 179- April 1873-
- R.M. Williams VS H.C. Groseclose. In debt
- Rufus M. Williams VS H.C. Groseclose. In debt.
- The following allowed the sum of $1.00 for services as petit jurors. Robt. L. Newberry, J.C. Painter, A.B. Pauley, John R. Bird, S.M. Hamilton, John P. Roach, Elias Harman, James M. Corner, H.G. Davis and Wm. Kitts.
- Louisa Lamb VS Ballard P. Wilson. Breach of marriage contract. Wilson denies Lambs assumption. Case continued.

Page 180- April 1873-
- James M. French, for benefit of Locke & Thompson, VS I.K. Price. In debt. French to recover from Price the sum of $20.00.
- On motion of C.G Crockett, road commissioner of Mechanicsburg district view route for a new road from the house of John C. Crockett to the Walkers Creek & Holston Turnpike at Harvey Nicewanders and make report thereon.

Page 181- April 1873-
- $10.00 allowed Samuel W. Williams, Prosecuting Attorney, certified to the Auditor of Public Accounts.
- William T. Hamilton, Clerk of the County Court, presents claim for $12.50. Examined and allowed.
- Ordered that all cases not otherwise disposed of be continued until next term of Court.

Page 182- OFFICE JUDGEMENTS, April 1873-
- Thomas Shannon for benefit of Hezekiah Harman VS Stephen Lambert. In debt. Plaintiff to recover from Lambert, $50.00 plus interest and costs. Credits noted.
- Thomas Shannon for benefit of Hezekiah Harman VS Uriah Bean. In debt. Bean failed to appear. Plaintiff recovers from Bean, $25.00 plus interest and costs.
- James M. French for benefit of Locke & Thompson VS John M. Cassell. In debt. Plaintiff recovers from Cassell, $100.00 plus interest & costs. credits noted.

Page 183- Office judgements, continued.- James D. Johnston VS Ellen J. Cecil & John Cecil.

In debt. The Cecils did not appear in court. Plaintiff recovers from the Cecils, $50.00 plus interest & costs.
- C.H. McCormick & Bro. VS Wm. N. Harman & J.W. Finley. In debt. Plaintiffs to recover from Harman & Finley, $130.00 plus interest from November 1868 and costs.
- Robert Sayers, executor of Joseph Crockett, deceased, VS Samuel C. Davis. In debt. Davis failed to appear in court. Plaintiff to recover from Davis, $93.50 plus interest from July 21, 1861 & costs.

Page 184- Office judgements, continued.®)1⁻
- Guynn, Oglesby & Co. VS Wm. H.H. Niswander. In debt. Niswander did not appear in court. Plaintiffs to recover from Niswander $32.20, plus interest from May 8, 1869 and costs.
- John C. Crockett VS Harry James. In debt. James did not appear in court. Crockett to recover from James, $72.50 plus interest from February 10, 1872 and costs.
-All cases signed by William T. Hamilton, Clerk.

Page 185- At a monthly term of Court, Monday May 5, 1873 - P.W. Strother, Judge.
- A list of deeds presented and recorded in the Clerk's office, viz-
- Wm. N. Harman to William T. Hamilton, trustee. Book 3, pg. 62.
- Elias Harman with Wm. N. Harman, agreement.   Book 3, pg. 64.
- Hiram Pauley to Addison B. Pauley.   Book 3, pg. 65.
- Hiram Pauley to Louisa V. Roach.   Book 3, pg. 66.
- Margaret T. Crockett to Abraham Wampler.   Book 3, pg. 68.
- Abraham Wampler to Ephraim Wampler.   Book 3, pg. 69.
- Wm. Wynn to Harvey Gross.   Book 3, pg. 71.
- W.W. Harman to Cloyd Adkins.   Book 3, pg. 72.
- Wm. Wilkinson & wife to D.W. Dunn.   Book 3, pg. 73.
- James Bruce to Harman Newberry.   Book 3, pg. 74.
- Dower of Malinda Cooley.   Book 3, pg. 75.
- B.D. Graves to Thomas J. Munsey, trustee.   Book 3, pg. 76.
- Phineas Thruston to Wm. Hounshell, a copy.   Book 3, pg. 77
- Report of settlement by William Kitts, guardian of Florence A. Bogle, infant child of L.D. Bogle, with John H. Hoge, Deputy Commissioner. Confirmed and recorded.
- Report of settlement by Elias Harman and Richard Moore, admrs. of Samuel McGuire, deceased. Confirmed and recorded.
- Report of settlement by Adam Waggoner, guardian of Margaret and Foster Waggoner, children of George E. Waggoner, deceased. Filed for exceptions.
- Report by A.T. Suiter, guardian of infant heirs of James T. Gills. Filed for exceptions.

Page 186- May 5, 1873.
- Report by H.C. Groseclose, gaurdian of Wm. R. Tilson. Filed for exceptions.
- Harman Newberry VS Hezekiah Tickle. This day came the parties and their attorneys and Charles Forbs, a garnishee, who acknowledged a debt to Hezekiah Tickle of $200.00. Ordered that $132.10, of this money be given to Harman Newberry. Forbes to pay interest and costs.
- Elias Harman VS D.W. Dunn, Treasurer. Case continued. (2 cases)

- Wm. P. Bogle & others VS Wm. Deaver & others. Case continued.
- Cloyd Adkins VS Miles Roland et al. Unlawful detainer. Continued.
- Cloyd Adkins VS D.M. Neel. On a motion, a rule is awarded against N.B. Stimoson, a garnishee, who failed to appear. Case continued. until next term of Court.

Page 187- May 5, 1873-
- A.G. Updyke VS James McCulley. Case dismissed.
- F.I. Suiter, deputy fro Eli F. Groseclose, has leave to amend his return on an execution issued from the Clerk's Office, in favor of Jas. R. Witten, , executor of Jas. C. Davidson, for benefit of Wm. H. Hughs, and against B.D. Graves, L.D. Bogle and Newton Waddle.
- John F. LOcke, T.N. Finley and C.H. Forbs appointed judges of the election in the Seddon District of Bland County. To serve until the April term 1874 of this court.
- The Court certifies that Thomas J. Munsey, Gentleman, who wishes to obtain a license to practice as an attorney in the courts of this Commonwealth, has resided in this county for the last preceeding twelve months; that he is a person of honest demeanor and upwards of twenty one years of age.
- John M Neel, makes motion that the Road Commissioners of Rocky Gap District, go on and view the ground and report on expediency of a new road from Pine Grove Church to the top of Rich Mountain.

Page 188- May 5, 1873-
- H.C. Newberry, Road Commissioner for Seddon Township, makes report on proposed new road leading from the Raleigh & Grayson Turnpike down Little Walkers Creek to the Mechanicsburg and Wytheville Turnpike. Ordered that, Samuel Davis, David King, Moses Akers, E.C. Wampler, Wm. Shelly, Mrs. E.W. Collins, James Collins, Abraham Wampler, Miss Margaret Crockett, James Jones, G.W. Hancock, Wm. Hounshell and M.F. Hill, owners of the land through which road will pass, be summonsed here to show cause if any the said road should not be established as proposed.
- John C. Crockett VS Harry James. Henry Dowling, summonsed by Crockett, and on interrogation, there being some uncertainty as to the amount due from Dowling, said Dowling is restrained from paying any of said funds but to hold same subject to the order of the court.
- R. Dodd makes application for a certificate to keep an ordinary and also for Merchant's Liquor license at his residence. Samuel H. Newberry, Franklin Grayson and John W. McGinnis opposed such license. Case continued until tomorrow.

Page 189- Tuesday Morning, May 6, 1873. - P.W. Strother, Judge.
- D.W. Dunn, Treasurer of the County, presented a list of delinquents in the license taxes for the year of 1872 in Rocky Gap Township. A.R. Bogle, assessor in said Township. List examined and corrected and sent to the Auditor of Public Accounts.
- George Wohlford, collector for Mechanicsburg District, presents a list of delinquent tax-payers for Real Estate for the year of 1872. Certified and sent to Auditor of Public Accounts.
- George Wohlford, collector for Mechanicsburg, presents a list of persons delinquent in paying Capitation and Personal Property Tax for the year of 1873. Certified and sent to Auditor of Public Accounts.

Page 190- May 6, 1873-
- D.W. Dunn, Treasurer, presented a list of property in the assessor's land book which is improperly assessed. For year of 1872.
- H.A. Chandler, Collector for Seddon Township, presents list of delinquent Real Estate Taxes in district of P.H.M. Bird, assessor.
- D.W. Dunn, treasurer, presents list of delinquent taxes in district of P.M.H. Bird, for the year of 1872.

Page 191- May 6, 1873-
- Jas. Robinett, Jr., makes motion fer the Road Commissioner to go on and view road leading from a point where the road crosses the branch above the house of James Robinett near the lines of Wm. E. Hoge through the lands of James Robinett and others. The most acceptable route from A.W. Millers to Walkers Creek and Holston Turnpike. Ordered that said road be established.
- Reece Crabtree, Road Commissioner for Sharon Township, appointed to go on and view road from Groseclose & Tilson's Mill to Walkers Creek and Holston Turnpike. There being no objections from land owners, road is ordered to be built.
- D.W. Dunn, treasurer, presented a list of delinquent tax payers in the district of A.R. Bogle, assessor for Rocky Gap .

Page 192- May 6, 1873-
- John R. Johnston, collector for Rocky Gap Township, presents a list of delinquents in capitation and personal property taxes.
- The assessor for Rocky Gap Township, having erroeously assessed the County of Bland with the "Poor House Property" and the said having been returned to the collector of said township, the said property being exempt from taxation. Commonwealth's Attorney moved that the facts be certified to the Auditor of Public Accounts.
- B.Dodd with his attorneys withdrew his application for a certificate to operate an ordinary and for Merchants Liquor License.
- Court is adjourned until next term.

Page 193- June 2, 1873. - P.W. Strother, Judge.
- Following is a list of deeds in the clerks office since last term of court. Admitted to record.
- Elender C. Maxwell to Margaret Waddle.   Book 3, pg. 75.
- Isaac E. French to Wm. T. Hamilton, trustee.   Book 3, pg. 79.
- B.D.Graves to H.A. Chandler, trustee.   Book 3, pg. 80.
- Wm. A. Evans to Ephraim Woodyard, trustee.   Book 3, pg. 81.
- John Mustard to Wm. P. Mustard & others, trustees. Book 3, pg. 82.
- Bankruptcy of Samuel I. Patterson. Assignments.   Book 3 pg. 83.
- Bankruptcy of Samuel C. Davis. Assignments.   Book 3, pg. 84.
- Samuel Emmert to E.G. Booth.   Book 3, pg. 85.
- J.M. French, comm., to Samuel H. Bernard.   Book 3, pg. 88.
- Thompson E. Gregory, with Colby Stowers, his surety, gives bond in sum of $1,000.00 and took oath of office as a Road Commissioner for the Rocky Gap Township.
- James A. Repass, with John R. Compton and John Repass, his surities, posted bond for

$1,000.00, having been elected Supervisor for the Sharon Twonship.
- Colby Stowers, elected Overseer of the Poor, in Rocky Gap Township, with John W. Harman, his security, posts bond of $500.00.

Page 194- June 2, 1873- P.W. Strother, Judge.
- Rees Crabtree, who was elected Road Commissioner for Sharon Township, with H.F. Bruce, his security, posts bond for $1,000.00
- James S. Robinett, who elected Supervisor of Mechanicsburg Township, with J.M. Fanning, Z.T. Weaver & Harvey R. Mustard, his securities, posted bond for $1,000.00.
- F.G. Helvey who was elected Overseer of The Poor for Mechanicsburg Township, with Jas. H. Munsey, his security, posts bond for $500.00.
- H.C. Fanning, who was elected Road Commissioner for Mechanicsburg Township, with J.M. Fanning, his security, posts bond for $2,000.00.
- J.W. Compton, who was elected Township Clerk for Rocky Gap Township, with Thos. H. Kinser, security, posted bond of $2,000.00.

Page 195- June 2, 1873.
- Thomas H. Kinser, who was elected Supervisor for Rocky Gap Township, with J.W. Compton, his security, posts bond for $1,000.00.
- Gordon Wohlford, who was elected Collector for Mechanicsburg, with Harvey R. Mustard, his security, posts bond for $5,000.00.
- T.G. Hudson, who was elected Clerk for Sharon Township, with John Repass, his security, posts bond for $2,000.00.
- Geo. M. Tibbs, wah was elected Assessor for Sharon Township, with Sam'l. H Newberry, his security, posts bond for $2,000.00.

Page 196- June 2, 1873-
- Z.T. Weaver, who was elected Assessor for Mechanicsburg Township, with Harvey R. Mustard and James S. Robinett, his securities, posted bond for $2,000.00.
- J.H. Thompson, who was elected Assessor for Seddon Township, with A.J. Grayson and W.M. Bird, his security, posted bond for $2,000.00
- J.D. Honaker, who was elected Assessor for Rocky Gap Township, with Peter C. Honaker, his security, posts bond for $2,000.00.

Page 197- June 2, 1873-
- James M. Stowers, who was elected Supervisor of Seddon Township, with H.C. Newberry and Eli F. Groseclose, his secuties, posted bond for $1,000.00.
- Samuel W. Williams, who has been appointed and commissioned by the Governor of Virginia, a Notary Public, with Samuel H. Newberry and George Wohlford, his securities, posts bond for $500.00.
- Allen Mustard, who was elected Justice of the Peace for Mechanicsburg Township, takes oath of office as prescribed by law.
- Paul James elected Justice of the Peace for Seddon Township, takes oath of office as prescribed by law.

- Jacob Wagner elected Justice of the Peace for Seddon Township. Takes oath of office as prescribed by law.
- P.C. Honaker elected Justice of the Peace for Rocky Gap Township, takes oath of office as prescribed by law.

Page 198- June 2, 1873-
- On motion of A.T. Suiter, ordered that H.C. Newberry, Road Commissioner for Seddon Township, to view and find best route for a road leading from a fence at Hiram Robinett's house through the said Robinett's, Lidda Waddle and Alex Suiter and land of J. Meek on Round Mountain to the Tazewell line in the low gap east of Jno. Sprakers.
- Geo. W. Kinser presents an account against the County for $3.00. Allowed and certified to the board of Sharon Township Supervisors.
- Hezekiah Harman, best friend of Wm. R. Tilson, infant son of G.D. Tilson, deceased, files exceptions to the report of John H. Hoge, Deputy Commissioner of this County, of a settlement made by him with H.C. Groseclose, guardian of said Wm. R. Tilson. Exceptions, sustained and said report to be recommitted to Hoge for a new settlement. Hoge is directed to use regular form adopted by Chancery.
- B. Dodd applies for permission to keep a hotel in Town of Seddon. Court determines that Dodd's house is a suitable place and Dodd a respectable person to have such an endeavor.

Page 199- June 2, 1873-
- The Court certifies Acles Fannon to have a hotel at his residence in Seddon Township.
- Court relieves Joseph Waddle from working on the Public Roads.
- Peter C. Honaker, elected Justice of The Peace for Rocky Gap Township, takes oath of office.

Page 200- June 2, 1873-
- George W. Fanning says he does no owe $9.07 taxes erroneously charged to him on a tract of land on Kimberling Creek, is exonerated from said tax, if already paid to be refunded.
- Alex Umbarger exonerated from paying tax erroneously charged to him by G.W. Tibbs, assessor. If already paid, to be refunded.

Page 201- June 2, 1873-
- Sally Jones exonerated from paying tax erroneously charged to her by A.A. Ashworth, assessor of Mechanicsburg Township.

Page 202- June 2, 1873-
- H.C. Newberry, to report on the expediency of building a new road from Raliegh & Grayson Turnpike down Walkers Little Creek to Mechanicsburg and the Wytheville Turnpike. Ordered that the road be established.
- Thomas J. Muncy, has leave to practice Law in Bland County.
- D.W. Dunn, Treasurer of Bland County, presents a list of delinquent tax payers of Licenses for the year of 1872 in the Sharon Township.
- John C. Stowers presents a list of delinquents in the capitation and property taxes in Sharon Township. G.M. Tibbs, assessor.

Page 203- June 2, 1873-
- D.W. Dunn, treasurer of the County, presents a list of delinquent tax payers of real estate in Sharon Township for the year of 1872. G.M. Tibbs, assessor.
- Hiram Peery, assignee of Thos. Cook VS John R. Compton. Compton failed to appear in court. Peery to recover from Compton, $242.48 and costs.
- D.W. Dunn VS John R. Johnston & sureties. Motion for county levy.
Ordered that this case be dismissed.
- Cloyd Adkins VS D.M. Neel.

Page 204- June 2, 1873.
- Elias Harman VS Treasurer of Bland County. Notice.
- Cloyd Adkins VS Miles Roland et al. Unlawful detainer.
- Wm. P. Bogle VS Wm. Deaver et al.
- Elias Blankenship VS H.P. Wheeler. Notice.
- Wm. B. Foster VS Wilkinson.
- John C. Crockett VS Harry James.
(Ordered that the forgoing cases be continued.)
- Cloyd Adkins VS D.M. Neel. Case continued.
- Robt. C. Green, G.H. Morgan, Geo. Wohlford, Wm. P. Mustard and Wm. E. Hoge, oppose Nye Bogle's motion to obtain a certificate to obtain a liquor license to sell ardent spirits away from the premises in the Town of Mechanicsburg. Motion is continued to next term of court.
- On vacation, June 2, 1873. This day Isaac J. Davis, who was elected Township Clerk for Mechanicsburg, appeared and took the oath of office and posted bond with Geo. Wohlford, John R. Compton, A. Davis and Allen Mustard, his securities, posted bond for $2,000.00. Qualification to be entered as a vacation order.

Page 205- In vacation, June 3, 1873.
- John F. Locke who was elected Justice of the Peace for Seddon Township, took the oath of office as prescribed by law. P.W. Strother, Judge.

Page 206- July 7, 1873- P.W. Strother, Judge.
- A list of deeds recorded since last term of Court:.
- H.G. Thompson to John F. Locke, trustee.   Book 3, pg. 89.
- R.S. Hicks & wife to P.R. Hicks.   Book 3, pg. 90.
- Wm. Mustard to J.J. & S.P. Mustard.   Book 3, pg. 91.
- Wm. N. Harman to W.J. Shufflebarger.   Book 3, pg. 92.
- Wm. Mustard, Sr. to H.R. Mustard & others.   Book 3, pg. 93.
- John Compton & wife to John Baugh.   Book 3, pg. 94.
- Wm. Terry to James M. French, power of attorney.   Book 3, pg. 96.
- Aaron McDonald to Jmaes M. French.   Book 3, pg. 95.
- Wm. H. Boling to Sam'l H. Newberry.   Book 3, pg. 95.
- Allen T. Newberry & others to H. Newberry.   Book 3, pg. 95.
- Corla? Spangler to Michael Waddle.   Book 3, pg. 98.
- R. Grayson & wife to John C. Crockett.   Book 3, pg. 99.
- A report of settlement of Adam Waggoner, guardian of Margaret and Foster Wagner,

children of George Waggoner, deceased, with J.H. Hoge, Deputy Commissioner. Filed for exceptions, and recorded.

- A report of settlement of A.T. Suiter, guardian of infant heirs of Jas. T. Gills, with J.H. Hoge, Deputy Commissioner of accounts. Filed for exceptions and recorded.

- Elias Foglesong, appointed Overseer of the Poor for Sharon Township, with Joseph Foglesong, his security posted bond for $500.00 and took the oath of office.

Page 207- July 7, 1873-

- Rees Crabtree is allowed the sum of $6.00 for services rendered as Road Commissioner for Sharon Township.

- Elias Harman VS Treasurer of Bland County. Case dismissed.

- Commonwealth VS James Tolbert. Violation of the Revenue Law. Tolbert is acquitted.

- Commonwealth VS Emeline Repass. Misdemeanor. Repass is acquitted.

- Allen Mustard VS Wm. N. Harman. Settled by mutual agreement.

Page 208- July 7, 1873.-

- Franklin Grayson & others VS A. Fannon. On a notice to revoke hotel license. Order is quashed. Fannon to recover from Grayson his costs.

- Wm. P. Bogle VS Wm. Devor's estate. F.I. Suiter, garnishee, summonsed to court to answer the plaintiff's question of whether or not he owes anything to Devor. Suiter says he is indebted to F.F. Repass in an amount greater than the amount which Bogle asks for. Case continued.

- John Repass VS H.G. Thompson. On a notice. Thompson to recover from Repass his costs. Notice is quashed.

- Cloyd Adkins VS D.M. Neel.

- Wm. B. Foster VS John Wilkinson.

- John C. Crockett VS Harry JAmes.

- Jas. M. Fanning, admr. VS Wm. N. Harman.

- Reuben Hughes VS Wm. N. Harman.

- Aaron Criss? & son VS Wm. N. Harman.

    (Ordered that the above 6 cases be continued.)

Page 209- July 7, 1873-

- James M. French VS N.B. Dodson & W.J. Hubble. Case continued.

- James Tolbert made motion that Dr. J.M. Lovell and Dr. L.J. Miller, be appointed to examine Wm. F. Tolbert, a lunatic, now confined in the Bland jail and report to the court tomorrow morning.

- Grand Jury members: H.C. Groseclose, Andrew Hanshew, Joshua Thompson, Hiram Davis, Wm. M. Bird, Jas. C. Painter, Thos. Wohlford, Daniel Muirhead, I.K. Price, Henry Mustard, Addison Davis, Thos. Franklin, Jno. A. Davidson and Thos. F. Walker.

- Overseer of the Poor VS H.J. Kitts & others. Motion on a bastardy bond. Ordered that motion be docketed and continued.

- T.E. Gregory, Road Commissioner for Rocky Gap Township, presented claim against the said township for $8.00, which was allowed.

- Thos. F. Walker presents a claim against Rocky Gap Township for $11.00, for surveying

road. Allowed and ordered certified to the Township board.
- Ordered that Court be adjourned until tomorrow at 9:o'clock AM.

Page 210- Tuesday morning, July 8, 1873.
- Harman Newberry VS Hezekiah Tickle. On motion of Gordon Tickle, defendant has leave to file his petition. Granted.
- James M. French VS N.B. Dodson & W.J. Hubble. Defendants failed to appear in court. French to recover from defendants.
- James Tolbert makes motion to remove his son, Wm. F. Tolbert, a lunatic, from the County Jail. After hearing evidence from Dr. L.J. Miller and Dr. J.M. Lovell, it was decided that the jail was no suitable place for him and that James Tolbert is willing and able to care for him. Ordered that the jailor turn over said lunatic to James Tolbert.

Page 211- July 8, 1873-
- Commonwealth VS Sallie & Ellen Jones. On an indictment for keeping a house of ill fame. Came the jury consisting of- Wm. B. Ashworth, Frank Kitts, B.D. Graves, Wm. Crutchfield, R.L. Newberry, J.H. Moyers, Harvey Gross, A.B. Brown, Jas. H. Bruce, Jas. E. Maxwell, A.B. Pauley and W.W. Ashworth. Jury rendered a guilty verdict, fining defendants $18.75, each.
- The Grand Jury adjourned yesterday returned today. Reported that Thomas Franklin was unable to attend. Samuel H. Newberry appointed in his place. Jury reported that the case of Commonwealth VS Sophia Dillow, indicted on a felony, was not a true bill.
- In case of Sophia Dillow, confined in the County Jail on a felony charge, the grand jury having returned the indictment, not a truebill, jailer is directed to release her from jail.
- Jos. T. Cooley's admr. VS S. I. Patterson. In debt.
- Peter Kinder VS T. Cooley's admr.
- Samuel H. Newberry VS E.G. Booth.

Page 212- July 8, 1873-
- Peter C. Honaker VS G.W. & J.M. Brown. Case continued.
- J.J. Harner's admr. VS John A. Bennett. Case continued.
- Isaac P. Lambert, Jr. & others VS Mary Cooper's admr. Case continued.
- Zachariah Cook VS William Hedrick. Case of slander. Case dismissed by consent of parties.
- Robert Crockett VS Isaac Kegley. In debt. Kegley has filed his petition in bankruptcy court. Crockett has leave to file again.
- Marion Robinett VS Isaac Kegley. In debt. Same verdict as above.
Michael Waddle VS Isaac Kegley. In debt. Same verdict as above.

Page 213- July 8, 1873-
- Sallie and Ellen Jones made motion to set aside the verdict against them and grant them a new trial.
- Ordered that the court stand adjourned until tomorrow morning at 9 O'clock AM.

Page 214- July 9, 1873- P.W. Strother, Judge.
- L.D. Bogle appointed Road Commissioner to fill a vacancy. With H.C. Newberry & W.N..

44

Mustard, his securities, posts bond in the amount of $500.00.
- The Grand Jury found the following indictments:
- Commonwealth VS Winton Jackson. Misdemeanor.
- Commonwealth VS S.W. Williams. Unlawful gaming.
- Commonwealth VS Henry Dowling, Nye Bogle, B. Dodd, and H. Chandler. Indicted for unlawful gaming. A true bill.
- Commonwealth VS B.Dodd. Misdemeanor.
- Commonwealth VS Hiram Chandler, H.B. Estill, and Z.T. Weaver. Indicted for unlawful gaming. A true bill.
- Commonwealth VS S.R. Crockett, T.S. Blair, John G. Crockett, and Z.T Weaver. Unlawful gaming. A true bill.
- Commonwealth VS Joseph Stras, B. Dodd, R.S. Hoge. Misdemeanor.
- Commonwealth VS Z.T. Weaver, Hiram Chandler, H.B. Estill, D.W. Dunn, and Nye Bogle. Misdemeanor.
- Commonwealth VS B. Dodd, Z.T. Weaver, D.W. Dunn and Nye Bogle. An indictment for unlawful gaming.
- Commonwealth VS B. Dodd. Midemeanor.
- Commonwealth VS B.Dodd. Allowing unlawful gaming at his ordinary.
- Commonwealth VS Joseph Sublett. Larceny. A true bill.

Page 215- July 9, 1873.
- Overseers of The Poor VS William Wilkinson and George W. Suiter. Motion on Bastardy. Defendants did not appear in Court. Overseers to recover from the defendants the sum of $15.00 plus interest due on August 1, 1872 from their bonds executed March 12, 1868, for the maintenance of a bastard child of Polly Lambert.
- R.M. Williams VS H.C. Groseclose. Withdrawn. (2 cases)
- Elias Blankenship VS H.P. Wheeler. Wheeler moves to quash. Motion is Considered.
- The following are allowed $1.00 for ther services as Grand Juroras- Wm. Stowers, H.C. Groseclose, Andrew Hanshew, Joshua Thompson, Hiram Davis, Wm. M.Bird, Jas. C. Painter, Thos. Wohlford, Daniel Morehead, I.K. Price, Henry Mustard, Addison DAvis, Geo. W. Brown, Thos. Franklin, Jno. A. Davidson, S.H. Newberry and Thos. F. Walker.

Page 216- Robert C. Green & others VS Nye Bogle. On application to obtain a liquor license. Case dismissed at cost of Nye Bogle.
- Franklin Grayson & others VS B. Dodd. On a notice to revoke hotel license. Court, after hearing evidence took time to consider.
- Ordered that a rule be issued agaimst Thomas Franklin to show cause why he should not be fined for failing to appear for jury duty.
- Court stands adjourned until tomorrow morning at 9:0'clock AM.

Page 217- Thursday, July 10, 1873.
- Ida Neidermaire applies for certificate to obtain a license to keep a house of entertainment at her home at Booth's Springs. Granted.
- K.C. Thornton, jailer, presents claim for $18.00. Allowed.
- Dr. J.M. Lovell presents claim for $26.00. Allowed.

- H.C. Newberry makes motion for L.D. Bogle, Road Commissioner for Seddon Township, to examine the road leading from said Newberry's gates to R.L. Newberry's Mill, particularly where the road strikes the line at Newberry's gate between the lands of G.W.K. Green. W.N. Mustard's land mentioned.
- R.M. Williams VS H.C. Groseclose. In debt. (2 cases)

Page 218- July 10, 1873-
- Peter C. Honaker VS Geo. W. & J.M. Brown. Both parties agree that W.W. Compton and E.A. Davis be umpires and settle their differences. Court agrees.
- John R. Compton and John W. McGinnis, surviving partner VS Henry Dowling. Jury heard evidence and adjourned until tomorrow.
- Cloyd Adkins VS Miles Roland & Raiborn Neel. Unlawful detainer. Miles Roland had failed to plea at an earlier hearing and was pleaded "not guilty" by the court. Cloyd Adkins accused Roland & Neel of holding possession of his lands. Surveyor ordered to go on lands and set lines & boundaries.

Page 219- July 10, 1873-
- John C. Crockett VS John R. Bird. Ejectment. County surveyor to go on land and enlarge survey and amend his report.
- H.C. Newberry, late Road Commissioner for Seddon Township, ordered to turn in his books, papers, money in his possession to the Township Board of Seddon.
- Court adjourned until tomorrow morning at 9:o"clock AM.

Page 220- Friday morning July 11, 1873-
- John R. Compton & John W. McGinnis, surviving partner, VS Henry Dowling. Jury found in favor of the defendant the sum of $21.53 being the amount of the defendants set-offs over and above the plaintiffs demands.
- F.I. Suiter, deputy for Eli Groseclose, makes claim for $5.90. Allowed and certified to the auditor for payment.
- Wm. J. Richardson VS Eli F. Groseclose. In debt. Case continued.
- R.M. Williams VS H.C. Groseclose. (2 cases) Continued.

Page 221 and page 222 missing from book.

Page 223- July 11, 1873.
- Eli F. Groseclose VS A.C. Wagner. Verdict for the defendant for $86.29. plus interest. Each party to pay their own costs.
- John F. Locke VS Hiram Munsey. In debt. Case continued.
- James F. Hoge, surviving partner of himself and D.H. Hoge, decd. VS W. N. Harman. In debt. Defendant and plaintiff agree that plaintiff have judgement against the defendant for $75.00 with interest and costs except for Attorney's fees.

Page 224- July 11, 1873-
- Wilson Burns & Co. VS G.H. Morgan. Dismissed by agreement.
- J.W. Compton VS John R. Compton. Dismissed by agreement.

- Wm. P. Davis VS John R. Compton & J.W. McGinnis & Co. surviving partners. In debt. Defendants have leave to file a special plea and the plaintiffs likewise. The cause is continued.

Page 225- July 11, 1873-
- Wm. C. Williams VS Wm. N. Harman. On warrant. Continued.
- K.C. Thornton, jailor, presents claim for $38.00, for care of Wm.F. Tolbert, a lunatic. Certified to auditors.
- W.B. Brooks, assignee, VS John R. Compton. In debt. Continued.
- Kimberley & Morehead VS John R. Compton. In debt. Continued.
- K. Mosby DAvis VS John R. Compton. In debt. Continued.
- John R. Compton VS John R. Bird. In debt. Continued.
- Elias Harman VS John Moyers & others. In debt. Continued.
- Michael Waddle VS Isaac Kegley & Geo. Robinett. Isaac Kegley has filed for bankruptcy. Case continued as to defendant Robinett.
- A.C. Waggoner VS F.M. Harman. In debt. Jurors were: J.H. Moyers, B.D. Graves, J.M. Neel, R.L. Newberry, J.W. Finley, E.W. Eagle, James McCuley, Wm. Kitts, J.S. French, W.F. Thornton, J.P. Roach and C.H. Forbs. Jury heard evidence and adjourned until tomorrow at 7:0'clock AM. (Part on page 226)

Page 226- July 11, 1873-
- F.M. Branden VS Melvina Cubine. In debt. Further hearing adjourned. until tomorrow.
- H.C. Newberry, Road Commissioner for Seddon Township, whose term of office has expired, has leave to turn in his money, books, papers, etc. to Board of Seddon Township.
- Court adjourned until tomorrow at 7:0'clock AM.

Page 227- Saturday, July 12, 1873-
- A.C. Waggoner for Adam Waggoner VS F.M. Harman. In debt. Verdict for the plaintiff for $188.33. Credits noted.
- Names of jurors allowed $1.00 each for services on petit jury. Wm. B. Ashworth, Frank Kitts, B.D. Graves, Wm. Crutchfiels, R.L. New- berry, J.H. Moyers, Harvey Gross, A.B. Brown, Jas. H. Bruce, Jas. E. Maxwell, A.B. Pauley and W.W. Ashworth.

Page 228- July 12, 1873-
- Same jurors as listed above with amounts of money paid to each. (Over $1.00)
- Armstead Cloud VS Henry Newberry. Verdict for Cloud in the sum of $68.40, the amount of damages plus interest and costs. (verdict on page 230)

Page 229- July 12, 1873-
- F.M. Branden for Richard M. Hopper VS Melvina Cubine. In debt. Plaintiff to recover from defendant the sum of $124.00 plus interest and costs. Exceptions noted.
- Elias Blankenship & others VS H.P. Wheeler. Cause considered from last Wednesday, and the motion was quashed. Wheeler to recover from Blankenship, his costs.
- Commonwealth at the relation of Eli F. Groseclose VS A.C. Waggoner & surities. In debt. Case continued.

- Commonwealth VS Sallie & Ellen Jones. Misdemeanor. Court sustained the motion of the defendants to have former verdict set aside. New trial granted.
- This day was presented an agreement by Wm. Hederick and Zachariah Cook dated April 9, 1873 which was proved by J.M. French and S.W. Williams, witnesses thereto ordered to be recorded.

Page 230- July 12, 1873-
- Henry Newberry took exception to the ruling of the court. Said exceptions signed sealed and ordered made part of the record.
- Louisa Lamb VS Ballard P. Wilson. Case continued.
- Court adjourned until first day of next term. P.W. Strother.

Page 231- OFFICE JUDGEMENTS, July 12, 1873.
- J.M. Brower & Bro. VS John R. Compton & John W. McGinnis, surviving partners. In debt. Defendants failed to appear in court. Plaintiffs to recover the sum of $164.00. Credits noted.
- I.E. Chapman VS S.T. Gibson. In debt. Gibson did not appear. Verdict for Chapman in amount of $20.11.
- Crockett & Blair for benefit of R.C. Kent VS Wm. E. Neel & A.J. Honaker. In debt. Defendants did not appear. Verdict for plaintiffs.

Page 232- July 12, 1873- OFFICE JUDGEMENTS, Continued-
- Crockett & Blair for benefit of R.C. Kent VS Z.T. Weaver. In debt. Weaver did not appear. Verdict for plaintiffs.
- Wm. H. Howe VS James H. Mustard. In debt. Mustard did not appear. Verdict for Howe in amount of $21.52 plus interest & costs.
    - Signed by William T. Hamilton, Clerk

Page 233-Monthly Term of Court- August 4, 1873- P.W. Strother, Judge.
- List of deeds recorded at Courthouse since last term of Court.
- Wm. G. Mustard to Harman Newberry.   Book 3, pg. 101
- Jacob Waggoner & wife to Joseph Kitts.   Book 3, pg. 102.
- G.N. Pegram & wife to Joseph A. Fanning.   Book 3, pg. 104.
- William Hederick agreement with Zachariah Cook. Book 3, pg. 105.
- John Fanning makes motion that Road Commissioners of Mechanicsburg Township view road leading from or near house of William Helvey down south side of Kimberling Creek through the lands of Wn.N. Harman, J.W. Finley and I.K. Price near a point near the house of I.K. Price and report to the Court the expediency of such a road.
- Wm.P. Bogle VS Wm. Deavor.
- Cloyd Adkins VS D.M. Neel.
- Wm. B. Foster VS John Wilkinson.
- Harman Newberry VS Hezekiah Tickle.
- John C. Crockett VS Harry James.
- James M. Fanning, admr. VS Wm.N. Harman.
- Reuben Hughes VS Wm. N. Harman.
- Aaron Criss & Son VS Wm. N. Harman.
- W.C. Williams VS Wm. N. Harman.

- Overseers Of Poor VS B.P. Wilson. Case of Bastardy.
- Franklin Grayson & others VS Acles Fannen.
(The above eleven cases to be continued.)

Page 234-August 4, 1873-
- Franklin Grayson & others VS B. Dodd. On motion to revoke Hotel license. Court found not enough evidence to revoke license. Dodd to recover from Grayson his costs in this endeavor.
- L.D. Bogle, having been appointed Road Commissioner for Seddon Township, takes oath of office.
- Court adjourned until first day of next term. P.W. Strother, Judge.

Page 235- In Clerk's Office of Bland County, August 2, 1873.
- Jas. L. Cooley's admr. VS S.I. Patterson. In debt.
- Peter Kinder VS Jas. Collet's admr.
- Samuel H. Newberry VS E.G. Booth.
- Robt. C. Green VS William Stuart.
- Peter C. Honaker VS Geo. W. & J.M. Brown.
- W.J. Richardson VS Eli F. Groseclose. In debt.
- R.M. Williams VS H.C. Groseclose. In debt.
- Allen Mustard VS Wm. N. Harman.
- W.B. Brooks, assignee, VS Compton, McGinnis & Co. In debt.
- John C. Crockett VS John R. Bird. Ejectment.
- J.J. Harner's admr. VS John A. Bennett.
- Kimberly & Morehead VS Compton McGinnis & Co. In debt.
- J.Mosby Davis VS John R. Compton. In debt.
- John R. Compton VS John R. Bird. In debt.
- John F. Locke, exor. VS Hiram Munsey estate. In debt.
- Issac P. Lambert, Jr. & others VS Mary Cooper's exors.
- Louisa Lamb VS Ballard P. Wilson.
- Robert Crockett VS Isaac Kegley. In debt.
- Marion Robinett VS Isaac Kegley. In debt.
- Michael Waddle VS Isaac Kegley. In debt.
- Michael Waddle VS Isaac Kegley & Geo. Robinett. In debt.
- Elias Harman VS John Meyers. Covenent.
- Wm. P. Davis VS Compton McGinnis & Co.
- Wm. P. Davis VS Compton McGinnis & Co. In debt
[In compliance with the 6th section of an act of the General
- Assembly of Virginia "In force April 2, 1873" entitled "An act to regulate and define the jurisdiction of the County and Circuit Courts", & all the foregoing causes together (with) the papers belonging to same are removed to the Circuit Court of Bland County, there to be finally tried and determined.

Page 236- September 1, 1873- P.W. Strother, Judge.
- List of deeds presented and recorded since the last term of Court-
- 1- Anna Steel to Daniel R. Steel.   Book 3, pg. 106.

- 2- Daniel R. Steel to R. Grayson.   Book 3, pg. 107.
- 3- Henry Lambert & wife to SW VA Mining.   Book 3, pg. 108.
- 4- Franklin Grayson & wife to same.   Book 3, pg. 110.
- 5- F.M. Harman & wife to same.   Book 3, pg. 112.
- 6- Isaac HUdson to same.   Book 3, pg. 114.
- 7- Charles J. Hudson to same.   Book 3, pg. 115.
- 8- James Lambert & wife to same.   Book 3, pg. 117.
- 9- Daniel Waddle & wife to same.   Book 3, pg. 119.
- 10-Samuel I. Patterson & wife to same   Book 3, pg. 121.
- Ordered that L.D. Bogle, Road Commissioner for Seddon Township go on and report the expediency of making changes in the road from a gate at H.C. Newberry's to R.L. Newberry's Mill. H.C. Newberry and G.W.K. Green owners of land.

Page 237- September 1, 1873.
- Reuben Hughes VS Wm. N. Harman. George Fanning, garnishee, failed to appear in court. Hughs makes motion for a rule awarded him against Fanning for contempt of Court. Continued until next term of court.
- There was no opposition to a motion made by A.W. Miller, for establishing a new road from H.C. Fanning's land, changing from a wagon road to a road 4 feet wide and the same be sertified to the Township Board of Mechanicsburg.
- James M. Fanning, Adme. VS Wm. N. Harman. A rule is awarded to Harman against George Fanning who was summonsed to appear and did not. Show cause why George Fanning should not be fined fro contempt of Court. Returnable here next term of Court.
- Aaron Criss(Crisp)? VS Wm. N. Harman. Same rule as in above suit.

Page 238- September 1, 1873.
- It appearing to the Court that due notice of a motion by Harman Newberry, has been posted on the front door of the courthouse for the last two terms of Court. Due notice given to Sarah Groseclose, Henry Foglesong, Jonus Umbarger, John S. McNutt, John Kincel, A.W. Shewey, Henry Lambert, Wm.P. Cecil, Joel Spangler and John Cassell, the owners of the lands adjoining the lands of Harman Newberry. Motion to make plat showing whether ot not owners will be harmed by said new road and present it to the court.
- It appearing the Wm. F. Tolbert, a lunatic, has been refused entry to any of the Asylums, ordered that James Tolbert be paid the sum of $1.50 per day from July 9, 1873, for maintaining the said Wm. Tolbert. Now due the sum of $76.50 for 51 days. Certified to the Auditor of Public Accounts.
- Wm. P. Bogle VS F.F. Repass & others.
- Cloyd Adkins VS D.M. Neel.
- Wm. B. Foster VS John Wilkenson.
- Harman Newbeery VS Hezekiah Tickle.
- John C. Crockett VS Harry James.
- W.C. Williams VS W.N. Harman. (Warrant)
- Overseers of Poor VS Jacob Waggoner. Bastardy.
- Ordered that the foregoing 7 cases be continued.

- Louisa Lamb VS Ballard P. Wilson. A warrant on Bastardy. Case dismissed by consent of both parties.

Page 239- September 1, 1873.
- Franklin Grayson & others VS A. Fannon. On motion to revoke Hotel license. Case dismissed on motion by plaintiffs.
- In the case of the infant child of Sophia Dillow, found dead. John F. Locke, Justice of the Peace acting as coroner. The following were jurors at the inquisition- J.W. Kitts, Henry Dowling, John A. Bennett,
Randolph Hall, Lewis Hall, J.H. Myers, G.W. Deaver, Wm.W. Hicks, Dock Thomas, A.N. Thompson, and J.N. Fannon. The following were witnesses, Dr. J.M. Levell, Margarett Chandler, Hannah Chandler, Ellen Jones, J.H. Hoge, and Sallie Jones. Amounts paid to them is after their names.
- John F. Locke, a Justice of the Peace and acting Coroner in the case of an infant found dead in the town of Seddon on March 28, 1873, certifies names of jurors who are to be paid $1.00 each for their services. C.H.C. Fulkerson, Henry Dowling, J.B. Thompson, Nye Bogle, J.N. Fannon, Gregg Ewald, Harman Leady, Wm. M. Bird, Isaac Kegley, E.A. Mills and J.H. Moyers.
- Hiram Rider appointed Registrar for Mechanicsburg precinct in room of A.J. Nye. Took the oath of office.
- Court adjourned until first day of next term.

Page 240- This is a blank page.

Page 241- November 3, 1873- Philip W. Strother, Judge.
- Following is a list of deeds recorded in the Clerk's Office since last term of Court-
- 1- Berry Blankenship to G.C. Thorn.   Book 3, pg. 122.
- 2- R.A. Richardson to D.O. McNiel.   Book 3, pg. 123.
- 3- Robert Doake to Jas. W. Doake.   Book 3, pg. 124.
- 4- R.S. Hoge, Commr. to S.W. Williams.   Book 3, pg. 125.
- 5- Geo.W.Martin & others to Geo.A. Kidd & others. Book 3, pg. 126.
- 6- Jas. H. Muncy to Wm. B. Ashworth & others.   Book 3, pg. 128.
- 7- Zachariah Cook to A.J. & Thomas Neel.   Book 3, pg. 129.
- 8- Zachariah Cook to Frederick Cook.   Book 3, pg. 131.
- 9- Malinda Cooley to M. Sanders.   Book 3, pg. 133.
- 10-R. Grayson to J.M. Hicks.   Book 3, pg. 132.
- 11-Robert Dillow to Wm. Dillow. (POA)   Book 3, pg. 134.
- 12-Robert Dillow, by & to A.A.Ashworth.   Book 3, pg. 135.
- 13-Wm.P. Hornbarger to George Walters.   Book 3, pg. 136.
- 14-B.S. Walker,(Bankrupt, assignment)   Book 3, pg. 138.
- 15-Phineas Thurston to Hiram Stinson.   Book 3, pg. 139.
- 16-John Bogle & wife to Hiram Stinson.   Book 3, pg. 140.
- A report of Joel Spangler, guardian of Maggie J. Hudson, John H. Hoge, Deputy Commissioner. Filed for exceptions.
- A report of a settlement made by George W. Brown, Trustee, presented and filed fro exceptions.

51

- Margaret Wilson has been dead for more than 3 months, and no one having having applied for letters of administration, Samuel Dilman makes motion that the estate be turned over to the Sheriff.

Page 242- November 3, 1873.
- A report of settlement by James Robinett, admr for George Melvin, deceased, with J.H. Hoge, deputy Commissioner. Filed for exceptions.
- Due to vacancies in some of the voting places in the county, the following are appointed- Isaac Kegley as judge of Election in Seddon Precinct in place of Franklin Grayson who failed to serve at last election; A.D. Lambert to be Judge at Rocky Gap Precinct in place of W.W. Compton who failed to serve as such in the last election; Abram Frye to be Judge of the Election for Sharon Precinct in place of Elias Foglesong who failed to serve in the last Election.
- H.C. Fanning, Road Commissioner, viewed the route for a new road from the house of W.B. Helvey through the lands of Wm. N. Harman and J.W. Finley to a point near the house of I.K. Price, and reported to the Court. Ordered that the land owners show cause why road should or should not be built.
- George Wohlford, Collector for Mechanicsburg Township, presents clain against the Commonwealth for $30.00. Examuned and allowed.

Page 243- November 3, 1873.
- On motion of Mrs. Julia Tolbert, wife of Wm. F. Tolbert who has been adjudged a lunatic, John H. Hoge is appointed a committee to take charge of the estate of said lunatic. Hoge with A.A. Ashworth his security enters bond of $500.00.
- John R. Johnston renders his resignation in writing, as Collector for Rocky Gap Township. Accepted and Johnston released.
- Wm. P. Eakens, having shown satisfactory evidence that he is an ordained minister in the Methodist Episcopla Church South, on his motion is authorized to celebrate the rites of matrimony in Bland County, and with J.M. French, his security posts bond for &1,500.00.
- John C. Crockett VS Alex Havens. Unlawful detainer. Havens has left the property mentioned and case is dismissed.
- Wm. B. Foster VS John Wilkinson. Case dismissed.

Page 244- November 3, 1873.
- Wm. P. Bogle VS F.F. Repass.
- Cloyd Adkins VS D.M. Neel.
- Harman Newberry VS Hezekiah Tickle.
- John C. Crockett VS HArry James.
- J.M. Fanning, Admr., VS Wm. N. Harman.
- Aaron Crisp(Criss) VS Wm. N. Harman.
- Reuben Hughes VS Wm. N. Harman.
- W.C. Williams VS Wm. N. Harman. (Warrant)
- Overseers of Poor VS Jacob Waggoner. Bastardy.
- Wm.N. Harman VS W.C. Williams. (Warrant)
- Peter C. Honaker VS A.J. Keeling. Unlawful detainer.
- School District # 4 VS Prudence Robinett. Unlawful detainer.

- Ordered that the 12 foregoing cases be continued.
- H.C. Fanning, Road Commissioner for Mechanicsburg Township, reports on route for a new road leading from the house of John C. Crockett to the Walkers Creek and Holston Turnpike near the house of Harvey Nicewander. Ordered that the same be established as a public road.
- Case continued upon the application to change the road from near H.C. Newberry's to R.L. Newberry's Mill which came upon the report of L.D. Bogle, Road Commissioner.

Page 245- November 3, 1873.
- Joshua B.Thompson who was at last September term of Court appointed and qualified as guardian for Mary Jane, James Henry and Lucy McCoy, No order having been entered in regard thereto it is ordered that the same be entered. This day Mary Jane McCoy, uder 21 and over 14, infant of Newton McCoy, selected Joshua B. Thompson as her guardian. He is also appointed guardian of James Henry McCoy and Lucy McCoy, children of the said Newton McCoy, under the age of 14.
- Ordered that the Court adjourn until the first day of next term.

Page 246- December 1, 1873- P.W. Strother, Judge.
- List of deeds recorded in Clerk's Office since last term of Court.
- 1- Russell Patton & wife to Sam'l. H. Bernard.   Book 3, pg. 141.
- 2- E.G. Booth with Wm. Kelsay. (An agreement)   Book 3, pg. 142.
- 3- J.N. Tickle & wife to Jas. H. Muncy.   Book 3, pg. 144.
- 4- Cenna Devor & others to Ephraim Waddle.   Book 3, pg. 145.
- A report of a settlement by Joel H. Spangler, guardian of M.J. Hudson, with J.H. Hoge, Deputy Commissioner of Accounts. Filed at former term for exceptions and none being taken, same is confirmed and ordered to be recorded.
- A report of settlement by George W. Brown, trustee for Geo. W. Crump, decd. is confirmed and ordered to be recorded.
- Settlement made by James Robinett, Admr. of Jezreal Robinett, decd. presented in Court and ordered to be recorded.
- Wm. P. Bogle VS F.F. Repass. On motion, case dismissed.

Page 247- December 1, 1873.
- James M. Fanning, Admr., VS Wm. N. Harman. Case dismissed at cost to the defendant. No attorney fee to be taxed in the cost.
- Aaron Crisp(Criss) & Son VS Wm. N. Harman. Same verdict as above.
- Reuben Hughes VS Wm. N. Harman. Same verdict as above.
- Harman Newberry VS Hezekiah Tickle. The claim of interpleader, Gordon Tickle is not sustained and is dismissed at cost of said Tickle. Newberry asks for judgement against Charles Forbs for $100.00 due June 1, 1873 subject to credit of $53.69 offset of Forbs against Hezekiah Tickle. All without prejudice on Tickle's land. Newberry to recover his cost.

Page 248- December 1, 1873.
- James Tolbert makes motion for an allowance for maintaining Wm. L. Tolbert, a lunatic. Mrs. Julia Tolbert, wife of said lunatic makes motion for part of this allowance. She is allowed $40.00 of this money which was assigned to her by James Tolbert.

- This day James Tolbert makes claim for $140.00 for maintaining Wm. L. Tolbert, a lunatic. Allowed and certified to the Auditor of Public Accounts for payment.
- F.I. Suiter, elected as Sheriff of the County for a term of three years, commencing January 1, 1874, together with Henry Newberry, W.N. Mustard, Harman Newberry, A.J. Grayson, James M. Stowers and H.C. Newberry, his securities, posted a bond in the amount of $20,000.00. F.I. Suiter then took the oath of office as requuired by law.
- D.W. Dunn, elected County Treasurer, on November 4, 1873- (continued on next page)

Page 249- -December 1, 1873 --- to serve a term of three years commencing January 1, 1874, together with Harman Newberry, A.J. Grayson and James M. Stowers, his securities, posted bond in the amount of $20,000. D.W. Dunn then took the oath of office as required by law.
- Samuel W. Williams, elected as Commonwealth's Attorney for Bland County, offered to post bond which was not taken, the Court being of the opinion that it was not required by law. He then took the oath of office as required by law.
- George W. Kinzer, elected Surveyor of the County, for a term of three years, qualified as such by taking the oath of office as required by law.

Page 250- December 1, 1873-
- George W. Stowers, elected Superintendant of the Poor for Bland County for a term of three years, together with Wm. Stowers and John C. Stowers, his securities posts bond in the amount of $2,000.00. He then took the oath of office.
- A.W. Shewey, this day appointed Collector for Sharon Township until July 1, 1874. He with Harman Newberry, Samuel H. Newberry and Henry Newberry, his securities, enters into bond in the amount of $2500,00. A.W. Shewey took the oath of office as prescribed by law.
- John W. Johnston VS Andrew J. Honaker. In debt. Came the plaintiff by his attorney and was granted leave to withdraw the bond on note filed in this cause by leaving a copy thereof.
- J.H. Bruce tendered his resignation as Justice of the Peace for Seddon Township. Resignation was accepted and Bruce was released.

Page 251- December 1, 1873-
- James M. Stowers foreman, John Havens, A.N. Thompson, J.G. Kegley, Mitchell Kegley, H.C. Newberry, Henry Foglesong, John S. McNutt, Jas. N. Justice, N.B. Stimson, A. Barnett, John P. Roach, Jas. S. Robinett, S.S. Melvin, Wm. Stowers and John C. Carpenter, were empaneled and sworn a grand jury of Inquest in the case of Commonwealth VS Charles Brown for a felon. Returned a true bill.
- Oliver E. Wright made motion that H.C. Fanning, Road Commissioner for Mechanicsburg Township, report on the expediency of changing the location of the road leading from Stower's Shop (No Business Road) to Rock Lick near the house of said Wright, and report to the Court.
- On motion of Paul James, ordered that L.D. Bogle, Road Commissioner for Seddon Township, go on road and report on expediency of building a new road from south side of Hunting Camp Creek, up the valley through the lands of W.P. Hornbarger, J.N. Justice, Paul James, Jas. Kidd, Geo. W. Martin, J.M. Irving, Crockett Shelton, Morgan Eagle and Alex Suiter to the house of said Suiter. To report to the Court.

Page 252- December 1, 1873.
- On motion of T.N. Finley, ordered that L.D. Bogle, Road Commissioner for Seddon Township, report on any changes he may deem necessary in the public road leading from at or near McGuire's Branch to and past French's Mill. Changes to begin where road first crosses Crab Orchard Creek. Report to next term of Court.
- List of Grand Jurors to be paid the sum of $1.00.
- Settlement made by H.C. Groseclose, guardian of W.R. Tilson, with J.H. Hoge, Deputy Commissioner, presented and filed for exceptions.
- Court adjourned until tomorrow morning at 9:0'clock AM.

Page 253- Tuesday Morning, December 2, 1873.®)1⁻ P.W. Strother, Judge.
- L.D. Bogle, reports on changes in road. Said changes ordered to be made as set forth in his report.
- By agreement with H.C. Newberry and G.W.K. Green, George W. Kinzer, County Surveyor located the line between said parties which report of survey has been returned to the Court. Ordered that location of road be changed from Walker's Creek to R.L. Newberry's Mill.
- Hicks & Newberry VS H.A. Chandler, Collector. On Notice. Ordered to be docketed and continued.
- Wm. Ray VS Hiram A. Chandler, Collector for Seddon Township and A.J. Grayson and James Stowers his securities. On notice of motion. Defendants failed to appear in court. Plaintiff to recover from the (Continued on next page)

Page 254- December 2, 1873.
----------- ---- -- defendants the sum of $15.00 with interest and costs.
- Peter C. Honaker VS A.J. Keeling. Unlawful detainer. Keeling pleads "not guilty". Robt. C. Green, H.R. Mustard and S.M. Hamilton were empaneled and sworn as a jury to decide if Keeling is holding possession of property mentioned against the will of Honaker. They found that Keeling did hold premises against the will of Honaker and ruled that Honaker recover from Keeling his property plus costs of this suit.

Page 255- December 2, 1873.
- Henry Newberry VS Bower Pauley. Unlawful detainer. Newberry to recover from Pauley his property. A writ is granted to Newberry for the sheriff to get possession from Pauley, Newberry's property.
- I.K. price makes motion that the report of H.C. Fanning, Road Commissioner for Mechanicsburg Township, concerning expediency of building a new road from Wm. B. Helvey's to I.K. Price's, be recommitted to Commissioner Fanning and L.D. Bogle, Commissioner for Seddon Township, who are directed to go upon and view the road and report the facts to the court.

Page 256- December 2, 1873-
- A.J. Grayson and James M. Stowers, sureties for H.A. Chandler, ask to be relieved of said surety. Said relief is granted and Chandler refusing to give other security is removed as Collector.

- Rule against Thomas Franklin for contempt of court, in absenting himself from the grand jury is hereby discharged.
- The following persons and the amount paid to them for service as petit jurors: H.A. Chandler, $2.00; A.J. Grayson, $2.00; T.E. Gregory, $2.00; R.C. Green, $2.00; S.E. Stinson, $2.00; Marion Robinett, $2.00; J.H. Mustard, $2.00; J.M. Fanning, $2.00; C.H. Forbs, $2.00; H.R. Mustard, $2.00; S.M. Hamilton, $2.00; H.P. Mustard, $2.00; John H. Bird, $2.00; Wm. P. Eakin, $1.00; Wm. C. Williams, $1.00; I.K. Price, $1.00; A.W. Miller, $1.00 and B. D. Graves, $1.00. Certified to Board of Supervisors.
- Petition of Wm. Davis and others from Wythe County, an order was made by Wythe County Court directing the Road Commissioners in Black Lick Township, to view the route for the unfinished portion for the Black Lick and Plaster Bank Turnpike and said commissioner having made his report to court and said county court- (Continued on page 257)

Page 257, December 2, 1873-
---of Wythe County having certified to this court that the completion of this road will be a great convenience both to Wythe County and to Bland County. Ordered that Reese Crabtree, Commissioner for Seddon Township go onto and view road and confer with Black Lick Commissioner and report back to this court.
- Simms Stowers makes motion that Mechanicsburg Road Commissoner make report of expediency of changing the location of the road leading from the old ford east of Wm. N. Harman's house to to the east side of the creek on the Tazewell Road, and report to the Court.
- It appearing to the court that due notice has been posted on the front door of the courthouse and due notice given to A.J. Grayson, Wm. Kitts, J.M. French, James Bruce, William Wilkinson, James Burton, Ralph Wyrick, Geo. Bogle, Wm.P. Bruce, Hiram Pauley, Henry Deavor and Phineas Thruston, owners of the lands adjoining Harman Newberry. It is ordered that George W. Kinzer, County Surveyor resurvey lands of said Newberry and be careful not to intrude on the rights of others and return a fair plat whether or not it be fair, to the court.

Page 258- December 2, 1873-
- K.C. Thornton took oath of office as Deputy Sheriff under newly elected, F.I. Suiter, Sheriff.
- Upon the motion of Dr. L.J. Miller, it is ordered that the Township Board of Mechanicsburg meet and show cause if any, why they shall not be compelled to levy a tax for the completion of the new road leading from the west end of H.C. Fanning's land to near A.W. Miller's.
- Commonwealth VS Fulton French. In debt. Case dismissed by consent.
- Commonwealth VS Winton Jackson. Indictment for misdemeanor. Case continued.
- H.C. Fanning, Road Commissioner for Mechanicsburg, appointed to locate a road leading from James Robinett's house to the turnpike near James Fannings, having returned his report to the court--- (Continued on next page)

Page 259- December 2, 1873.
----- and to the proprieters of said lands through which the proposed road will pass. There being no objection it is ordered that said road be established as a public highway according to the report of Commissioner Fanning.
- Ordered that all cases be continued until neat term of Court.
- Ordered that Court be adjourned until first day of next term.

Page 260- Blank page.

Page 261- Monday February 2, 1874- P.W. Strother, Judge.
- Following, a list of deeds presented and recorded in the Clerk‚s Office since the last December term of court:
- Dec. 9, 1874- Joseph & Margaret Bogle, to the heirs of John Bogle, Jr., being their interest in the lands of their father, John Bogle, Sr., deceased, on Walkers Creek.
- December 10, 1873- A deed of B&S for Real Estate bearing date of Nov. 17, 1874, from Phineas Thruston, by J.B. & J.S Wygal, attorneys in fact, to John Bogle, Jr. heirs for 50 or 60 acres of land on the north side of Walkers Mountain.
- Dec. 10, 1874- Deed of Trust on Real Estate from John M. Neel to F.I. Suiter, trustee, to secure A.L. Suiter, the sum of $86.25. Bearing date of December 9, 1873.
- Dec. 10, 1874- John C. Crockett & others to Peter C. Honaker, deed of B&S for land on Wolf Creek. Bearing date of July 7, 1873.
- Dec. 11, 1874- A deed of trust on real and personal property from H.A. Chandler to J. Meek Hoge, trustee, to secure A.J. Grayson, & J.M. Stowers, his sureties in his official bond as Collector of Seddon Township. Bearing date of December 8, 1873.
- December 11, 1874- Deed of B&S from W.W.Harman, October 19, 1869, to heirs of J.C. Davidson. Quantity unknown, on waters of Wolf Creek.
- December 11, 1874- Randolph Grayson to J.G. Kegley, 13 acres on north side of Walkers Mountain. Bearing date of November 12, 1873. December, 16, 1874- Andrew Havens & others to Wm. M. Bird, 55 acres on Walkers Creek. Deed of B&S. Bearing date of July 4, 1873.
- December 16, 1874- S.W. Williams, Sub. Trustee, in a deed of trust executed by Reuben Repass to John H. Hoge. 300 acres lying on Kimberling Creek. Bearing date of November 29, 1873.

Page 262- February 2, 1874 (Deeds continued)
- December 16, 1874- A.J. Grayson, trustee, to Sanuel W. Williams, bearing date of December 8, 1873. 7+ acres on west side of Seddon.
- December 18, 1874- Assignment of effects of W. McGinnis, bankrupt, to John Walsh, assignee, bearing date of November 24, 1873.
- January 3, 1874- R. Grayson & wife to J.W. Kitts, house and lot in Seddon, bearing date of April 22, 1873.
- January 3, 1874- J.W. Kitts & wife to C.H.C. Fulkerson & Co. for house & lot in Seddon. Dated January 3, 1874.
- January 13, 1874- JOhn H. HOge to S.H. Bernard, for a 1\2 acre lot near Mechanicsburg. Bearing date of December 8, 1873.
- January 13, 1874- T.J.B. Spangler to MIchael Waddle, for interest in estate of Wm. Deaver, deceased, bearing date of December 30, 1873.
- January 15, 1874- A deed of trust from George W. Suiter to A.T. Suiter, trustee, to secure Alex Suiter the sum of $300.00, on Real Estate on Walkers Creek, bearing date of January 5, 1874.
- January 15, 1874- Elias Spangler & wife to Jacob Waggoner, 123 acres on north side of Walkers Mountain. Dated March 4, 1873.
- January 19, 1874- Assignment of effects of L.D. Bogle, Bankrupt, to George D. Smith, assignee, bearing date of September 5, 1873.

- January 19, 1874- Assignment of effects of A.J. Honaker, Bankrupt, to George D. Smith, assignee, dated July 25, 1873.
- January 22, 1874- S.W. Williams, Commissioner, to Mary Patton, 25 acres on Walkers Creek, bearing date of September 24, 1873.

Page 263- February 2, 1874-
- January 26, 1874- An agreement concerning Kimberling Springs, between E.G. Boothe and William Kelsey, dated --- -- 1873.
- January 26, 1874- A deed of Homestead by Francis M. Harman, including real estate on Little Wolf Creek valued at $800.00 and Personal property valud at $217.00. Dated January 1874.
- January, 27, 1874- S.L. Kitts & wife to S.H. Newberry, for interest in the land of Wm. Deaver, deceased. Dated December 24, 1873.
- January 27, 1874- D.O. McNiel & wife to John H. Hoge, for part of lot # 25 in Seddon. Dated October 8, 1873.
- January 29, 1974- Assignment of effects of Jacob Muncy, Bankrupt, to George D. Smith. assignee, bearing date of June 7, 1873.
- January 29, 1874- Assignment of effects of Burriss D. Graves, Bankrupt, to George D. Smith, assignee, dated August 25, 1873.
- January 29, 1874- Assignment of effects of John M. Neel, Bankrupt, to John Walsh, assignee, dated January 22, 1874.
- A report of settlement by John H. Hoge, admr. of E.A. Sheppard, deceased, with J.M. French, Commissioner of Accounts. Ordered to be filed for exceptions.
- A report of settlement by John F. Locke, executor of Wilburn Harman, deceased, with John H. Hoge, Deputy Commissioner of Accounts, ordered to be filed for exceptions.
- A report of settlement by D.F. Thompson, guardian of Marietta E. Thompson with J.H. Hoge, deputy Commissioner of Accounts, ordered to be filed for exceptions.

Page 264- February 2, 1874.
- A report of settlement by H.C. & J.A.T. Groseclose, executors of William Groseclose, deceased, with John H. Hoge, Deputy Commissioner of Accounts, fild for exceptions.
- A report of settlement by John H. Hoge, admr. of John Bogle, deceased. Filed for exceptions.
- A report of a settlement by James Robinett, admr. of Jezreal Robinett, deceased, with J.H. Hoge, having been presented at a frmer term of court and filed for exceptions, is now confirmed and ordered to to be recorded.
- A report of a settlement by James Robinett, admr. of George Melvin, deceased, ordered to be recorded.
- A report of a settlement by Randolph Waddle, admr. for Robinett Waddle, deceased, ordered to be filed for exceptions.
- H.G. Thompson, Constable of Bland County, makes a claim for $3.25, for arresting Wm. P. French on a bastardy charge. Claim allowed.
- Eli F. Groseclose qualifies as deputy to F.I. Suiter, Sheriff of Bland County and takes the oath of office.
- Samuel H. Newberry & others VS H.G. Thompson. On notice. Plaintiffs are sureties on the official bond for defendant as constable of Bland County. (Continued on nextpage)

Page 265- February 2, 1874.
--Plaintiffs are hereby releived of
further liabilities as sureties for H.G. Thompson. Thompson refused to give other security and
was relieved of his office as Constable.
- William Dillow appointed Collector for Seddon Township. Together with W.N. Mustard & T.N.
Finley, his securities, posted bond for $4,000.00. Dillow took the oath of office.
- School District # 4 VS Prudence Robinett. Unlawful detainer.
Case dismissed at cost of defendant.
- Harman Tilson VS H.G. Thompson & Sureties. On notice. Case dismissed atcost of the Plaintiff.

- Cloyd Adkins VS D.M. Neel. N.B. Stimson, the garnishee, appeared in court and was
interrogated under oath. Attorney for plaintiff withdraws said summons on suggestion.

Page 266- February 2, 1874.
- Overseers of The Poor VS Jacob Waggoner. On a warrant. Both parties appeared in court.
Waggoner was granted a rule against Catherine Johnston and the Overseers of the Poor. The
former for failing to appear in court as a witness. Defendant asks that case be dismissed for
want of prosecution.
- Eli F. Groseclose VS Wm. Groseclose's Executor. Plaintiff makes motion that he be relieved as
one of the sureties for the bonds of H.C. & A.L. Groseclose, executors of Wm. Groseclose,
deceased.
- J.C. Painter presents account against Seddon Township, for $4.00, as viewer for locating a road.
Certified for payment.
- H.C. Newberry presnts claim for $3.00 against Sharon Township for locating a road. Certified
for payment.
- The following are appointes as registrars for the following election precincts- Hiram Rider for
Mechanicsburg; Wm. Kitts for Seddon; John Davidson for Rocky Gap.

Page 267- February 2, 1874.
- On motion of James D. Honaker, Road Commissioners of Rocky Gap to report on the
expediency of making changes in the road leading from the forks of the road at Rocky Gap to the
house of Peter C. Honaker and make report to the court.
- H.C. Fanning, Road Commissioner for Mechanicsburg, reports there is no opposition to changes
in the road leading from the Walkers Creek and Holston Turnpike and that Simms Stowers owner
of the land says there is no damage. Ordered that changes be made as set forth.
- Robert Crockett VS J.W. & L.N. Finley. Motion on bond. The Finleys did not appear in Court.
Crockett to recover from the Finleys the sum of &168.40. Credit of $84.20 noted.

Page 268- February 2, 1874.
- D.W. Dunn, Treasurer in the name of the Commonwealth, for benefit of Bland County VS H.A.
Chandler, Collector of Seddon Township and his sureties. The defendants failed to appear.
Plaintiff to recover from defendants (H.A. Chandler and A.J. Grayson & James M. Stowers, his
securities) the sum of $453.52. Credits noted .
- Hicks & Newberry for benefit of John P. Hicks VS H.A. Chandler, Collector of Seddon
Township. Plaintiffs to recover from defendant and his sureties, A.J. Grayson & James M.

Stowers, the sum of $6.90.

Page 269- February 2, 1874-
- George W. Brown, foreman, Arch Barnett, Wm. Stowers, Joel H. Spangler, John F. Locke, Joshua B. Thompson and Mitchell Kegley empaneled and sworn a special grand jury, found the following--
- Commonwealth VS R.C. Green, indictment for felony, a true bill.
- Commonwealth VS Samuel Stuart, on indictment for felony. Not a true bill.
- Not having completed the business before them, the grand jury stood adjourned until tomorrow morning at 10 o'clock.
- Wm. F. Tolbert, who has been adjudged a lunatic and who was taken to the County jail and was taken therefrom by James Tolbert. It appearing that it impossible for said lunatic to be received at either of the asylums. The court contracts with James Tolbert to keep said lunatic at the rate of $1.50 per day. Certified.
- On motion of Joel H. Spangler, it is ordered that George W. Kinzer, Wm. L. Yost and JOhn H. Lindamood, do lay off and assign to Elizabeth S. Hudson her dower in the lands of her late husband, G.T.M. Hudson, deceased and makr report to the court.

Page 270- February 2, 1874-
- George Wohlford, Collector for Mechanicsburg Township presents a claim for $ 27.92, which was examined and allowed.
- John F. Umbarger made oath that he lost a jury claim issued to him in the case ofCommonwealth VS Wm. Waddle, for a misdemeanor. A duplicate is issued to him.
- Commonwealth VS M.D Robinett & others, for misdemeanor. A rule awarded against Robert Robinett who was summoned as a witness but failed to appear.
- J.H. Bruce VS D.W. Dunn, guardian of the infant heirs of Joseph Dunn, deceased. Bruce asks to be relieved of his surety for D.W. Dunn. Dunn refused to give other security. Ordered that D.W. Dunn be relieved of his guardianship where upon F.P. Dunn, & C.W. Dunn, infants of Joseph Dunn, deceased selected Ganam Kitts as their guardian, which was approved by the court. Ganam Kitts with D.W. Dunn his security posted bond for $2,000.00. Kitts took oath as prescribed by law.
- Court adjourned until tomorrow morning at 10 o'clock.

Page 271- February 3, 1874- P.W. Strother, Judge.
- Commonwealth VS Sallie & Ellen Jones. Misdemeanor. Case continued.
- The following persons appointed as registrars of elections in the following precincts- John Deavor for Sharon Precinct; Joseph Cameron for Cameron's precinct.
- Commonwealth VS R.C. Green. Indictment for felony. Green refused to make a plea. A.J. Nye, John W. Bruce, Wm. Rider and Samuel Stuart, posted bond in the amount of $50.00 each, for Green's appearance in next term of court. (Continued on page 272--)

Page 272- February 3, 1874.
-- These same bondsmen to give evidence in case of Commonwealth VS R.C. Green.

- John F. Locke makes claim as viewer of the road in Seddon Township, in the amount of $4.00. Allowed and certified.
- Commonwealth VS Winton Jackson. Misdemeanor. A rule is awarded the defendant against Claiborn Green for failure to attend court as a witness for the defendant. Case continued.

Page 273- February 3, 1874-
- The Grand Jury empaneled and adjourned yesterday, came to court and rendered the following verdicts---
- We the grand jury present J.N. Fannon for selling ardent spirits by evidence of Harvey Thompson and Hiram A. Chandler, sworn in court to give evidence.- G.W. Brown, foreman.
- We the grand jury present J.N. Fannon for selling brandy to Jas. Lambert, on evidence of H.A. Chandler. G.W. Brown, foreman.
- --And the grand jury having nothing further before them were discharged.
- The following jurors allowed $2.00 for their services- F.C. Bogle, John H. Bird, H.C. Groseclose, C.V. Ashworth, J.C. Carpenter, Jr., Elias Repass, Geo. W. Lambert, P.R. Suiter, Samuel Stimson and Thos. F. Walker.
- The following jurors allowed $1.00 for their services--- Geo. W. Brown, Arch Barnett, Joel H. Spangler, Wm. Stowers, John F. Locke, Joshua B. Thompson and Mitchell Kegley.

Page 274- February 3, 1874-
- John H. Hoge, Justice of the Peace, this day tendered his resignation as such which was accepted by the court.
- Ordered that all cases not disposed of be continued until next term of court. P.W. Strother, Judge.

Page 275- March 2, 1874- P.W. Strother, Judge.
- A list of deeds recorded in Clerk's office since last term of court-
- Feb. 9, 1874- Hiram Rider & wife to Jas. T. Taylor. A house and lot in Mechanicsburg. Dated Nov. 5, 1873.
- Feb. 10, 1874- An assignment of effects of Ballard P. Stafford, Bankrupt, to George S. Smith, assignee. Dated June 20, 1873.
- Feb. 10, 1874- An assignment of the effects of Randolph Waddle, Bankrupt, to George S. Smith, assignee. Dated Aug. 7, 1873.
- Feb. 12, 1874- Deed of Trust from John R. Compton & wife for 210 acres on Walkers Creek to secure debt to I.A.T. Painter. To John Baskerville, Trustee.Dated Jan. 10, 1874.
- Feb. 13, 1874- An assignment of effects of Daniel A. Walker, Bankrupt, to George S. Smith, assignee. Dated July 25, 1873.
- Feb. 14, 1874- Randolph Hall & wife to John M. Hicks. A house & lot in Seddon. Dated ??? 2, 1874.
- Feb. 17, 1874- Wm. Page, assignee in bankruptcy of H.L. Muncy, to A.J. Muncy, for 275 acres on Wolf Creek. Dated Jan. 27, 1874.

Page 276- March 2, 1874-
- Feb. 17, 1874- Deed of B&S from H.A. Chandler to D.W. Dunn. Interest in real estate. Dated Feb. 11, 1874.

Feb. 18, 1874- Assignment of the effects of Jacob Waggoner, bankrupt, to George S. Smith, assignee, bearing date of June 27, 1873.

Feb. 18, 1874- Assignment of the effects of Elias Repass, bankrupt, to George S. Smith, assignee, dated Sept. 4, 1873.

- Feb. 18, 1874- John H. Hoge & wife to D.O. McNiel, a tract of 8 acres lying on Walkers Creek. Dated Oct. 8, 1873.

- The will of John Grayson, deceased, was presented and proven by the oaths of A.A. Ashworth and John F. Locke, the witnesses. Wm. Bane one of the executors refused to act and Franklin Grayson the other named executor posted bond for $16,800.00, with James M. Stowers and Harman Newberry, his securities.

- Mary Cundiff, daughter of Betsy Cundiff, being over the age of 14, selected Randolph Hall as her guardian. Hall posted bond for $50.00, with Wm. M. Bird his security.

- J. Meek Hoge, justice of the Peace for Mechanicsburg Township, resigned as such at the last term of court and recommended that James H. Muncy be appointed. Muncy took the oath of office.

Page 277- March 2, 1874.

- James M. French VS John H. Hoge, admr for E.A Sheppard, deceased.
French removed himself as surety for Hoge. Hoge refused to give other security and was removed as administrator.

- T.E. Greggory, road commissioner for Rocky Gaop, returned his report on the expediency in making changes in the road leading from Rocky Gap to the house of Peter C. Honaker. Ordered that changes be made. There was no opposition to said changes.

- On motion of John H. Hoge, admr. of J.C. Shannon, desceased. It appearing that Wm. Suiter has been dead over 3 months and no one has applied for letters of administration, ordered that the estate be turned over to the Sheriff of this county.

- Report of settlement by H.C. Groseclose, guardian of W.R. Tilson, with J.H. Hoge, deputy commissioner. Had been filed for exceptions and report not confirmed, case continued until next term of court.

Page 278- March 2, 1874.

- A report by John F. Locke, executor of Wilbern Harman, deceased. Files for exceptions in the last terem of court and none being taken, is ordered to be recorded.

- A report of settlement by D.F. Thompson gardian of M.E. Waggoner, having been filed for exceptions at last term of court and none being taken, is ordered to be recorded.

- A report of settlement by H.C. & J.A.T. Groseclose, executors of Wm. Groseclose, deceased, files for exceptions, none being taken, ordered to be recorded.

- A report of settlement by John H. Hoge, admr. of E.A. Sheppard, deceased, filed for exceptions, none being taken, ordered recorded.

- A report of settlement by John H. Hoge, admr. of John Bogle, deceased, filed for exceptions at last term of court and none being taken was ordered to be recorded.

- Report of settlement by Randolph Waddle, admr. of Robinett Waddle, deceased, ordered to be recorded.

- Report of settlement with Adam Waggoner, guardian of Margaret and Foster Wagner, ordered filed for exceptions.

Page 279- March 2, 1874-
- Settlement by James M. Fanning, admr. of Joseph Fanning, deceased, ordered filed for exceptions.
- H.C. Newberry & others VS L.D. Bogle, Road Commissioner for Seddon.
H.C. Newberry & W.N. Mustard, securities for L.D. Bogle, are relieved from further liability as such sureties. Bogle refused to give a new bond and is hereby removed as Road Commissioner.
- Special Grand Jury Of Inquest jurors, Harmen Newberry, foreman, J.A.T. Groseclose, George Wohlford, A.G. Updike, Henderson Bruce and James D. Honaker, rendered the following indictment-
- Commonwealth VS Joseph Kindrick. Felony, a true bill.
- William F. Tolbert allowed $141.00 for keeping James Tolbert, a lunitic.

Page 280- March 2, 1874-
- A paper signed by H. & Henry Newberry, sureties for A.W. Shewey, Collector of Sharon Township, is approved and sent to the auditors.
- A paper signed by James M. Stowers and H. Newberry, sureties for D.W, Dunn, Treasurer of Bland County. Approved & sent to auditors.
- Overseers of The Poor VS Jacob Waggoner, in case of bastardy. Rule against Catherine Johnston, returnable here at next term of Court.
- John C. Crockett VS Harry James. Case ontinued.
- F.M. Branden VS Melvina Cubine. Case continued.
- J.T. & C.R. Burton VS B. Dodd, Trustee. Case continued.

Page 281- March 2, 1874-
- Joseph Groseclose, Geo. L. Hudson and Thos. O. Wilson, appointed to appraise the personal estate of the late Margaret Wilson, deceased.
- H.C. & J.A. T. Groseclose, together with N.B. Dodson & P.W. Strother, posted a new bond as executors of Wm. Groseclose, deceased.
- The following jurors allowed $1.00 for their services on Grand Jury. Harman Newberry, J.A.T. Groseclose, George Wohlford, A.G. Updike, J. Henderson Bruce and James D. Honaker.
- Exceptions to settlement by J.H. Hoge, admr. of E.A. Sheppard, deceased, noted. Order confirming same, is set aside and case continued.
- Court adjourned until next term of Court.

Page 282- April 6, 1874- S.C. Graham, Judge.
- List of deeds admitted to record since last term of court-
- Assignment of the effects of Jacob Groseclose, Bankrupt, to George S. Smith, assignee, dated April 8, 1873.
- Assignment of effects of Geo. S. Ritter, Bamkrupt, to George S. Smith, assignee, dated Oct. 14, 1873.
- E.C. Shelton & wife to Thomas G. Coburn for 45 acres on Hunting Camp Creek. for $300.00.
- John H. Hoge, Commissioner, to Jas. H. Munsey being the dower interest in the lands of George Waggoner, deceased. For $500.00
- John H. Hoge, commissioner, to Randolph Grayson, conveying a house & lot in the town of

Seddon, for $1,250.00.

- B.H. Oxley & wife to John H. Hoge, 80 acres on Helvey's Mill Creek, for $500.00.
- A deed of trust from James Tolbert to T.J. Munsey, trustee, to secure J.M. French in the amount of $100.00. Personal property.
- Wm. Bane to Allen Mustard for house & lot # 2 in Mechanicsburg, for $125.00.

Page 283- April 6, 1874-
- Commonwealth VS M.D. Robinet & others. Misdemeanor. The jury found the defendants, M.D. Robinett & Christopher Neel, not guilty.
- Commonwealth VS S.W. Williams. Indictment for misdemeanor. Defendant is acquitted and discharged.
-Zachariah Cook is permitted to qualify as deputy for D.W. Dunn, Treasurer of Bland County. Cook takes oath of office.
- A.W. Shewey, with Eli Groseclose and James Lampert, his securities, posts bond for $2,000.00 as administrator of the estate of Henry Kitts, deceased.

Page 284- April 6, 1874-
- Wm. A. Evans to Thomas J. Munsey, trustee, to Ephriam Woodyard, trustee to secure John W. Harman, dated May 7, 1859. It appearing that Ephriam Woodyard has died.
- Sallie Jones has leave to bind out her daughter Frances Jones to C.H.C. Fulkerson until she reaches the age of 18.
- The last will of Amos Thompson, deceased this day presented in court and proved by oaths of A.J. Muncy and Jacob Muncy. Ordered to be recorded.
- Overseers of the Poor VS Jacob Waggoner. A rule granted against John F. Umbarger, Wm. H. Cooley and Melinda Cooley, for failing to appear as witnesses for the defendant. Case continued at the cost of the defendant.
- K.C. Thornton, jailer, makes claim for $4.60 which is allowed.
- J.N. Fannon VS J.D. Thorn. (Continued on page 285)

Page 285- April 6, 1874-
------------------------------------- Fannon came with R.L. Newberry who was to answer suggestions of Fannon, whether he was indebted to Thorn or not. Case dismissed without cost or damages. Fannon tendered his bill of exceptions.
- Commonwealth VS B. Dodd. Indictment for misdemeanor.
- Commonwealth VS H. Chandler & others. Indictment for misdemeanor.
- Commonwealth VS F.S. Blair & others. Indictment for misdemeanor.
- Commomwealth VS B. Dodd (2) & others. Indictment for misdemeanor.
- Commonwealth VS Joseph Stras & others. Indictment for misdemeanor.
- Commonwealth VS Z.T. Weaver & others. Indictment for misdemeanor.
- Commonwealth VS B. Dodd (3). Indictment for misdemeanor.
- Commonwealth VS B.Dodd (4). Indictment for misdemeanor.
- Commonwealth VS Winton Jackson. Indictment for misdemeanor.
- Commonwealth VS J.N. Fannon. Violation of revenue laws.
- Attorney for Commonwealth says he will not prosecute the foregoing 11 cases. Therefore they are acquitted and discharged thereof.

- J.J. Openchain for the benefit of Joseph Wohlford VS Wm. N. Harman and Jacob Waggoner. Harman & Waggoner failed to appear in court. Verdict for the plaintif in the amount of $337.84, the penalty of said bond. Judgement may be discharged by payment of &168.92, plus interest and costs.

Page 286- April 6, 1874-
- Wm. L. Bridges & others VS H.G. Thompson & others. Case continued.
- J.M. Hicks VS Sam'l. H. Newberry & A.N. Thompson. Hicks to recover from Newberry & Thompson the sum of $4.78 plus interest & costs.
- J.M. Hicks & Co. VS H.G. Thompson & sureties. Hicks to recover from defendants the sum of $41.50 plus interest and costs.

Page 287- April 6, 1874-
- J.W. Compton VS Jno. R. Compton. Matters of difference submitted to Gordon Wohlford and P.C. Honaker for arbitration.
- John C. Crockett VS Harry James. The death of the plaintiff, John C. Crockett was suggested in court.
- Commonwealth VS Charles Brown. Indictment for felony. A writ of Capias against Brown is issued.
- Settlement by A.T.Suiter, guardian of infant heirs of Jas. L. Gills, filed for exceptions.
- Settlement by Adam Waggoner, guardien of Margaret & Foster Waggoner, infants of F.P. Waggoner, deceased. { These children were not children of Franklin P. Waggoner. Foster and Margaret were children of George Waggoner and Mary Elizabeth Hearn Waggoner. They were Adam Waggoner's grandchildren. George died during the Civil War. }
- Settlement by James Fanning, admr. of Joseph Fanning, deceased. Filed for exceptions.

Page 288- April 6, 1874-
- The following are allowed &1.00 for their services as petie jurors: J.H. Bird, J.H. Thompson, Harvy Gross, J.H. Myers, B.H. Penley, J.B. Thompson, J.P. Roach, S.M. Hamilton, Wm. Leady, H.A. Pauley, P.C. Honaker and A.B. Pauley.
- F.I. Suiter, presents claim for &11.65. Allowed and certified.
- Commonwealth VS Henry Dowling. Misdemeanor. Indictment quashed and Dowling is set free.
- Court adjourned until tomorrow morning at 9:0'clock AM.

Page 289- Tuesday Morning, April 7, 1874- S.C. Graham, Judge.
- Wm. C. Williams VS Wm. N. Harman. Warrant. Case continued at cost to Harman.
- Wm. N. Harman VS Wm. C. Williams. Warrant. Case continued.
- J.T. & C.R. Burton VS B. Dodd, trustee for Annie E. Banks & heirs. Case dismissed. Plaintiffs tender bill of exceptions to said ruling.
- Ordered that all causes not otherwise disposed of, be continued until the next term of court. Court is adjourned.

Page 290- On vacation, May 6, 1874-
- Judge P.W. Strother appoints the following persons as judges of Election for the ensuing year for their respective voting places, to wit:

Sharon Precinct- Isaac Hudson, Elias Foglesong & A.W. Shewey.
Seddon Precinct- Henry Newberry, William Hederick & Isaac Kegley.
Mechanicsburg Precinct- Wm. E. Hoge, Isaac Davis & Hiram Rider.
Rocky Gap Precinct- W.W. Compton, G.W. Brown & A.D. Lambert.
Camerons Precinct- Duncan Cameron, A.R. Bogle & John A. Smith.
Commissioners appointed were- Henry Newberry, Wm. E. Hoge, Geo. W. Brown, A.W. Shewey and A.R. Bogle.

Page 290- ON VACATION, May 6, 1874- In compliance with Section 16, Chapter 54, code of Virginia, the following appointees-
Wm. Kitts, registrar for Seddon Township.
John F. Locke, James Painter & W.W. Hicks, judges of elections to be held in the Town of Seddon on the 4th Thursday of May 1874.
Hiram Rider, appointed as registrar and Allen Mustard & John H. Hoilman to act as judges at the municipal election to be held there on 4th Thursday next. (Signed by Judge P.W. Strother)
- Allen Mustard tenders his resignation as Justice of the Peace for Mechanicsburg Township. Ordered that the sheriff post notice thereof, that the voters of Mechanicsburg Township may (Continued on next page)

Page 291- May 4, 1874-
proceed to the election of a successor to the said Allen Mustard. Given under my hand this 25th day of May, 1874. Judge G.W. Easley.
- At a County Court held Monday June 1st, 1874- G.W. Easley, Judge.
- List of deeds admitted to record since April term of Court.-
- R. Patton & wife to E.M. Melvin. House & lot in Mechanicsburg for $300.00, dated Oct. 20, 1872.
- Mrs. Ida Neidermaier, a deed of Homestead, for personal property included, amounting to $384.45. Dated April 20, 1874.
- F.S. Blair, commissioner, to Martha Edwards. 205 acres on Wolf Creek. Dated Aug. 27, 1873.
- Wm. A. Hill & H.C. Dalton to Elisha Bond. 100 acres on Dry Fork of Laurel for $251.00. Dated July 19, 1873.
- James M.C. Wilson & others to Thomas Snider. 162 1/2 acres in Rich Valley for &2,437.50. Dated Feb. 14, 1874.
- Elias Foglesong & wife to John H. Crabtree. 46 acres in Sharon Township for $950.oo. Dated Feb. 6, 1874.
- Jonas Umbarger to John M. Cassell& others, trustees. A lot of 2 acres for church. Deed of gift. Dated Oct. 10, 1868.

Page 292- June 1, 1874- G.W. Easley, Judge.
- Assignment of the effects of Uriah Bean, Bankrupt, to Geo. D. Smith, assignee. Dated June 24, 1973.
- John S. Crockett, took oath to practice law in Bland County.
- H. Rider, elected, took oath as prescribed by law.
- James T. Taylor, elected, took oath as prescribed by law.
- George Bogle VS Josiah Thompson. A.G. Thompson says he is indebted to the defendant for

$85.00 but same is not due for 5 years. Bogle to recover from A.G. Thompson the amount of $57.58, the amount of debt owed to Bogle by Josiah Thompson, plus interest and costs.
- A claim by Samuel W. Williams for $10.00 was allowed and certified.

Page 293- June 1, 1874-
- William Dillow, Collector and Constable of Bland County, makes claim for $2.10, which is allowed and certified.
- Colby Stowers, Captain of Police in this county, makes claim of $6.40, which is allowed and certified.
- Overseers of The Poor VS Jacob Waggoner. A Warrant for Bastardy.
A rule ordered against John F. Umbarger,Wm. H. Cooley and Malinda Cooley, witnesses for the defendant, is discharged. Ordered a rule against Catherine Johnston who was summonsed and failed to appear as witness for the plaintiff. Returnable here next term of court.
- A.A. Ashworth appointed administrator of the estate of Amos Thompson, deceased, on motion of A.G. Thompson, son and heir. Certificate granted him with the will annexed, and recorded.

Page 294- June 1, 1874-
- On motion of John Havens, Wm. M. Bird and W.A.B. Bird, are appointed appraisers of the estate of Amos Thompson, deceased.
- William Dillow, was elected Collector for Seddon Township, on May 28, 1874, with T.N. Finley and Newton Waddle, posted bond in the amount of $4,000.00 and took oath of office prescribed by law.
- Eli F. Groseclose, elected Collector for Sharon Township, with H.H. Tislon, T.G. Hudson and S.M. McNutt, his sureties, posted bond for $5,000.00, and took the oath of office as prescribed by law.
- Gordon Wohlford, elected Collector for Mechanicsburg Township, with George Wohlford and John R. Compton, his sureties, posted bond for $4,000.00 and took the oath of office..
- James S. Robinett, elected supervisor of Mechanicsburg Township, (Continued on page 295)

Page 295- June 1, 1874-
to serve for one year. With F.I. Suiter, J.G. Kegley and Dunn B. Newberry, his securities, made bond in the amount of $1,000.00. He then took the oath of office as prescribed by law.
- Wm. L. Yost, elected as Supervisor of Sharon Township, with Eli F. Groseclose, his security, made bond for $1,000.00 and took the oath of office.
- Thomas H. Kinser elected Supervisor of Rocky Gap Township, with J.W. Compton, his security, posted bond for $!,000.00 and took the oath of office.
- James M. Stowers elected Supervisor for Seddon Township, with F.I. Suiter and D.W. Dunn, posted bond for $1,000.00 and took oath of office.
- T.G. Hudson,y elected by the voters of Bland County, for Sharon (continued on next page)

Page 296- June 1, 1874
Township, as Supervisor, with A.J. Grayson, his security posted bond for $1,000.00 and took the oath of office.
- J.W. Compton elected Clerk for Rocky Gap Township, with Thomas Kinser, his security
- posted bond in the amount of $1,000.00 and took the oath of office.

- Z.T. Weaver who was elected Assessor for Mechanicsburg Township, with S.H. Bernard and George Wohlford, his sureties, posted bond for $2,000.00 and took the oath of office
- George M. Tibbs, elected Assessor for Sharon Township , with H.H. Tilson, his security, posted bond for $2,000.00 and took the oath of office.

Page 297- June 1, 1874-
- J.H. Thompson, was elected Assessor for Seddon Township, with A.J. Grayson, A.G. Thompson and Wm. M. Bird, his securities, posted bond for $2,000.00 and took oath of office.
- H.C. Fanning, elected Road Commissioner for Mechanicsburg Township, with A.F. Miller, his security, posted bond for $1,000.00 and took oath of office.
- Rees Crabtree, elected Road Commissioner for Sharon Township, with Eli F. Groseclose, his security, posted bond for $1,000.00 and took oath of office.

Page 298- June 1, 1874-
- Levi S. Woodyard elected Road Commissioner for Rocky Gap Township, with John H. Bird and J.G. Kegley, his securities, posted bond for $1,000.00 and took oath of office.
- F.G. Helvey elected Overseer of The Poor for Mechanicsburg Township, with Hugh C. Fanning, his security, posted bond for $500.00 and took oath of office.
- S.S. Reeder, elected Justice of the Peace for Seddon Township, took oath of office.
- An error in the number of acres conveyed from Franklin Grayson to H.C. Newberry. 103 and ½ acres were deeded and by recent survey there were only 93 ¾ acres. Recorded.

Page 299- June 1, 1874-
- J.N. Fannen VS John C. Stowers. Motion dismissed.
- J.W. Compton VS John R. Compton. Warrant. Dismissed.
- A report of settlement by A.T. Suiter, guardian of the heirs of Jas. T. Gills, deceased. No exceptions filed. Ordered to be recorded.
- A report of settlement by James M. Fanning, admr. of Joseph Fanning, deceased. No exceptions noted. Ordered to be recorded.
- A report of settlement by Adam Waggoner, guardian for Margaret and Foster Waggoner. Filed for exceptions at a prior term of court, none being taked, ordered to be recorded.
- A report of settlement by J.H. Hoge, admr. of E.A. Sheppard, deceased, filed for exceptions. Ordered that W.T. Hamilton, one of the commissioners, make settlement and report to the court.
- A report of settlement bly L.D. Bogle, admr. of Robert J. Raines, deceased. Continued.

Page 300- June 1, 1874-
- Wm. L. Bridges, for benefit of Wm. E. Compton VS H.G. Thompson& others. Other defendants, S.H. Newberry & A.N. Thompson failed to appear in court. Plaintiffs to recover from the defendants the sum of $15.00 plus interest. Credit of $8.58 noted.
- D.W. Dunn, County Treasurer, presents list of delinquent real estate taxes for the year of 1873. By Z.T. Weaver, Collector for Township of Mechanicsburg.
- D.W. Dunn, receives list of delinquent personal property taxs for Mechanicsburg Township.

Page 301- June 1, 1874-
- Gordon Wohlford, collector for Mechanicsburg Township, presents a list of delinquent

capitation taxes. Z.D. Weaver was the assessor.
- A.W. Shewey, Collector for Sharon Township, presents list of delinquent capitation and personal property taxes. G.M. Tibbs, Assessor.
- A.W. Shewey, presents list of delinquent real estate taxes. George M. Tibbs, Assessor.

Page 302- A list of delinquent real estate taxes in the Rocky Gap Township, James D. Honaker, assessor.
- William Dillow, Collector for Sharon Township, presents list of delinquent capitation and property taxes. J.H. Thompson, Assessor.
- Certificate of exemption granted to Alexander F. Miller, from working on the public road, because of physical disability.
- Certificate of exemption granted to Gordon Saunders, from working on the public road because of physical disability.

Page 303- June 1, 1874-
- F.M. Brandon VS Melvina Cubine. On suggestion. Case continued.
- John C. Crockett VS Harry James. On suggestion. Case continued.
- George W. Easley, presented certificate of his qualications as judge, to act in the counties of Bland and Giles. Takes oath as prescribed by law.
- Ordered that the court stand adjourned until first day of next term. Geo. W. Easley.
- Court in vacation- Isaac Davis elected Clerk for Mechanicsburg Township and with Addison Davis and John R. Compton, his securities, posts bond for $2,000.00 and took oath of office.

Page 304- July 6, 1874-
- A list of deeds presented and recorded in the Clerk's Office since last term of court:
- Deed of trust from Hickman Stowers to Joseph H. Thomason, trustee, on 300 acres of land on Clear Fork, to secure Wm. M. Bishop in the amount of $519.00. Dated April 23, 1874.
- Deed of Homestead, including personal property only, valued at $50.30 , by Ida Neidermeir. Bearing date of June 12, 1874.
- A.T. Suiter & others to Joseph H. Thomason, a tract on Clear Fork , for $300.00. Dated December 23, 1873.
- J.B. Wygal to John Havens, a boundry on north side of Walker's Mountain. No consideration mentioned. Dated February 18, 1874.
- James B. Honaker, appointed Assessor for Rocky Gap Township. He, with P.C. Honaker, his security, posts bond for $2,000.00 and takes oath of office.

Page 305- July 6, 1874-
- Elias Foglesong appointed Overseer Of The Poor for Sharon Township. He, with John C. Stowers, his security, posts bond for $500.00 and takes oath of office.
- W.W. Ashworth appointed Justice of The Peace for Rocky Gap Township.
- Jas. H. Muncy, appointed Justice of The Peace for Mechanicsburg Township.
- James W. St.Clair, has leave to practice Law in Bland County.
- Jno. W. McGinnis, appointed Clerk of Seddon Township. He, together with James M. Stowers, F.I. Suiter and C.H.C. Fulkerson, his securities, posts bond for $2,000.00.

Page 306- July 6, 1874-
- Colby Stowers appointed Overseer Of The Poor for Rocky Gap Township, together with I.F. Stowers, his security, posted bond for $500.00.
- Commonwealth VS Hannah Chandler. Misdemeanor. A jury consisting of, Elias Blankenship, Geo. W. Kinser, G.H. Tickle, John Havens, Henry Dowling, D.L. Tickle, Wm. Kitts, J.H. Thompson, Jas. H. MUncy, Peter Kitts, Newton Waddle and John W. Harman, could not agree on a verdict. New trial granted at next term of court.
- Henry M. Pruitt, appointed Collecter for Rocky Gap Township, together with Jno. A. Davidson, his security, posted bond for $2,000.00 and took oath of office.

Page 307- July 6, 1874-
- Wm. E. Compton VS John Myers. Unlawful detainer. Case continued.
- Commonwealth VS John R. Walker. Misdemeanor. A jury consisting of, S.I. Patterson, B.H. Penley, James H. Bruce, James Hederick, Wm. Crutchfield, Jas. W. Thompson, Wm. M. Bird, A.J. Kitts, L.D. Helvey, W.G. Painter, Stephen Kitts and Stephen Lambert, after hearing the evidence, were adjourned until tomorrow at 9 0'clock AM.
- Overseers Of The Poor VS Jacob Waggoner. Case of Bastardy. For satisfactory reasons appearing to the court, case was dismissed.

Page 308- July 6, 1874-
- Supt. Of Poor VS Geo. W. Suiter. Motion on a Bastardy Bond. Ordered to be docketed and continued until tomorrow.
- H.H. Tilson VS H.G. Thompson & others. Continued until tomorrow.
- Colby Stowers appointed Captain of Police in this county, has leave to resign his office.
- I.K. Price asks for leave to erect gates across the public road leading from Harvey Nicewanders to the Tazewell Road at a point of his own land on Kimberling Creek. Notice posted.
- Ordered that the Court be adjourned until tomorrow morning at 9: 0'clock AM.

Page 309- July 7, 1874- Hon. Geo. W. Easley, Judge.
- Commonwealth VS J.N. Fannen. Violation of revenue laws. Not guilty, case dismissed.
- John F. Umbarger appointed guardian for Ada B. Repass and Corlia L. Repass, infants under the age of 14, children of Emeline Woods and Winfield Repass. Umbarger with M.L. Baumgardner, his security, posted bond for $400.00 and took oath prescribed by law.
- Commonwealth VS Ellen Chandler. Misdemeanor. Case continued.

Page 310- July 7, 1874-
- Common wealth VS Sallie Jones. Misdemeanor. Jones fined $5.00 and to imprisonment in the custody of the jailer for 50 minutes.
- Commonwealth VS Ellen Jones. Misdemeanor. Defendant is acquitted.
- Wm. C. Williams VS Wm. N. Harman. Continued at cost of Williams.
- Wm. N. Harman VS Wm. C. Williams. Continued at cost of Williams.
- Eli F. Groseclose presents claim against Commonwealth for $25.00. Allowed.
- S.W. Williams, attorney for commonwealth of this county, presents claim for $5.00. Allowed.

Page 311- July 7, 1874-

- Commonwealth VS John R. Walker. Misdemeanor. Jury could not agree on verdict. New trial ordered.
- A report of settlement by L.D. Bogle, admr. for Robert I. Raines, deceased. Exceptions made by Charles M. Rudder, which today he withdrew. Report confirmed and ordered to be recorded.
- Wm. N. Harman, made motion that the Estate of E.A. Sheppard be turned over to the sheriff. Ordered that the Sheriff take over and administer said estate.
- A rule is awarded against T.N. Finley by Seddon Township board, to show cause why he has not worked on the road leading from McGuire's Branch to French's Mill, as he agreed to do.
- A rule against Randolph Grayson and Henry Newberry by Seddon Township Board, to show cause why they have not done work on roads leading from R.L. Newberry's to near Henry Newberry's and from Newberry's to Jas. M. Stowers.

Page 312- July 7, 1874-
- Superintendant Of The Poor VS Geo. W. Suiter, Acles Fannon, & H.A. Pauley. Motion on Recognizance. Plaintiffs to recover from defendants the amount of $14.75 plus interest from August 1, 1872 until paid and the costs.
- The following persons and the amount paid to them for serving as Petit Jurors: John Havens, $2.00; Henry Dowling, $2.00; Elias Blankenship, $2.00; Geo. W. Kinser, $2.00; G.H. Tickle, $2.00; D.L. Tickle, $2.00; Wm. Kitts, $2.00; J.H. Thompson, $2.00; Jas. H. Muncy, $2.00; Peter Kitts, $2.00; Newton Waddle, $2.00; John W. Harman, $2.00; S.I. Patterson, $2.00; B.H. Penley, $2.00; Jas. H. Bruce, $2.00; James Hederick, $2.00; William Crutchfield, $2.00; Jas. W. Thompson, $2.00; Wm. M. Bird, $2.00; A.J. Kitts, $2.00; L.D. Helvey, $2.00; Wythe G. Painter, $2.00; Stephen Kitts, $2.00 and Stephen Lambert. Certified to auditor for payment.
- A report of settlement by J.H. Hoge on estate of E.A Sheppard. Filed for exceptions.
- Commonwealth VS J.N. Fannon. 2 cases of violation of Revenue laws. Commonwealth's Attorney says he will not prosecute. Fannon is acquitted. (Verdict is on page 313)

Page 313- July 7, 1874-
- H.H. Tilson VS H.G. Thompson. On a motion. Case continued.
- John C. Crockett VS Harry James. Case continued.
- F.M. Branded VS Melvina Cubine. Case continued.
- On motion of J.M. abd I.F Pruett, ordered tha Road Commissioners for Mechanicsburg Township, go on and view the ground and determine the expediency of changing the location of the road known as the Wilderness Road. Said changes to be made on lands of J.M. and I.F. Pruett.
- Court adjourned until first day of next term. Signed by Geo. W. Easley.

Page 314- August 3, 1874- George W. Easley, Judge.
- A list of deeds presented and recorded in the Clerk's Office since last term of Court-
- John F. Lambert & wife to Wm. P. French, 100 acres+- north Wolf Creek Mountain. For $125.00. Dated ?? December, 1871.
- S.J. Dunbar to J.H. Hoge. Conveying the dower interest of Dunbar in a tract of land on Kimberling on which G.C. Thorn resides. For a "valuable consideration". Dated April 13, 1874.
- A deed of trust on personal property from R.N. Wheeler, B.L. Nunn to H.P. Pruett, to secure H.M. Pruett the sum of $106.31. Dated May 22, 1874.

- Josiah Bruce & wife to Wm. P. Bruce, 122 acres on Big Walkers Creek,. Dated June 17, 1874. No consideration given.
- James M.C. Wilson & wife to Samuel Hanshew, their interest in 284 acres in Rich Valley. For $2,000.00. Dated April 25, 1874.
- Alex Umbarger & wife to Elizabeth McNutt, 772 acres in Rich Valley of Walkers Creek. In exchange for land in the State of Tennessee. Dated September 18, 1870.
- Robert Wylie, given leave to practice law in Bland County.

Page 315- August 3, 1874-
- Overseers Of The Poor VS H.G. Kitts, Wm. Wilkenson and G.W. Suiter. The defendants failed to appear in court. Verdict for James Maxwell, J.B. Thompson, R. Hall and Wm. Heneger, Overseers of The Poor, recover from the defendants the sum of $15.00 and interest from August 1, 1873, the amount due on the bond executed March 13, 1868 for the maintinance of a Bastard child of Polly Lambert and the costs of this motion
- John C. Crockett VS Harry James. The plaintiff being dead, case continued by his executors.
- J.N. Fannen VS H.A. Chandler & others. The defendants to recover from plaintiff their costs.
- Peter R. Hicks, refuses to act as trustee in a deed of trust executed by Jacob & Ann Wimmer to secure Peter H. Dills . Ann Wimmer makes motion that James D. Honaker be substituted in place of Hicks. Honaker accepted same.

Page 316- August 3, 1874-
- Township Board of Seddon Township VS Randolph Grayson. The rule awarded at last term of court against the defendant now to be and is discharged.
- Felix Buck, late Road Commissioner for Sharon Township, presents claim of $2.00.
- Wm. C. Williams VS Wm. N. Harman. The jury found for Williams in the amount of $35.00 plus interest from April 30, 1872 till paid. Harman objected and jury reconsidered it's verdict. A new trial was ordered.

Page 317- August 3, 1874-
- Wm. N. Harman VS Wm. C. Williams. The court sustained a motion by Harman to dismiss this case. Case remanded back to former court.
- Wm. E. Compton VS John Myers. A rule is awarded against W.W. Blankenship, a witness for Myers who was summonsed and failed to appear. Case continued at cost of Myers.
- A rule awarded against Eli F. Groseclose by Sharon Township Board to show cause why he should not have a tax levied on him or else work on the road leading from Groseclose's Mill through the lands of Andrew Handshew to the Walkers Creek & Holston Turnpike.
- I.K. Price granted leave to erect gates across the public road as he asked for in last term of court.

Page 318- August 3, 1874-
- On motion of W.S. Repass, by his attorney, a rule is awarded against John F. Umbarger, to show cause if any why the order made at the July term of court, making him guardian of Ada B. and Corlia L Repass, infants under the age of 14, should not be set aside and his powers revoked. and annulled.
- John F. Locke appointed Justice Of The Peace for Seddon Township, qualified by taking the

oath of office.

- J.G. Kegley appointed Road Commissioner for Seddon Township. He with James M. Stowers and Samuel W. Williams, his securities, posted bond for $1,000.00 and took oath of office.
- Eli F. Groseclose VS H.G. Thompson & others. Ordered to be docketed and continued.
- John M. Hicks VS Mechanicsburg Township Board. Docketed and continued.

Page 319- August 3, 1874-
- The following persons are allowed $1.00 for their services as Petit Jurors-
James Hederick; J.H. Myers; Jno. C. Carpenter, Jr.; A.G. Thompson; A.N. Thompson; Wm. Kitts; James M. Corner; H.G. Thompson; George Pegram; Marion Robinett and Felix Buck.
- Joseph Umbarger VS H.G. Thompson, Constable & securities. Case dismissed and defendants to recover form plaintiff their costs. Plaintiff granted 60 days to enable him to apply to the Circuit Court. At cost of plaintiff.
- Court adjourned until tomorrow at 8: 0'clock AM.

Page 320- Tuesday Morning August 4, 1874-
- Harman Tilson VS H.G. Thompson, Constable and securities. Plaintiff to recover from the defendants, H.G. Thompson, S.H. Newberry, A.N. Thompson & J.B. Thompson, securities of H.G. Thompson, the sum of $45.61 with interest at 6% from January 1, 1872 till paid. & costs.
- Wm. N. Harman asks leave to erect gates across the public road, 1st leading from Harvey Nicewander's to the Tazewell Road near the line of said Harman's land now occupied by Simeon Stowers and 2nd at the foot of the hill between I.K. Price's and the house occupied by James W. Harman. Notice ordered to be posted.
- Superintendant Of The Poor VS George W. Suiter & others. Plaintiffs to recover from defendants, George W. Suiter, Acles Fannon and H.A. Pauley, the sum of $25.00. Set-offs allowed to defendants. (Part on page 322)

Page 321- August 4, 1874-
- F.M. Branden VS Melvina Cubine. On suggestion. Case continued.
- Township Board of Seddon VS Henry Newberry. Case continued.
- Township Board of Seddon VS T.N. Finley. Case continued.
- Eli F. Grosclose VS H.G. Thompson, Constable & sureties.. Court sustained the defendants motion to quash the notice. Case dismissed and defendants to recover from Groseclose their costs in this matter.
_ Court adjourned until the first day of next term of Court. Signed by Judge Geo. W. Easley.

Page 322- Monday, September 7, 1874.-
- A list of deeds presented and recorded in the Clerk's Office since last term of Court-
- John R. Compton & wife to School Trustees. 1 ½ acres on Kimberling Creek for $15.00. Dated May 25, 1874.
- John H. Hoge & wife to Wm. P. Mustard. 175 acres near Mechanicsburg, for $2,500.00. Dated December 9, 1873.
- Margaret Carper to Jacob Carper. He dower interest in a tract of land on Clear Fork. No consideration given. Dated May 14, 1874.
- Geo. W. Martin & wife to James M. Kidd. 20+- acres on Hunting Camp Creek. For $90.00.

Dated August 17, 1874.

- Report of settlement by F.I. Suiter, Sheriff, and as such admr. of Stephen Gose, deceased, with J.H. Hoge, Commissioner of Accounts. Ordered filed for exceptions.

- Report of settlement by F.I. Suiter, Sheriff, admr. of Samuel Muncy, deceased. Ordered filed for exceptions.

- Report of settlement by I.S. Harman, trustee for Polly Parsons. Filed for exceptions.

- Harman Newberry's application for a new survey of his several tracts of land. G.W. Kinzer, surveyor for the county, returned a fair plat which the court deemed just and reasonable. Ordered to be certified to the land office.

-

Page 323- September 7, 1874-
- Report of settlement by E.S. Kidd, guardian of the infant heirs of William H. Muncy, deceased. Ordered filed for exceptions.

- Wm. E. Compton VS John Myers. Unlawful detainer. Both parties agree to the determination of Peter C. Honaker, Jacob McNeil and A.F. Miller. Agreed that their judgement will be that of the Court.

- F.I. Suiter, Sheriff makes claim for $4.30. Examined and allowed.

- Report of settlement by John H. Hoge, admr. for E.A. Sheppard, deceased, with W.T. Hamilton, one of the Commissioners of this court which was made under a previous order of this court and exceptions taken. Exceptions were overruled. The report ordered to be recorded.

- Wm. N. Harman VS Joseph Wohlford & Bro. On notice to quash an execution. Continued.

Page 324- September 7, 1874-
- H.C. Groseclose appointed Justice Of The Peace for Sharon Township. Took oath of office.

- The Court certifies that Wm. L. Yost who wishes to practice law in Bland County is a person of good character, is over age 21 and has lived in the county for 12 months.

- Jno. S. McNutt is appointed a Commissioner to contract with some person or persons to keep in order that portion of the road leading from Wytheville to Jeffersonville in Tazewell County. From the top of Walkers Mountain to Garden Mountain. To contract for the best terms that can be obtained for the county.

- Leave is granted to Wm. N. Harman to erect gates across the public road. Case started in last term of court.

- On motion of L.J. Miller, Jas. Robinett and H.C. Fanning, ordered that the Road Commissioners of Mechanicsburg, go onto and view the ground and determine the expediency of changing the road from H.C. Fanning's land near A.W. Miller's . Obidiah Smith and Susan Helvey;s land mentioned.

Page 325- September 7, 1874-
- W.S. Repass VS John F. Umbarger, guardian. Ordered thatthe order appointing Umbarger as guardian be set aside and declared void. Repass to recover his costs from Umbarger.

- W.C. Williams VS Wm. N. Harman. On Warrant. Case continued.

- G.W.K. Green VS Winton Jackson. Unlawful detainer. Cause docketed and continued.

- John C. Crockett's Executor, VS Harry James. Case continued.

- F.M. Branden VS Melvina Cubine. Case continued.

- Township Board of Sharon VS T.N. Finley. On a rule. Case continued.

- John M. Hicks VS Township Board of Mechanicsburg. On an appeal. Case continued.
- Eli F. Groseclose VS Township Board of Sharon. On a rule. Case continued.

Page 326- September 7, 1874-
- Gordon Wohlford, Collecter for Mechanicsburg Township, makes claim for $1.80.
- On motion of S.A. Bridges, it appearing that he is physically unable to work on the public road and is therefore exempt.
- Court adjourned until first day of next term of Court. Signed, G.W. Easley, Judge.

Page 327- Monday October 5, 1874-
- A list of deeds presented in the Clerk's Office since last term of court-
- Granville Jones & wife to Wm. M. Bishop. 400 acres on Clear Fork of Wolf Creek. Deed made in pursuance of a decree from th Bland Circuit Court.
- John Lambert & wife to Henry Hounshell. 8 acres, being dower interest. On waters of Walkers Creek. For $75.00.
- D.A. Whitman, Special Commissioner, to W.A. Bird. 400 acres on south side of Brushy Mountain. Deed made in pursuance of a decree from Wythe Circuit Court.
- P.R. Spracher, Special Commissioner, to Peter C. Honaker, 50 acres on north side of Rich Mountain. Deed made in pursuance of a decree from Tazewell Circuit Court.
- Jas. W. Hill & wife to Henry Newberry, their interest in the lands of Wm. Hearn, deceased. Consideraton, $150.00.
- Wm. T. Hamilton, Special Commissioner, to John M. McNeil, 150 acres on Wolf Creek. Deed made in pursuance of a decree from Bland Circuit Court.
- Ordered that the motion of John Fanning, made at last term of court, ordering the Road Commissioners to go on and view lands of Wm. N. Harman, J.W. Finley and I.K. Price so as tyo determine what damages if any will result from road changes, is amended to allow J.G. Kegley, Road Commissioner from Seddon Township to accompany them and make report. (Part of this item is on page 328)

Page 328- October 5, 1874.

- On motion of J.S. Wyrick, ordered that the Mechanicsburg Township Road Commissioner go onto and view the ground to determine the expediency of building a new road, 10 feet wide, leading from Wyrick's house to a point leading from J.M. French's Mill to D.O. McNiel's Mill at or near the house of James Muncy. Report on any damages that might occur.
- Wm. L. Yost, has leave to practice Law in Bland County and takes the oath prescribed by law.
- Ordered that the changes in the road (from J.M. & I.F. Pruett's motion at last term of court) will only be on J.M. Pruett's land. Pruett is ordered to do all the work on this portion of the road caused by making said changes.

Page 329- October 5, 1874-
- On motion of L.J. Miller & others, made at last term of court, it is ordered that T.J. Munsey, Obediah Smith and Sarah B. Helvey, owners of land through which road will pass, be summonsed her to show cause why the road should not be changed as set forth in said report.

- Wm. N. Harman VS Joseph Wohlford & Bro. and John Williams. On a notice. Defendants moved the court to quash the notice which the court sustained. Defendants to recover from Harman their costs.
- Wm. E. Compton VS John Myers. Unlawful detainer. Case was mutually submitted to arbitrators, A.W. Miller, Peter C. Honaker and Jacob McNeil, at the last term of this court. Ordered that both parties be called back to court to show cause if any why said award should not be entered up as the judgement of the court. (Does not say what the award was)
- Martin D. Robinett appointed Committee of the person and estate of Prudence Robinett a lunatic. Leave is granted him until next term of court to give such bond and security as the court deems sufficient.

Page 330- October 5, 1874-
- The court certifies that Martin D. Robinett is allowed $1.00 per day for taking care of and supporting Prudence Robinett, a Lunatic. To be paid out of the estate of said Lunatic.
- The sale and appraisement bills of the esatte of John C. Crockett, deceased. A list of personal property which was set aside for his widow, S.J. Crockett. Ordered recorded.
- Wm. C. Williams VS Wm. N. Harman. On Warrant. Jury finds in favor of the defendant.
- The following Jurors allowed the sum of $1.00 for their services as Petit Jurors:- Jas. C. Painter; Wm. Hederick; R.L. Newberry; J.R. Neel; H.A. Chandler; M.L. Bumgardner; Isaac G. Pauley; P.H.M. Bird; Stephen S. Kitts; J.W. Thompson; James Lambert and Jas. S. French.
- The last will and testament of Calvin G. Crockett, deceased, with codicil thereto, this day produced in Court and proven by the testimonies of John H. Hoge & John P. Roach, the subscribing witnesses. Codicil continued for further proof.

Page 331- October 5, 1874-
- G.W.K. Green VS Winton Jackson. Unlawful Detainer. Case continued.
- Jno. C. Crockett's Exors. VS Harry James. Case continued.
- F.M. Brandon VS Melvina Cubine. Case continued.
- Seddon Townshp Board VS T.N. Finley. On rule. Case continued.
- Eli F. Groseclose VS Sharon Township Board. On rule. Case continued.
- John M. Hicks VS Mechanicsburg Township Board. Cause dismissed.
- J.N. Fannen VS H.H. Chandler, Collector & Sureties Case docketed and continued.
- Court adjourned until first day of next term. Signed, G.W. Easley, Judge.

Page 332- Monday, November 2, 1874-
- A list of deeds presented and recorded in the Clerk's Office since last term of Court.
- Thomas F. Crow & others to James M. Crow. 112 acres on north side of Walker's Mountain head waters of Holston River, for $200.00. Dated August 18, 1874.
- James M. Crow & others to Daniel Crow, 60 acres on head waters of North Fork of Holston River, for $125.00. Dated October 2, 1874.
- Joseph Foglesong & wife to Henry Foglesong, their right, interest and title in 142 ½ acres lying in Rich Valley, for $400.00. Dated Februery 7, 1874.
- H.N. Keightley & wife by Wm. N. Harman, their attorney in fact, to John H. Bland, 38 acres on Walker's Creek. (No consideration given) Dated September 15, 1873.
- Eli F. Groseclose VS Sharon Township Board. Plaintiff to recover his costs from Defendants.

- On motion of George P. Price, ordered that Road Commissioner of Mechanicsburg Township
go upon and view the ground and report on the expediency of establishing a new road leading
(Continued on page 333)

Page 333- November 2, 1874-
from the Turnpike near Geo. W. Fanning's down the creek through lands of said Fanning and
Geo. P. Price to the County line. To report if any orchard, yard or garden will be damaged.
- On motion of A.J. Songer, ordered that the Rocky Gap Road Commissioners, report on the
expediency of building a new road from the Turnpike road near the house of Samuel L. Gibson
up the Dry Fork to a point near the house of the upper Settler, east of where A.J. Songer now
lives. Report on damages if any to yards, gardens and orchards.
- On motion of Isaac Pruett, ordered that Mechanicsburg Road Commissioner, go on and view
land and report on expediency of changing road . Make report as in above item.
- G.W.K. Green VS Winton Jackson. Unlawful detainer. Ordered that Jackson recover from
Green his costs. Green has leave to take his case to a higher court if he can execute a bond of
$20.00

Page 334- November 2, 1874-
- On motion of Giles County Iron Co., by it's attorney, it is ordered to be certified that it appears
to the satisfaction of the court that said Company owns land in Bland County at the assessed
value of $14,500.00 and that the said Company pays taxes in the County of Bland.
- On motion of the Commonwealth's Attorney, ordered that no person be allowed to turn his
stock into the courthouse yard or to trespass on public property. The Sheriff is hereby ordered to
enforce this order.
- Ordered that Colby Stowers, Overseer of The Poor, bind out Andrew Jackson Robinett a poor
orphan. {The child's parents are not listed nor the exact date of his birth} until he attain the age of
21 years
. William Vest, Orphan son of Flemming Vest, deceased, over 14 years of age and under age 21,
made choice of Wm. N. Harman as his guardian, whereupon the said Harman took the oath
required by law. No bond being required.

Page 335- November 2, 1874-
- Wm. E. Compton VS John Myers. Unlawful detainer. It appearing that the award made by the
arbitrators, makes it improper for the Court to rule in this matter. Ordered that the case be
remanded back to the Circuit Court and be determined.
- Ordered that H.C. Fanning, Road Commissioner of Mechanicsburg who upon motion of J.S.
Wyrick, was to go on the ground and report the expediency of building a new road, from
Wyricks to near Jas. Muncys, go on and find any other route for location of the road to go and
report on the practicality of same.
- Ordered that Gordon Kegley, Road Commissioner for Seddon Township, go on the new road
reviewed by said Kegley & H.C. Fanning, beginning at Wm. Helvey's, passing wood lands of J.W.
Finley & W.N. Harman to the house of I.K. Price. Lands of Micajah Saunders & Jas. Miller are
mentioned. Would any orchard, yard or garden have to be taken?

- J.G. Kegley & H.C. Fanning, Road Commissioners return report on above road establishment. Ordered that the land owners of said property be summonsed to court to show cause if any why road should not be established. (Part of item on page 336)

Page 336- November 2, 1874-
- Ordered that all causes not otherwise disposed of be continued until the next term.
- Court adjourned until first day of next term. Signed, G.W. Easley, Judge.

Page 337- Monday, December 7, 1874-
- Following is a list of deeds presented in the Clerk's Office and certified to be recorded-
- John Deaver & wife to Geo. W. Kinzer, 81 ½ acres on waters of North Fork of the Holston, for $890.00. Dated October 30, 1874.
- L.J. Miller & wife to Jacob F. Kitts, 100 acres+- on Kimberling Creek, for exchange of a lot in Seddon. Dated February 20, 1874.
- Jacob F. Kitts & wife to James H. Bruce, a house and lot in Seddon in exchange for land in Kimberling. Dated March 10, 1874.
- Geo. Bogle to Polly M. Tickle, for love and affection, deed of gift, land on waters of Walkers Creek. Amount of acerage not given. Dated November 9, 1874.
- A Deed of Trust from Wm. Dillow to J.G. Kegley, trustee, to secure debt to C.H. Fulkerson. Dated November 23, 1874.
- E.G. Boothe to John H. Hoge.
- E.G. Boothe to Geo. W. Hines.
- A Deed of Trust from Joseph H. Thomason to I.F. Stowers, land on Clear Fork and personal property, too secure Wm. M. Bishop in amount of $800.00. Dated September 1, 1874.
- Jonas M. Crow & others to Joseph Kimberling, all their interest in lands lying on head waters of the Hoslton, for $125.00. Dated October 2, 1874.
- Geo. W. Fanning to M.A. Fletcher, 90 acres+- on Walkers Creek, for $600.00. Dated February 21, 1874.
- Rachell Harman to Mitchell Kegley, land (no amount given) on Crab Orchard Creek, for $50.00. Dated December 1, 1874. {Part of item on page 338}.

Page 338- December 7, 1874-
- P.A. Ewald & wife to F.I. Suiter, conveying house & lot # 7, in Seddon for $1,300.00. Dated November 7, 1874.
- The last will and testament of Elizabeth Robinett, deceased, was presented and proven by the oaths of Jas. C. Painter and David S. Painter, the subscribing witnesses and ordered to be recorded. George Robinett, the named executor, qualified as such and with F.I. Suiter & Newton Waddle, posted a bond for $1,000.00, as required by law.
- Isaac F. Stowers is authorized to serve a subpoena on Watson Neel.
- A report by Jno. Repass, H.H. Tilson and Samuel H. Newberry, Commissioners appointed to divide the Real Estate of Wm. Groseclose, deceased. No exceptions noted and report was confirmed and recorded.
- Wm. H. Nicewander, Jacob H. Nicewander and Alex Nicewander, make deed of gift to Nancy Nicewander on May 10, 1860 and was partially proven by the oath of G.C. Thorn as to the signature of M.A. Thorn now deceased. Continued until next term of Court.

- Martin D. Robinett makes claim for upkeep of Prudence Robinett, {Continued on page 339}

Page 339- December 7, 1874-
a lunatic, for $52.00 under a contract made in the October term of Court. The personal property of Prudence Robinett amounted to $25.00. M.D. Robinett is allowed his account minus the $25.00. Certified to the Auditor for payment.
- David M. Baugh appointed guardian for Eve, Nikati and Alex Baugh, infants under the age of 14 years. Baugh with Peter Litz, his security posts bond for $200.00 and took oath as prescribed by law. { The children's parents names were not given}
- The last will and testament with codicil attached, of Calvin G. Crockett, deceased was again presented and was fully proven by the oath of Samuel Stuart, one of the subscribing witnesses. The said will and codicil is ordered to be recorded.
- Catherine C. Crockett is appointed administratrix of the will of Calvin G. Crockett, deceased. She, with J.M. Lovell and George Wohlford, her securities, posts bond for $1,000.00.
- The sheriff of the county has contracted with James Tolbert for taking care of William F. Tolbert, a lunatic, at the rate of $1.00 per day. Ordered that same be ratified.
- James Tolbert presents an account against the Commonwealth for $11.00 for taking care of and supporting Wm. F. Tolbert, a lunatic. Certified to auditors for payment.

Page 340- December 7, 1874-
- H.M. Pruett tendered his resignation as Collector of Rocky Gap Township. It was accepted and Pruett was relieved of his office as Collector.
- Harman Newberry VS Eli Repass Unlawful detainer. Case dismissed at cost of defendant and to be without damage to the rights of the plaintiff.
- Wm. N. Harman VS Joseph Wohlford & Bro. and Sam'l. C. Williams, admr. of Jno. Williams, deceased. Settled by payment of $33.25 in interest.
- James A. Repass appointed Supervisor of Sharon Township in place of Wm. L. Yost who this day resigned. Repass, with F.I. Suiter & Isiah Henderson his securities, posted bond for $1,000.00 and took the oath of office.

Page 341- December 7, 1874-
- Wm. L. Yost this day appointed a Coomssioner in Chancery for this court in place of William T. Hamilton, resigned.
- Isaac S. Harman, Z.T. Weaver and George Wohlford appointed to appraise the personal estate of Calvin G. Crockett, on motion of Catherine C. Crockett, admr. of Calvin Crockett,s will.
- James H. Muncy is aggrieved because he has been assessed for 75 acres when there are only s 32 acres in the tract mentioned. Muncy is exonerated from paying the excess tax.

Page 342- December 7, 1874-
- William T. Hamilton, was elected as Clerk of the Bland County Court, on November 3, 1874 and this day qualified to enter upon the discharge of his duties. He, with Samuel W. Williams and Wm. E. Hoge, his securities, made bond for $5,000.00 and took the oath of office.
- The appraisement bill of the personal property of Amos Thompson, deceased, was presented in court. Appraised by John Havens, Wm. A.B. Bird and Wm. M. Bird. Ordered to be recorded.

- The appraisement bill for the personal estate of J.M. Brown, deceased, was presented in Court. Appraisers were, Thos. F. Walker, I.F. Stowers and Jos. H. Thomason. Ordered recorded.
- The sale bill of the personal property of Amos Thompson, deceased, was presented and ordered to be recorded.
- A report of settlement by F.I. Suiter, admr. of Samuel Muncy, deceased, having been filed for exceptions at a former term of court and no exceptions taken, same ordered to be recorded.
- A report of settlement by F.I. Suiter, admr. of Stephen Gose, deceased, conformed and ordered to be recorded.

Page 343- December 7, 1874-
- A report of settlement by Isaac S. Harman, Trustee for Polly Parson & her children Confirmed and ordered to be recorded.
- A report of settlement by E.S. Kidd, guardian of the heirs of Wm. H. Muncy, deceased. Confirmed and ordered to be recorded.
- John S. McNutt appointed a Commissioner to let to contract that portion of Fancy Gap and Tazewell Turnpike, from top of Walkers Mountain to the Garden Mountain. His report was satisfactory and was ordered to be confirmed and that John Franklin, the contractor mentioned, be permitted to collect tolls upon said road.
- Ordered that all causes on the docket not otherwise disposed of be continued until the next term.
- Ordered that the Court be adjourned until the first day of the next term. Signed by G.W. Easley.

Page 344- January 4, 1875-
- A list of deeds presented in the Clerk's Office since last term of court-
- John Fanning, a deed of Homestead dated November 2, 1874. Real Estate value-$500.00 and personal property value $879.00
- John G. Crockett, exor. of John C. Crockett, deceased, to Robert Wylie, a Power Of Attorney, dated November 20, 1874.
- A deed of release from J.H. Hoge, trustee, and J.M. Stowers and A.J. Grayson the beneficiaries in the deed of trust, to H.A. Chandler. Dated February 11, 1874.
- John M. Hicks & wife to A.J. Grayson, 2 lots in the town of Seddon, for &500.00. Dated September 25, 1874.
- D.O. McNeil & wife to William T. Hamilton, lot # 11 in the town of Seddon, for $125.00. Dated November 19, 1874.
- L.J.B. Spangler & others to C.C. Bales, 3 acres on head waters of the Holston, for $21.00. Dated September 19, 1874.
- R.C. Kent, trustee, to W.N. Mustard, 209 acres on Walkers Creek for $2,325.00. Dated November 21, 1874.
- Randall Grayson & wife to J.G. Kegley, lot # 21, in town of Seddon. Made under decree from the Court. Dated December 21, 1874.
- George W. Easley presented the certificate of his qualifications as Judge. {Part of his vows on page 345}

Page 345- January 4, 1875-
- On motion of D.W. Dunn, ordered that the Sedon Road Commissioners go on and view the

ground and report on the expediency of establishing a new road from said Dunn's saw mill to as near the town of Seddon as possible, connecting with the Wakers Creek and Holston Turnpike and report on whether any garden, yard or orchard will be taken.
- On motion of Henry Newberry, ordered that the report made by Mechanicsburg Road Commissioner on the proposed road leading from J.S. Wyrick's to Jas Muncy's., be recommitted to said Commissioner. H.C. Fanning having returned another report, it is ordered that James Thompson and Adam Waggoner the land owners, appear and show cause if any why road should not be established as a public highway.
- Geo. P. Price makes motion that H.C. Fanning, Road Commissioner, report on expediency of a new road from G.W. Fanning's to the County line. (Mechanicsburg Township)

Page 346- January 4, 1875-
- Commonwealth VS Ralph B. Wyrick. religious worship. James Jones failed to appear as a witness for Wyrick. and is summonsed to appear at next term of court.
- Commonwealth VS Ralph B. Wyrick. Assault & Battery. Case continued.
- Commonwealth VS Joseph Moss. Misdemeanor. Case continued.

Page 347- January 4, 1875-
- Commonwealth VS J.S. Wyrick. Misdemeanor. Defendant is acquitted.
- Commonwealth VS Isaac F. Stowers. Misdemeanor. Case continued. On motion of Wyrick, a rule is awarded against John R. Walker, Wm. C. Walker & Thos. J. Muncy should not be put upon the record as prosecutors in this cause and be liable for the cost.
- Commonwealth VS John R. Walker. On motion of Walker, a rule against Isaac F. Stowers, returnable next term, to show cause why he should not be put upon the record as prosecutor in this case and be made liable for the costs.

Page 348- January 4, 1875-
- John W. Harman, Jr. who was appointed Justice of The Peace for Rocky Gap Township in place of Peter Honaker, deceased., took the oath of office as prescribed by law.
- In the matter of the application of Harman Newberry for an inclusive survey on several tracts of land adjoining each other. This day Geo. W. Kinzer, surveyor of the county presented a fair plat which was certified to the Register of the land office.
- Commonwealth VS M.S. Pool. Violation of revenue law. Case continued.
- Commonwealth VS Rufus Robinett. Misdemeanor. Defendant not found, writ of capias awarded against him, returnable at next term of court.
- Commonwealth VS B. Dodd. Violation of revenue law. (# 1) Case continued.

Page 349- January 4, 1875-
- Commonwealth VS B. Dodd. Violation of revenue law. (# 2) Case continued.
- Commonwealth VS B. Dodd. Violation of revenue law. (# 3) Case continued.
- Assignment of dower to Elizabeth S. Spangler, her interest in the lands of her late husband, G.L. Hudson, deceased. Ordered to be recorded.
- Mary Ann Honaker relinquished the right to administer the estate of her late husband, Peter C. Honaker, deceased. On her motion James D. Honaker and John A. Davidson, appointed administrators of the said Peter C. Honaker, deceased, who together with Thos. J. Kinser, A.J.

Honaker, George Wohlford and Peter R. Stowers, their security, posted bond for $4,000.00.

Page 350- January 4, 1875-
- Thomas H. Kinser, Wm. W. Compton, John W. Harman and Wm. W. Ashworth, appointed as appraisers of the Personal Property of Peter C. Honaker, deceased.
- On motion of John R. Crawford, the Mechanicsburg Road Commissioners to go on and view ground and report on expediency of changing location of road leading from Kimberling Creek up Dismal Creek to the Giles County line.
- In matter of Geo. Price's application for a new road leading from Geo. Fanning's to the Giles County line. Ordered that the said road be established.
- B.R. Wilburn presented credentials of his ordination and communion with the Methodist Church and with A.N. Thompson & John Hoge, his securities, posted bond for $15.00, whereupon a certificate is issued to him to celebrate the rites of matrimony.

Page 351- January 4, 1875-
- Ordered that Fulton Rider and Julia Tolbert be summonsed to appear and show cause if any why charges should not be filed against them for lewdly cohabiting with each other contrary to law.
- Ordered that court be adjourned until tomorroe at 9 0'clock AM.
- Tuesday morning January 5, 1875-
- Commonwealth VS Austin French. Misdemeanor. Show why A.J. Honaker and Milton Farrington should not be put upon the record as prosecutors against the defendant and made liable for his costs. Granted and case continued.
- On motion of Newton Waddle, an heir of Rebecca Kyle, deceased, posts bond for $500.00 with T.N. Finley his security and is granted letters of administration for the estate of Rebecca Kyle.
- Commonwealth VS Daniel Robinett. In debt & violation of revenue laws. Robinett "not found". A writ of Capias awarded against Robinett.
Seddon Township Board VS T.N. Finley. On rule.(Continued on next page)

Page 352- January 5, 1875- ---------------------------- On motion of attorney for the plaintiff that the said issued (rule) be discharged.
- Nancy Neel VS John Myers. Case continued at cost of the Plaintiff.
- A report of settlement by A.J. Grayson, admr of the estate of Jas. W. Grayson, deceased, presented and ordered to be filed for exceptions.
- A report of settlement by A.J. Grayson, admr. of the estate of Emily Grayson, deceased, presented and ordered to be filed for exceptions.
- Names of Petit Jurors- E.S. Stowers, Wm. Perkey, E.S. Kidd, S.A. Melvin, Newton Waddle, J.N. Fannon, J. Wint Thompson, G.D. Havens, James Thompson, James Lampert, Jas. H. Bruce and J.H. Spangler.
- Commonwealth VS Ellen Chandler. Misdemeanor. Case continued.
- Commonwealth VS Hannah Chandler. Misdemeanor. Case continued.
- Commonwealth VS Melvina Cubine. Misdemeanor. Case continued.
- Jasper N. Fannon VS H.A. Chandler & others. Court overruled motion by defendants, to quash the notice. Both parties agree to put themselves upon the judgament of the court. Ordered that Fannon recover from Chandler the sum of $2.20 and each pay his own costs.

- Memorandum upon the above trial. The defendants tendered 10 bills of exceptions. Signed , sealed and made part of the record.
- Court adjourned until first day of next term. Signed by G.W. Easley, (Judge)

Page 354- Monday February, 1, 1875- Hon. Geo. W. Easley, Judge.
- A list of deeds presented in the Clerk's Office and admitted to record, since last term of court.-
- Wm. E. Hoge to Lucinda M. Sanders, 4 acres on Walkers Creek, for $25.00. Dated 6-7-1871.
- Gordon Sanders & wife to James Robinett, conveying a tract of land on north side of Walkers Mountain, being same land conveyed to Lucinda M. Sanders by her father, Henry Harman, containing 213 acres, a part of the Thruston Survey. For $3,750.00. Dated 12-25-1874
- George Bogle to Elizabeth V. Kitts, land (acreage not given) lying on Walkers Creek. Deed of Gift. Dated 12-3-1874.
- Simms M. Stowers & others to A.D. Burton, land on Laurel Branch. No acreage given, for $1.00. Dated 9-21-1874.
- A report of settlement by Joel H. Spangler, guardian of M.J. Hudson. Ordered to be filed for exceptions.
_ Commonwealth VS Ralph B. Wyrick. Indictment for disturbing religious worship. Jury found defendant guilty and fines him $43.00. Defendant by his attorney moved the court to set aside the verdict to which the court took time to consider. (Part on page 355-)

Page 355- February 1, 1875-
- On motion of James Jones, the rule against him for failing to appear as witness for James B. Wyrick, the same be discharged.
- Nancy Neel VS John Myers. On warrant. On motion of plaintiff, case is continued at her cost.
- On motion of A.W. Miller & others, they have leave to withdraw their application made at a previous term of court, to change the location of the road leading from west end of H.C. Fanning's land to land near A.W. Miller's. Said road to remain the same.
- Commonwealth VS John R. Walker. Misdemeanor. Court discharged a rule made against Walker against Isaac F. Stowers . A special jury after hearing the evidence adjourned until tomorrow at 10:O'clock AM.

Page 356- Tuesday Morning, February 2, 1875-
- Commonwealth VS Ralph B. Wyrick. Indictment for disturbing religious worship On the motion to set aside the verdict rendered yesterday, the court overrules said motion. Ordered that the defendant pay the sum of $43.00. Defendant made exceptions which were recorded.
- Commonwealth VS Ralph B. Wyrick. Indictment # 2, Assault & Battery. Acquitted.
- Commonwealth VS John R. Walker. Misdemeanor. The court took time to reconsider the guilty verdict passed down by the jury, on motion of the defendant.

Page 357- February 2, 1875-
- Commonwealth VS Isaac F. Stowers. Misdemeanor. A jury consisting of, Isaac Kegley, L.D. Bogle, Ganam Kitts, James C. Painter, Henry Dowling, I.K. Price, Jas. W. Harman, A.K. Kitts, Peter Tickle, J.N. Fannon, W.A. Bennett and C.C. Banks, were empannled and sworn and were adjourned until tomorrow.
- This day James Tolbert presented a claim against the Commonwealth for taking care of William

- James Tolbert makes claim for taking care of William Tolbert, a lunatic. Claim allowed.
- Court adjourned until tomorrow morning at 9: O'clock AM.

Page 358- Wednesday Morning, February 3, 1875-
- Commonwealth VS M.S. Pool. Violation of revenue laws. Case continued.
- Commonwealth VS Isaac F. Stowers. Misdemeanor. Jury finds defendant "not guilty".
- Commonwealth VS Rufus Robinett. Misdemeanor. Capias awarded against Robinett for not being found, returnable at next term of court.
- Commonwealth VS Austin French. Misdemeanor. Jury found the defendant guilty and fined him 1 cent. (Same jury as yesterday)

Page 359- February 3, 1875-
- Commonwealth VS Joseph Moss. Misdemeanor. Court overruled defendants motion to quash the indictment in this cause. The jury found him "not guilty".
- In the matter of the settlements of the accounts made by Jno. H. Hoge, appointed Commissioner of accounts, with Andrew J. Grayson, admr. of J.W. Grayson, decd. and A.J. Grayson admr. of Emily Grayson, decd. The exceptions A.J. Grayson to the actions of the Commissioner, were considered by the court. Ordered that the reports be recommitted back to the Commissioner who made them and he is hereby required to restate the said accounts showing the receipts and disbursements of the administrator annually in each case and stating said accounts in accordance with the principles and formula established by the Court of Appeals of Virginia and as set out and reported in "mathews Guide to the Commissioners in Chancery" and make report of his proceeding to Court at a future time.
- F.G. Helvey asks leave to erect a gate across the public road, passing Point Pleasant Academy and intersecting with the Walkers Creek & Holston Turnpike. Docketed and notices posted.

Page 360- February 3, 1875-
- Adam Waggoner, asks leave to erect gates across the public road leading from D.O. McNeil's Mill to the Raleigh Grayson Turnpike. Docketed and notices posted.
- Commonwealth VS B. Dodd. Violation of Revenue Laws. A special jury consisting of, Samuel Steel, L.D. Bogle, Henry Dowling, A.J. Kitts, Peter Tickle, E.S. Kidd, I.G. Pauley, James Thompson, Jno. Havens, Wm. Kitts, J.S. French and Jas. Lampert, rendered a "not guilty" verdict. Defendant is acquitted and discharged.
- Commonwealth VS B. Dodd. Violation of Revenue Laws. (Nos. 2&3) Acquitted.

Page 361- February 3, 1875-
- Commonwealth VS Daniel Robinett. Violation of Revenue Laws. The defendant still not being found so as to be served with warrant, a capias is issued agaist hi, and ordered returnable at the next April term of court.
- Commonwealth VS John R. Walker. Misdemeanor. The court overruled the motion to set aside the verdict of the jury in this cause. The defendant to be fined $25.00, the amount set by the jury in previous trial.
- William Dillow, Collector for Seddon Township, presents claim for $4.30. Allowed.
- Wm. N. Harman, plaintiff in an execution against Wm. C. Williams and John Fanning, and is dissatisfied with the property set aside by John Fanning in his deed of Homestead. Harman moved

the court to appoint three disinterested free holders to assess the value of said property, which motion Fanning resisted. Court overruled his objection and ordered Daniel F. Morehead, George Wohlford and John J. Mustard to assess the property of the said Fanning. They must give notice to Harman and Fanning as to the time and place at which they will execute this order.

Page 362- February 3, 1875

- Memorandum in the foregoing motion. John Fanning, by his attorney, took exception to the ruling of the court and tendered his bill of exceptions, which were made part of the record.
- Ordered that Court be adjourned until tomorrow morning at 9 ½ O'clock AM.

Thursday February 4th 1875-

- Commonwealth VS Hannah Chandler. Misdemeanor. The jury consisting of, Ganam Kitts, J.S. French, I.G. Pauley, A.J. Kitts, C.C. Thomas, H.A. Pauley, James Thompson, Peter Tickle, E.S. Kidd, J.S. Wyrick, James Lampert and Wm. A. Bennett, rendered a verdict of "Not Guilty".
- Commonwealth VS Ellen Chandler. Misdemeanor. The defendant is acquitted.
- By a former court order, Levi Woodyard, Road Commissioner for Rocky Gap Township, to view and report on expediency of building a new road from S.T. Gibson's up the Dry Fork to near A.D. Lambert,s farm. He returned his report today and A.J. Songer made motion that S.T. Gibson, Joshua Pruett, P.W. Hanks and A.D. Lambert, owners of said land through which the road will pass, be summonsed to appear and show cause if any why road should not be established.

Page 363- February 4, 1875-

- K.C. Thornton, jailor, makes claim for $6.10. Allowed and certified to the auditors.
- The following named persons named here with the amount allowed them for serving on the Petit Jury- E.S. Stowers, $1.00; J. Wint Thompson, $1.00; Isaac G. Pauley, $4.00; Wm. Leady, $2.00; James Lampert, $4.00; Hiram Hounshell, $1.00; E.S. Kidd, $4.00; Henry Hounshell, $1.00; John C. Stowers, $1.00; Joseph Waddle, $1.00; John Deaver, $1.00; Samuel Steel, $4.00; G.C. Thorn, $2.00; Wm. Kitts, $4.00; James Thompson, $4.00; John Havens, $4.00; H.A. Pauley, $4.00; H.C. Groseclose, $2.00; Adam Waggoner, $1.00; L.D. Bogle, $3.00; Ganam Kitts, $3.00; Isaac Kegley, $2.00; Jas. C. Painter, $3.00; Henry Dowling, $3.00; I.K. Price, $2.00; Jas. W. Harman, $2.00; A.J. Kitts, $3.00; Peter Tickle, $3.00; J.N. Fannon, $2.00; Wm. A. Bennett, $3.00; C.C. Banks, $2.00; A.J. Honaker, $1.00; J.S. French, $2.00 and C.C. Thomas, $1.00. Certified to the auditor of public accounts for payment.
- Gordon Kegley who was ordered to view another route for a road from Wm. B. Helvey's to near I.K. Price's at a former term of court, this day returned his report of the route viewed by him. Owners of land through which road will pass, J.W. Finley, Micajah Sanders, James B. Miller and John J. Wade to be summonsed to show cause if any why new road should not be established as a public highway according to said report.
- Commonwealth VS Fulton Rider & Julia Tolbert. On a Rule. (Continued on next page)

Page 364- February 4, 1875-

- ---The defendants moved the court to quash the rule on the ground that the affidavit was insufficient, which the court overruled. Case is returnable at next term of court.

- Samuel W. Williams makes claim for $35.00 which was allowed and certified to the auditor for payment.
- James S. Wyrick VS Henry Newberry and Wythe C. Newberry. On an application for a new road. James Thompson and Adam Waggoner, through whose land the road will pass appeared in person. The application of Wyrick won the route proposed by him is dismissed. No allowance allowed to land owners for damages that may be done to them but they are granted permission to erect gates on the public road. (Continued on next page)

Page 365- February 4, 1875----- Henry and Wythe Newberry appeared in person and agreed to open the road as established for $50.00. Allowed and certified to the Mechanicsburg Board.
- Court adjourned until first day of next term. Signed by G.W. Easley, Judge.

Page 366- March 1, 1875- G.W. Easley, Judge.
- Following is a list of deeds presented in the Clerk's Office since last term of court and sertified and admitted to record-
- James Thompson & wife to Wythe C. Newberry, 13 acres on north side of Walkers Mountain. For $ 107.50. Dated 12-1-1874.
- Randolph Grayson & wife to Charles S. Grayson, deed of gift, lot in Seddon. Dated 1-23-1872.
- Joseph A. Fanning & others, to Wm. W. Fanning, Jr. land on Kimberling Creek, amount not given. For $725.00. Dated 8-16-1873.
- Randolph Graayson to Leonidas G. & Mary S. McGinnis, a lot in Seddon. Deed of gift, dated 8-31-1872.
- George Bogle to D.L. Tickle, trustee, land on south side of Walkers Creek. Deed of gift, dated 12-17-1874.
- Joseph Myers to Marvin Sehorn? , trustee, to secure Henry Simmerman & others. Dated 10-6-1875.
- Elizabeth Henderson to Ballard P. Stafford, her dower interest in lands of John Henderson, deceased. For his support of her. Dated 2-18-1875.
- Wm. Umbarger & wife to James A. Repass, trustee, land on Walkers Creek, no amount given.to secure AlexUmbarger. Dated 2-19-1875
- George Bogle to D.L. Tickle, land on Walkers Creek, no acerage given. For $500.00 in part. Dated 12-17-1874.
- Richard Moore & wife to Darthula W. Hamilton, deed of gift. 40 ½ acres on the north side of Walkers Creek. Dated 2-15-1875.

Page 367- March 1, 1875- (Deeds continued)
- A.J. Nye, Special Commissioner, to E.G. Booth, interest of A.J. and Jas. F. Muncey, in the "Allum Springs Tract. Consideration, payment of purchase money. Dated 6-2-1874.
- Molly Cregger to Paris Harman, 18 ½ acres on Walkers Creek, for $100.00. Dated 4-7-1873.
- James Robinett to Wm. E. Hoge, trustee, 218 acers on Walkers Creek, to secure Gordon Saunders. Dated 12-25-1874.
- On motion of John Dilman & Stephen Kimberling, that Elias Foglesong, Henry Foglesong & James Huddle be and are hereby appointed commissioners to lay off and divide the lands of Joseph Kimberling, deceased among his heirs.
- On motion of K.C. Thornton, the jailer, it is ordered that the sheriff be authorized to purchase

for the use of the jail and at the expense of the county, 18 yards of heavy goods for two straw beds, 2 pair heavy prison blankets, 20 yards of cotton cloth for sheets, 2 wash pans, 2 tin cups, 2 small water buckets, 2 chambers and ½ dozen tin plates.

- Leave is given to Adam Waggoner to erect a gate across the public road on his land near the Creek on the road leading from D.O. McNeil's Mill to the Raliegh Grayson Turnpike.

Page 368- March 1, 1875-

- Leave is given to F.G. Helvey to erect a gate in the public road, passing Point Pleasant Academy intersecting the Walkers Creek & Holston Turnpike, north of said Academy.
- Dr. James M. Hamilton presented an account against the Commonwealth for $20.00 for medical attention given to Wm. F. Tolbert, a lunatic Allowed.
- Thomas F. Walker appointed administrator of John W. Hatch, deceased. Walker with B.H. Penley, his security posts bond for $400.00 and took oath of office.
- Richard Gregory, Jacob Carper and Russell Stowers are appointed to appraise the personal estate of John W. Hatch, deceased. (On motion of Thomas F. Walker, admr.)
- On moton of James M. Pruett, ordered that the Mechanicsburg Road Commissioner go on the Wilderness road and report on the expediency of changing the location of the road and report on the inconveniences that might result from such change.
- James Tolbert presents claim for $28.00 for taking care of Wm. F. Tolbert, a lunatic. Allowed.

Page 369- March 1, 1875-

- Eli Steel appointed administrator of Samuel Steel, deceased and with I.G. Pauley & Samuel Dillow, his security, posts bond for $600.00. Certificates awarded for pbtaining letters of administration of said estste in due form.
- Eli Groseclose, Thomas Wilson and George Hudson appointed to appraise the personao estate of Samuel Steel, deceased.
- Samuel Kitts and John C. Stowers present claim for $2.20. Allowed.
- James M. Stowers, H. Newberry and A.J. Grayson, present a signed a paper agreeing to remain as sureties on the bond of D.W. Dunn, Treasurer of Bland County.
- H.H. Tilson, one of the sureties for official bond of Eli F. Groseclose, Collector for Sharon Township presents signed paper consenting to remain as surety on the bond. S.M. McNutt, another surety agrees also to remain as surety.

Page 370, March 1, 1875-

- On motion of A.J. Songer at an earlier term of court, Levi Woodyard, Road Commissioner for Rocky Gap Township was ordered to view a route for a new road leading from near S.L. Gibsons up the Dry Fork to near A.D. Lamperts. Ordered that the road be established.
- A settlement by A.J. Muncy, administrator of Wm. Hearn, deceased, was presented and ordered to be filed for exceptions.
- A report of settlement by Adam Waggoner, guardian for Margaret and Foster Waggoner, ordered filed for exceptions.
- John Fanning VS Isaiah K. Price. Application for a new road. Cause continued until next term of court. James B. Miller and Wm. N. Harman mentioned as land owners.
- Ordered that the Court be adjourned until the first day of the next term. Signed by G.W. Easley, Judge.

Page 371- April 5, 1875- George W. Easley, Judge.

- Following is a list of deeds presented at the Clerk's Office since last term of Court and admitted to record:-

- John Havens & wife to Wythe C. Newberry, a tract of land on north side of Walkers Mountain (acreage not given) for $200.00. Dated 2-26-1875.

- Jno. A. Kelley, com. to E.A. Davis, land in Bland County for payment of purchase money. Dated 1-25-1875.

- Wm. Page, assignee of Joshua Pruett to E.A. Davis, 400 acres +- in Bland County for $300.00. Dated 10-28-1874.

- A report and plat made by the Commissioners to divide the lands of Wm. Groseclose, deceased. Dated 3-9-1872. Confirmed by court 12-7-1874.

- Dower of Elizabeth S. Spangler in the lands of G.T. Hudson, deceased, as laid off by the commissioners. Dated 3-7-1874, confirmed by court 1-4-1875.

- Catherine Stafford & others to County School Board of Free Schools, a lot of land on Walkers Creek, for $15.00. Dated 12-5-1874.

- F.S. Blair, com. to Zarilda A. Davis, 242 acres of the lands of P.H. Dills, deceased. Dated 1-4-1872.

- Dower of Jane Dunbar, in the lands of L.D. Dunbar, deceased, laid off by the commissioners. Dated 12-4-1865, confirmed by the court of Wise County 12-25-1874.

- The will of Moses Akers, Sr. was presented this day and proven by the oath of Samuel C. Davis, one of the subscribing witnesses. W.B. Akers, the other witness, not present. Will is ordered to be recorded.

Page 372- April 5, 1875-

- A.G. Thompson VS D.F. Thompson. On Notice. Plaintiff asks to be relieved from all further liability as surety for the official bond of the defendant, as guardian for Marietta E. Waggoner. Relief was granted and D.F. Thompson with James Thompson and James H. Muncy, his sureties, posts bond for $1,600.00.

- A will purporting to be the last will of John Mustard, deceased, was produced in court by Bane Price & Sarah, his wife in order to be proved. Wythe Newberry and Elizabeth, his wife, opposed the proof thereof. Ordered that a jury be impaneled at next term of court to try whether the will is or is not the true will of John Mustard, deceased. Ordered that William Crawford be summonsed here the first day of next term, and to bring with him any papers in his custody purporting to be testamentary papers of the said John Mustard.

- Commonwealth VS M.S. Pool. Violation of Revenue Laws. Pool pleads "innocent" and puts himself on the court. Commonwealth does likewise. Pool posts bond for $50.00 to assure his appearance in court.

Page 373- April 5, 1875-

- John C. Crockett, Executor, VS George Wohlford, collector. On notice. Case continued.

- Joseph Wohlford VS John Fanning. On a removal, # 1. A rule is awarded to Fanning against Wohlford abd Ira D. Hall returnable here at next term to show why this case should not be dismissed.

Joseph Wohlford VS John Fanning. On a removal, # 2. On motion of Fanning, this case to be docketed and continued.

- John C. Hanshew & S.R. Williams VS James Bottomly. The plaintiffs, having obtained an attachment for $52.25, against the estate of the defendant. (The defendant having moved out of the Commonwealth) Eli Groseclose, collector, had levied on about 30 bushels of wheat, belonging to the defendant and in the care of Jonathan Bottomly. Ordered that the sheriff sell the 30 bushels of wheat and out of the proceeds, pay the plaintiff's judgment. (part of this item is on page 374)

Page 374- April 5, 1875-
- James Tolbert presents claim for $35.00. ALlowed.
- A.B. Honaker, appointed Registrar for Rocky Gap Precinct in the room of P.C. Honaker, deceased. He took the oath of office.
- On motion of Wm. N. Harman, Plaintiff in an execution against Wm. E. Williams and John Fanning. A rule is awarded him against George Wohlford, John J. Mustard and D.F. Morehead, who were by a former court ordered to appraise the property of said Fanning, claaimed by him in his Homestead Deed, returnable to the next term of court to show why thay should not be fined for contempt in disregarding the order of this court.
- Nancy Neel VS John Myers. On a removal. Case continued on motion of defendant.
- Jasper N. Fannon appointed Registrar of Town of Seddon in place of Williasm Kitts who has moved from this jurisdiction.

Page 375- April 5, 1875-
- The following persons are appointed as judges and commissioners of the elections in Bland County, to serve as such until April 1, 1876, Viz-
Elias Foglesong, Isaac Hudson and A.W. Shewey, for Sharon Sharon Precinct.
Henry Newberry, Wm. Hederick and Isaac Kegley, for Seddon Precinct.
Wm. E. Hoge, Isaac J. Davis and Hiram Rider, for Mechanicsburg Precinct.
W.W. Compton, Geo. W. Brown and A.D. Lambert, for Rocky Gap Precinct.
Duncan Cameron, A.R. Bogle and John A. Smith, for Cameron's Precinct.
Henry Newberry, Wm. E. Hoge, George W. Brown, A.R. Bogle and A.W. Shewey are designated as Commissioners.
- John F. Locke, W.G. Painter and ---- Thornton are appointed judges of election for the Corporation of the Town of Seddon.
- Allen Mustard, John H. Hoilman and S.H. Bernard appointed judges for the Corporation of the town of Mechanicsburg.
- Sale and appraisement bill of the personal estate of Samuel Steel, deceased, returned to court and ordered to be recorded.
- Report of settlement by A.J. Muncy, admr. of estate of Wm. Hearne, deceased. No exceptions made. Ordered to be recorded. (Had been filed for exceptions at former term of court.)
- Report of settlement by Adam Waggoner, guardian for Margaret and Foster Waggoner, having been filed for exceptions at a former term of court, ordered to be recorded.
- Report of settlement by D. Thompson, guardian of Marietta E. Waggoner, ordered to be filed for exceptions.
- John M. Hicks & Co. VS Jacob Waggoner. On a removal. { Concerning bankruptcy of the defendnat. Writing so bad, cannot decipher it. }

Page 376- April 5, 1875-
- James Lambert VS T.J. Doyle. on a notice to correct a judgement. { Cannot decipher }
- Thomas L. Howard, trustee in a deed executed by Thomas Clare on February 2, 1857, this day reports sale of certain Real Estate by virtue of a certain trust deed. Ordered filed.
- A list of the appraisement of personal property, bonds & accounts of Peter C. Honaker, deceased. Ordered to be recorded.

Page 377- April 5, 1875-
- A writing signed by James M. Stowers, Harman Newberry and A.J. Grayson, sureties on D.W. Dunn's bond as treasurer of the county, giving their consent for the extension of time for the collection of taxes and levies for the year of 1874. Writing ordered to be recorded.
- Commonwealth VS Fulton Rider & Julia Tolbert. On information of lewd and lascivious cohabitation. Defendants plead "not guilty" . Case continued.
- Court adjourned until first day of next term. Signed by G.W. Easley, Judge.

Page 378- May 3, 1875- George W. Easley, Judge.
- Following is a list of deeds presented in the Clerk's Office since last term of court:-
- Jane Dunbar, widow of L.D. Dunbar, deceased, deeds her dower interest in a 100 acre tract of land on Kimberling, as assigned by commissioners whose report confirmed by Wise County Court. Report dated 12-4-1865. Dated 12-25-1874 in Bland County.
- Wm. B. Ashworth & others to Wm. P. Bruce, 105 acres on north side of Walkers Mountain, for $800.00. Dated 3-6-1875.
- Samuel Wohlford's executors to Matilda Rider, lot # 10, in Town of Mechanicsburg , for $150.00. Dated 11-17-1873.
- T.J. Munsey to S.W. Williams, trustee, a deed of trust on personal property, to secure John M. Hicks and Spotts & Gibson. Dated 4-6-1875.
- James L. Burton to D.G. Bird, 44 acres adjoining the lands of B.V. Bird & others. For $440.00. Dated 4-7-1875.
- R. Grayson to M.G. Chandler & others, lot # 41 in Town of Seddon, for $30.00. Dated 4-3-1872.
- S.W. Williams, Special Commissioner, to Wm. P. Mustard, lots 3, 4 & 5 as laid off by the commissioners in the lands of Jacob Nicewander, deceased. Dated 9-24-1873.
- John H. Hoge, Special Commissioner to C.H.C. Fulkerson, a lot adjoining the hotel property (Crocketts) in the Town of Seddon. (No consideration given) Dated 11-17-1874.
- John H. Hoge, Special Commissioner, to Acles Fannon for a lot adjoining George Pegram's lot in the Town of Seddon. (No consideration given) Dated 11-17-1874.

Page 379- May 3, 1875-
- A deed from John H. Hoge, Special Commissioner, to Wm. M. Bird, for 500 acres of lane 2 miles north of the Town of Seddon. (No consideration given) Dated 11-17-1874.
- Commonwealth VS Rufus Robinett. Misdemeanor. "he "alias capias" issued against the defendant, not executed ordered tha a "Pluries Capias" be awarded against him returnable at next term of court.

- Commonwealth VS M.S. Pool. Violation of Revenue Laws. On motion of defendant, a rule is awarded him against W.W. Ashworth & Albert Linkious, for failure to appear in court. Pool posts bond for $50.00 and case continued at next term of court.
- James Tolbert presents claim for $28.00 for taking care of Wm. Tolbert, a lunatic. Allowed.

Page 380- Commonwealth VS Fulton Rider & other. For lewd and lascivious cohabitation. A rule awarded to Rider against Wm. Hawkins, a witness who failed to appear in court. Case continued.
- On motion of Thomas Wohlford and Catherine C. Crockett, Jno. H. Hoge, Jno. P. Roach and Z.T. Weaver are appointed Commissioners to make pertition of the tract of land which was the dower of Nancy Nicewander, deceased, in the Real Estate of her late husband, Abraham Nicewander, deceased. Between Thomas Wohlford, Catherine C. Crockett and the heirs of Sam'l. Wohlford, deceased, 1/5th and said Catherine Crockett, 3/5ths. Having regard to the quantity as well as the quality of the said land.
- Ordered that the Court be adjourned until tomorrow morning at 8: O'clock AM.

Page 381- Tuesday Morning, May 4, 1875-
- A.J. Grayson asks for an inclusive survey of his several tracts of land which adjoin each other. Ordered that George W. Kinzer, County Surveyor re-survey this land and make report and return plat, to the court, being careful not to infringe upon the rights of others.
- John G. Crockett, surviving executor of himself & C.G. Crockett, deceased, who were the executors of the last will of Jno. C. Crockett, deceased, plaintiffs, against George Wohlford, collector and as such Constable of Bland County. On a notice. Plaintiff to recover from the defendant the sum of $20.00, being the amount levied by the defendant by a distress warrant obtained by John C. Crockett in his lifetime against R.C. Green & Wm. J. Jackson, his tenants.
- Joseph Wohlford VS John Fanning. Case dismissed and Fanning to recover from Wohlford his costs for this case.

Page 382-May 4, 1875-
- Joseph Wohlford VS John Fanning . Same verdict as above.
- A.W. Miller desires changes to be made in the road known as Booth Springs Road, from M.A. Robinett's land to a point west of A.W. Miller's land. I. K. Price. Leonard Muirhead and Pendleton Burton ordered to go on said route and report to the court with a map of such route.
- Wm. N. Harman, appointed guardian of E. Harman Sheppard, Ann May Sheppad and John Shepperd, infants over the age of 14 and under age 21, children of E. A. Sheppard, deceased. Harman with Eli Groseclose, his security posts bond for $600.00.

Page 383- May 4, 1875-
- George B. Schmitz has been dead for over 3 months. A. Gooch makes motion that the sheriff take over and administer the estate of said Schmitz, deceased.
- A license is granted to John H. Bridges to sell religious material, from May 1, 1875 to April 30, 1876. For paymebt of $5.00 tax.
- John Fanning VS I. K. Price. Price asks court to quash a report of Commissioners J.G. Kegley and H.C. Fanning, concerning a new road. Motion overruled. The cout is of the opinion that neither route should be established. Price to recover from Fanning his costs.

- Bane Price & wife VS Wythe C. Newberry & wife. Ordered that Wm. Crawford appear in court bringing with him any papers of testamentary of John Mustard, deceased, that may be in his possession.
- A report of settlement by D.F. Thompson, guardian of Marietta E. Waggoner. Ordered to be recorded.

Page 384- May 4, 1875-
- The rule awarded at last term of court on application of Wm. N. Harman against Daniel F. Morehead, George Wohlford & John J. Mustard, who were appointed to value and return a report of the property of John Fanning in his Homestead Deed, for failure to execute said order. Fanning moves to discharge said rule which the court overruled. Ordered that the rule against Daniel F. Morehead be dismissed and the same be enlarged against George Wohlford & John J. Mustard. John Fanning tenders his bills of exceptions which were made part of the record.
- Ordered that the following persons be appointed to lay off their respective Magisterial Districts into Road Precincts and that they allot the hands to work the road-
In Mechanicsburg District- James Robinett, Daniel F. Morehead & John J. Mustard.
In Seddon District- James M. Stowers, Paul James & J. Henderson Bruce.
In Sharon District- James A. Repass, A. W. Shewey & H.C. Groseclose.
In Rocky Gap District- Thomas H. Kinzer, Thomas F. Walker & John A. Davidson.
- In County Court on vacation this 25th of May 1875- James M. Hamilton is appointed by Z.T. Weaver as assistant assessor of Seddon Township. Hamilton took the several oaths of office.

Page 385- Monday June 7, 1875- Geo. W. Easley, Judge.
- Following, a list of deeds presented in the Clerk's Office and ordered tro be recorded--
- John C. Carpenter, Sr. to Edward L. Carpenter. Real Estate on Wolf Creek. (No amount or consideration given) Dated 5-1-1875.
- A deed of Homestead by S.T. Gibson. Including real & personal property. Dated 5-1-1875.
- Catherine Melvin to E.M. Melvin. Her interest in the estates of John & George Melvin, deceased. Both real and personal property. Dated 11-22-1873.
- Wm. P. Hornbarger to James M. Starks. 26 acres lying on Hunting Camp Creek, for $181.00. Dated 5-14-1875.
- Wm. P. Hornbarger & wife to Paul James & others, trustees, ½ acre on Hunting Camp Creek for for a church. Dated 5-14-1875.
- T.N. Finley to Wm. Dillow, trustee, to secure T.E. Greggory. Dated 5-22-1875.
- Wythe C. Newberry & wife VS Bane Price & wife. Case is removed to the district court to be finally tried and determined.
- W.W. Ashworth elected Justice Of The Peace for Rocky Gap Township, took oath of office.

Page 386- June 7, 1875-
- John H. Lindamood, elected Justice Of The Peace for Sharon District, takes oath of office.
- Jacob Waggoner, elected Justice Of The Peace for Sharon District, takes oath of office.
- John W. Harman, elected Justice Of The Peace for Rocky Gap District, takes oath of office.
- F.C. Bogle, elected Justice Of The Peace for Rocky Gap District, takes oath of office.
- John F. Locke, elected Justice Of The Peace for Seddon District, takes oath of office.
- Paul James, elected Justice Of The Peace for Seddon District, takes oath of office.

- Jas. H. Munsey, elected Justice Of The Peace for Mechanicsburg District, takes oath of office.

Page 387- June 7, 1875-
- Alexander Nicewander, elected Justice Of The Peace for Mechanicsburg, takes oath of office.
- William T. Hamilton, duly elected Clerk Of The County Court, to serve a term of six years, together with Wm. Kitts, F.I. Suiter & T.N. Finley, his securities, posts bond for $5,000.00 and took the oath of office as prescribed by law.
- Samuel W. Williams, elected Commonwealth's Attorney for Bland County, together with A.J. Gryson and J.M. Fanning, his securities, posts bond for $500.00 and took oath of office.
- D.W. Dunn, elected County Treasurer, with F.I. Suiter, A.J. Grayson, George Wohlford, A.W. Shewey, Wm. Kitts & William Wilkerson, his surities, posts bond for $20,000.00 and toke oath.

Page 388- June 7, 1875-
- L.J. Miller, elected Commissioner Of Revenue, together with Thomas H. Kinser and F.I. Suiter, his securities, posts bond for $3,000.00 and takes oath of office.
- Thomas H. Kinzer, elected Supervisor for Rocky Gap District. Together with Henry G. Hicks, posts bond for $1,000.00 and takes oath of office as prescribed by law.
- Ganam Kitts elected as Supervisor of Seddon District, with Wm. Kitts, his security, posts bond for $ 1,000.00 and took oath of office. (Part of item on page 389)

Page 389- June 7, 1875-
- James M. Hamilton, elected as Supervisor for Mechanicsburg District, with L.J. Miller, his security, posts bond for $1,000.00 and took the oath of office.
- James A. Repass, elected as Supervisor for Sharon District, with H.C. Newberry, his security, posts bond for $1,000.00 and took oath of office.
- J.G. Kegley, elected Sheriff of the county. He, together with Gordon Wohlford, S.H. Newberry, B.V. Bird and H. Newberry, his securities, posts bond for $20,000.00 and took oath of office.

Page 390- June 7, 1875-
- George W. Stowers, appointed by the Board of Supervisors as Superintendent Of The Poor, to serve for a term of four years. He, together with Wm. Stowers, Colby Stowers and A.J. Grayson his securities, posts bond for $2,000.00 and took oath of office.
- Colby Stowers, elected Overseer Of The Poor in Rocky Gap District, for a term of two years, together with Geo. W. Stowers, his security, posts bond for $500.00.
- F.G. Helvey, elected Overseer Of The Poor in Mechanicsbur District, for a term of two years, together with James H. Muncy, his security, posts bond for $ 5,000.00. { Why was his bond so much higher than that of Colby Stowers? Perhaps a misprint. P. Bogle}
- W.W. Grayson appointed as Surveyor of the County for a term of four years. He, with H.C. Newberry, his security, posts bond for $500.00 and took oath of office,

Page 391- June 7, 1875-
- H.C. Fannig, elected Constable for Mechanicsburg District for a term of two years. He, with J.M. Fanning and George Wohlford, his securities, posts bond for $2,000.00 and took oath.
- A rule against W.W. Ashworth for failing to appear as a witness for M.S. Pool, is discharged.
- Commonwealth VS David B. Greever. On presentment of a nuisance. Greever is fined $5.00.

- Commonwealth VS M.S. Pool. Misdemeanor. Pool admits debt to Commonwealth. Posts bond for $50.00 for his appearance at next term of court. { Part of item on page 392}

Page 392- June 7, 1875-
- Z.T. Weaver, appointed by the court as Assessor, to assess the value of all lots and land of the County. He, with J.J. Mustard, George Wohlford and H. Newberry, his securities, posted bond for $5,000.00 and took oath of office as prescribed by law.
- L.J. Miller, appointed administrator of Wm. Crawford, deceased, the widow having waived her rights to administer, together with George Wohlford and John J. Mustard, posted bond for $2,000.00. Certificate granted him to obtain letters of administration.
- Geo. W. Robinett, having took the oath necessary, is appointed administrator of the estate of Hiram Robinett, deceased. He with A.J. Grayson, his security, posts bond for $2,000.00, and is granted certificate for obtaining letters of administration. { Part of item on page 393 }

Page 393- June 7, 1875-
- Jas. A. Repass, Geo. W. K. Green, Jno. F. Locke and F.M. Harman, appointed on motion of Geo. W. Robinett administrator of Hiram Robinett deceased, to appraise the personal estate of Hiram Robinett, deceased.
- Rees Crabtree, elected Constable for Sharon District, together with George W. Kinzer and Jno. M. Cassell, his securities, posts bond for $2,000.00 and took oath of office.
- Samuel W. William, Commonwealth's Attorney, presents claim for $5.00. Allowed.
- James Tolbert presents claim for $35.00, for taking care of Wm. Tolbert, a lunatic. Allowed.
- F.G. Helvey, Overseer of The Poor, is directed to make provision for Josephine Burgess, a pauper, at her place of abode until such time as she may be able to be removed to the Poor House or shall not need assistance. To be paid for out of County levy as other expenditures for the poor.

Page 394- June 7, 1875-
- Wm. Dillow, Constable, makes claim for $3.00. Allowed.
- S.S. Reader, elected, Justice Of The Peace for Seddon District and took oath of office.
- Gordon Wohlford qualified to act as deputy for J.G. Kegley, Sheriff and takes oath of office.
- K.C. Thornton qualified as deputy to Sheriff J.G. Kegley and took the oath of office.
- James M. Hamilton, qualified to be deputy to William T. Hamiltom, Clerk this Court, and took the oath of office.
- Geo. W. Kinser qualified as deputy to W.W. Grayson, Surveyor of the County.
- Thomas H. Kinser, produces physician's certificate which proves that he is unable to work on the public roads. Ordered that he be released.

Page 395- June 7, 1875-
- A deed with proper certificates attached, from John A. Kelly, Commissioner, to the Board of Supervisors of Bland County, the lands on which the buildings now used as a reception place for the paupers of this County. Deed is to be recorded.
- Gordon Wohlford, Collector for Mechanicsburg District, presents a list of delinquents in capitation and property taxes for 1874. A copy be sent to the auditors of Public Accounts.
- Gordon Wohlford, Collector for Mechanicsburg District, presents a list of real estate in the district of Z.T. Weaver, assessor, which is delinquent for non payment for 1874 taxes.

- Gordon Wohlford, Collector for Mechanicsburg District, presents a list of property on the Assessor's land book, improperly placed thereon.

Page 396- June7, 1875-
- The following persons were appointed at an earlier term of court to lay off their several districts into road precincts, returned their reports whih were ordered filed for exceptions.- James M. Stowers, J.H. Brucea and Paul James, for Seddon; Jas. S. Robinett, John J. Mustard and D.F. Morehead for Mechanicsburg; Thos. H. Kinser, John A. Davidson and Thos. F. Walker for Rocky Gap and James A. Repass, H.C. Grosclose and A.W. Wiley? for Sharon District.
- The inventory report of the Personal estate of Calvin G. Crockett, deceased, certified and ordered to be recorded.
- It is suggested to the court that there are two thoroughfares through tha County of Bland, the Raliegh & Grayson Turnpike leading from the Wythe County line to the Mercer County line. The other one, known as Walkers Creek & Hoslton Turnpike, leading from the Giles County line to the Cmith County line. Both could be used as toll roads. Ordered that Sam'l. W. Williams, James M. Stowers and D.W. Dunn, are appointed as Commissioners to receive bids for keeping them in repair as toll roads. { Part of item on page 397 }

Page 397- June 7, 1875-
- All cases not otherwise disposed of be continued until next term of court.
- Ordered that court stand adjourned until first day of next term. Signed, G.W. Easley, Judge.
- Isaac J. Davis, elected as a Justice of The Peace, this day appeared before me in vacation at Mechanicsburg and took the several oaths of office prescribed by law.
Memo to Wm. T. Hamilton, Clerk of Bland County Court, dated June 8, 1875 and signed by G.W. Easley, Judge.

Page 398- Monday July 5, 1875- George W. Easley, Judge.-
- Following is a list of deeds presented and recorded in the Clerk,s Office-
- Elisha Bond & wife to Martha A. R. Ford. A tract of land on Dry Fork of Laurel. For $400.00, dated 3-29-1875.
- James Jones to Abrham Wampler, 2 acres on Walkers Little Creek for $6.50. Dated 4-28-1875.
- E. T. Mahood, Commissioner, to Peter C. Honaker, 3 tracts on on Wolf Creek, 40 ½ acres; 84 acres and 12 acres. Dated 9-18-1873.
- Robert Doak & wife to Henry F. Doak, 192 acres in Rich Valley, for love & affection. Dated 2-24-1873.
- Wm. Mustard, Sr. to Harvey R. Mustard, 156 acres on Walkers Creek for $1,500.00. Dated 6-2-1873.
- Allen T. Newberry & wife to Henry Newberry, 250 ½ acres on Walkers Creek for $1,000.000 and natural love and affection. Dated 5-26-1875.
- A.J. Grayson & wife to Samuel W. Williams, house & lot # 23 in Seddon. For $300.00. Dated June 5, 1875.
- J.T. Myers & wife to E.M. Melvin, conveying their interest in the lands of John & George Melvin, deceased. For $200.00. Dated 3-25-1875.
- James Jones to Bryl Jackson, 100 acres on Walkers Little Creek, for $75.00. Dated 6-14-1875.

Page 399- July 5, 1875-
- Peter R. Hicks & wife to J.W. Compton, 106 acres on Hunting Camp Creek, for $1,200.00. Dated 2-23-1875.
- The sale bill for John W. Hatch, deceased is presented and ordered to be recorded.
- The appraisement bill of personal property of John W. Hatch, deceased, ordered recorded.
- A report of settlement with Jno. H. Hoge, by A.F. Suiter, guardian of J.F. ?????, on March 1, 1875. Ordered to be filed for exceptions.
- A report of settlement by Joel H. Spangler, guardian of M.J. Hudson. Ordered recorded.
- Sale and appraisement bills of personal estate of Wm. Crawford, deceased, ordered recorded.
- D.W. Dunn, acting Collector of Rocky Gap District, presents a list of properties improperly placed upon the land books for the year 1874. The list after being examined and corrected, a copy was sent to the auditors.
- D.W. Dunn, County Treasurer, presents list of delinquent real estate taxes in the district of James D. Honaker, Assessor, for the year 1874.

Page 400, July 5, 1875-
- D.W. Dunn, acting Collector for Rocky Gap District, presents list of delinquent capitation & personal property taxes. James D. Honaler, assessor.
- Eli F. Groseclose, collector for Sharon District presents list of delinquent capitation and personaal property taxes in the district of George M. Tibbs, assessor.
- Eli F. Groseclose, collector for Sharon, presents delinquent tax list for real estate taxes.

Page 401- July 5, 1875-
- Elias Foglesong, this day appointed Overseer Of The Poor for Sharon District, with Eli F. Groseclose, his security posts bond for $500.00 and took the oath of office.
- Ordered that the rule against Fulton Rider for failing to appear as a witness, is discharged.
- Moses Akers has been dead for more than 3 months. On motion of James F. Seagle, it is ordered that the Sheriff take over his estate and administer it according to law.
- Commonwealth VS M.S. Pool. Violation of Revenue Laws. On motion of Pool, a rule is issued against Albert Linkous and Robt. Cecil for failure to appear as a witness for the defendant. Case continued.
- A rule is awarded against J. Wharton Repass for failure to appear before the Grand Jury as a witness after being summonsed.
- Commonwealth VS Fulton Rider. For lewd & lascivious cohabitation. (Continued on page 402)

Page 402, July 5, 1875-
Rider moves the court to award a rule against James Tolbert, who is put upon the record as "prosecutor" and be liable for costs in this case. Case is continued and on further motion a rule is awarded to Rider against Thos. Wohlford, Newton Mustard and Charley Rider for their failure to appear as witnesses for the defendant.
- A report was made by the Commissioners who laid off the dower of Nancy Nicewander in the lands of Abraham Nicewander, her deceased husband. Ordered recorded.
- On motion of Isaac Repass, it is ordered that F.F. Repass, H.H. Tilson and Henry Groseclose, report on the expediency of establishing a new road from the mountain road on the west end of Bland County to a point near the mouth of Daniel Hanshew's lane, and make report on same at

next term of court. Other land owners mentioned were, Jonas Groseclose, Thos. A. Snider and James McWilson.

Page 403- July 5, 1875-
- Commonwealth VS James S. Wyrick. Misdemeanor. # 1. Wyrick pleads "not guilty". A jury consisting of, W.H.H. Atkins, Wm. Stowers, A.W. Miller, S.W. Bird, William A. Bennet, W.G. Painter, J.A. Repass, A. Fry, Jas. W. Thompson, Jos. A. Fanning, G.N. Pegram and J.H. Thompson found the defendant "not guilty". He is acquitted & discharged.
- On motion of Commonwealth's Attorney, ordered that the sheriff summons ten persons as a special Grand Jury to serve as such during this term of court.
- Names of Grand Jury members- Paul James, foreman; Ganam Kitts, J.S. French, A.G. Thompson, Jas. T. Taylor, Peter Kitts, H.C. Groseclose and Henry Newberry. They not having finished the business before them were adjourned until tomorrow at 9' clock AM.
- Commonwealth VS James S. Wyrick. Petit larceny, # 2.- {Continued on page 404}

Page 404- July 5, 1875- --Came the jury to wit: Jno. Havens, Wm. Kitts, T.N. Finley, J.C. Painter, Geo. Lindamood, J.N. Fannon, Jacob Waggoner, Wythe G. Waddle, Henry Repass, Jno. W. Harman, Sr., D.D. Graves and Robinett Waddle, who were impaneled and sworn and adjourned until tomorrow at 9 'clock AM.
- I.E. Chapman VS John R. Johnston, Collector & sureties. On a notice.- Johnston admits that Chapman has judgement . Defendant, J.N. Justice (surety) did not appear. Judgement for the plaintiff for $62.02 plus interest and costs.
- Yost & Peery for benefit of Jno. D. Peery VS John R. Johnston, Collector & surities. On a notice. Judgement for Plaintiffs for $9.49 plus interest & costs. Same defendnats as above.
- Ordered that Court be adjourned until tomorrow morning at 9:0'clock AM.

Page 405- Tuesday Morning, July 6, 1875- Geo. W. Easley, Judge.
- Wm. Dillow, Collector for Seddon District presents a list of the insolvents in the Capitation and Personal Property Taxes. List certified and ordered to be recorded.
- The rule against Wharton Repass, for not appearing as a witness is ordered that an attachment be issued against him returnable at next term of court.
- James Tolbert presents his claim for $27.00, for keeping Wm. Tolbert, a lunatic. Allowed.
- The Special Grand Jury, impaneled and sworn yesterday, found the following indictments- Commonwealth VS Charles Waddle, a true bill. Commonwealth VS Hannah Chandler, a true bill.

Page 406- July 6, 1875-
- Exceptions were made to the report of Jas. S. Robinett, J. J. Mustard and D.F. Muirhead, the commissioners appointed to lay off the the public roads in Mechanicsburg District and allot the hands to work said roads. Ordered that the following overseers see to keeping roads in repair-
- Precinct # 1- George W. Fanning, Overseer, from Mouth of Kimberling Creek to the Widow Allen's farm, thence to the top of Brushy Mountain to west end of John Mustard'd (decd) farm.
- Precinct # 2- Isaac Lambert, Overseer, from Brick Church to hollow on Slaty Bank. From top of Brushy Mountain . Mentions Nobusiness Creek, and Micajah Sander's land.
- Precinct # 3- Simms Stowers, Overseer. Mentions Stowers' Shp, Rock lick, Wolf Creek Mountain and Simms Stowers' land.

Page 407 - July 6, 1875-
Precinct # 4- Wm. N. Harman, Overseer. Mentions Kimberling Creek, lands of James Miller and John Fanning.
Precinct # 5- William C. Williams, Overseer. Mentions Tazewell Road, Widow Neal's, Short Mountain and J. Fanning.
Precinct # 6- I.K. Price, Overseer. Mentions Stowers' Shop, Harvey Nicewander's, John Mustard's farm, Nobusiness Creek, Widow Bogle's and Farley's.
Precinct # 7- A.W. Sublett, Overseer. Mentions, James Stafford, Kimberling Creek, J.H. Mustard's farm, top of Wakkers Mountain and the county line.
Precinct # 8- Harvey R. Mustard, Overseer. Mentions, Geo. W. Fanning, Compton's Mill, J.H. Mustard's farm, Addison Davis's land and Updike's land. (Part of item on page 408)

Page 408- July 6, 1875-
- Precinct # 9- James M. Fanning, Overseer. Mentions Corporation line of Mechanicsburg, Crockett's path, Pauley's farm, Miller's branch, James Fanning's, Gordon Wohlford's Bradham's, Compton's land and George Wohlford's.
- Precinct # 10- A.F. Harman, Overseer. Mentions Old County line above Jas. Fanning's, John Hoge's line, Bogle's road, Point Pleasant Academy, F.G. Helvy & John Hoge's Homestead and James Robinett's.
- Precinct # 11- Jno. P. Roach, Overseer. Mentions Jas. Fanning's, W & H Turnpike, Jas. Robinett's, A.I. Harman's land and Harman's Road. (Part of item on page 409)

Page 409- July 6, 1875-
- Precinct # 12- John W. Harman, Jr. Overseer. Mentions Isaac Harman's, and McNeil's Mill.
- Precinct # 13- Samuel C. Davis, Overseer. Mentions Henry Davis', top of Little Mountain, Widow Mustard's land and Pulaski County line.
- No exceptions made to the report of H.C. Groseclose, A.W. Shewey and Jas. A. Repass, regarding the laying off of Road precincts in Sharon District. The following Overseers are appointed to see that the roads are kept in repair.
Precinct # 1 R.B. Repass, Overseer. Mentions Grassy Branch, W.G. Repass, Daniel Perkey, Wm. Ingrahams and Austin M. Kitts.
Precinct # 2- John Deavor, Overseer. Mentions W.G. Repass, Daniel Perkey, Tazewell & Fancy Gap Turnpike and Henry Lambert.

Page 410, July 6, 1875-
- Precinct # 3- W.T. McNutt, Overseer Mentions "the Ball Alley" at Sharon to C.J. Hudson's, James Bales', Big Jonas Umbarger's and T.H. Groseclose.
- Precinct # 4- Thos. G. Hudson, Overseer. Mentions C.J. Hudson's to the bridge at James Cassell's and Joseph Groseclose's to Burks Garden.
- Precinct # 5- Jacob Kitts, Overseer. Mentions "the bridge" at James Cassell's, Smythe County line, A.D. & E.F. Groseclose's and Joseph Groseclose's. to Smythe County line.
- Precinct # 6- H.H. Tilson., Overseer Mentions "river at Susan Groseclose's", with all hands south of said river.
- Precinct # 7- Jno. F. Umbarger, Overseer. Mentions A. Hanshew's, F.F. Repasses Mill, all

hands west of the line between F.F. Repass, M.L. Bumgardner, Jacob Groseclose and Samuel Hanshew.
- Precinct # 8- H.F. Bruce, Overseer. Mentions F.F. Repasses Mill, Turnpike at Joseph Grosecloses, with all hands east of line between F.F. Repass, M.L. Bumgardner, Jacob Groseclose and Samuel Hanshew to the Mt. Airy Turnpike.
- Precinct # 9- Henry Foglesong, Sr., Overseer. Mentions T.J.B. Spangler's, line between J.R. Bales and Big Jonas Umbarger.
- Precinct # 10- I. M. Repass, Overseer. Mentions Little Jonas Umbarger, (with T.P Umbarger, Henry Groseclose, Jno F. Umbarger, I.M. Repass, J.M.C. Wilson, the two Snidows and Samuel Hanshew as hands to work the road.)

Page 411- July 6, 1875-
- No exceptions made to the report of Thos. F. Walker, Thos. H. Kinser and Jno. A. Davidson, to the laying off of Road Precincts in Rocky Gap District, and ordered that the following Overseers, be appointed to keep said roads in good repair.
- Precinct # 1- Richard Greggory, Overseer. Mentions Tazewell line on Clear Fork to Adkin's Store and Wm. Bishop's land., .
- Precinct # 2- Nelson B. Stimson, Overseer. Mentions "from Adkin's Store to Burton's Store", hands on Bishop's lands to Dill's old farm.
- Precinct # 3- Travis Burton, Overseer. Mentions "fron J. Burton's store to Giles County line on Wolf Creek", by the hands from A.J. Honaker's to Giles County line.
- Precinct # 4- Henry P. Pruett, Overseer. Mentions Laurel Fork to Raleigh Grayson Turnpike, near Gibson's with hands in same bounds.
- Precinct # 5- Samuel L. Gibson, Overseer. Mentions East River Mountain, Deer Hollow Ford of Wolf Creek, Dills old farm, Mrs. Fletcher's, with Juno. Honaker, Albert Linkious & son, Booker Nunn and the hands from Honaker's Mill including Gibson's hands and all on Dry Fork
- Precinct # 6- James D. Honaker, surveyor of the road. Mentions Deer Hollow Ford, hands from Mrs. Mary Honakers including John A. Davidson, all in and around the Gap.
- Precinct # 7- Wm. W. Compton, Overseer. Mentions "the divides in the Wilderness to Wm. W. Compton.s ford with the hands from John A. Davidsons to Newton Johnstons, including Joseph Wynn.

Page 412- July 6, 1875-
- Precinct # 8- Henry Hicks, Overseer. Mentions Ford near W.W. Comptons to J.W. Comptons, Pine Grove Church to Mark R. Bogle's, Rich Mountain and John Neel.
- Precinct # 9- Archibald Barnett, Overseer. Mentions " from Clay Bogle's to top of Rich Mountain in Crabtrees Gap".
- No exceptions made in the report of Paul James, James M. Stowers and J. Henderson Bruce, Commissioners to laying off roads into precincts in the Seddon District. Ordered that the following Overseers see to keeping the said roads in good repair.
- Precinct # 1- Edward Epperson, Overseer. Mentions "second artificial turn on south of Big Mountain." By hands south of the top of the big mountain.
- Precinct # 2- Newton Waddle, Overseer. Mentions line between Henry Newberry and J.G. Kegley and Randolph Grayson.
- Precinct # 3- James T. Burton, Overseer. Mentions artificial turn on north side of Walkers

Mountain to the Corporation line of Seddon.
- Precinct # 4- D.G. Bird, Overseer. Mentions "from Corporation line of Seddon to
Mechanicsburg Magisterial line". W. M. Bird mentioned.

Page 413- July 6, 1875-
- Precinct # 5- B.H. Penley, Overseer. Mentions "from Seddon line to head of Kimberling Road",
to be kept by the hands living from Wm. M. Birds to B.D. Graves including the hands at Dunns
Saw Mill..
- Precinct # 6- George Walton, Overseer. Mentions Kimberling Springs, Hunting Camp Creek,
Morgan Eagle's and Rocky Gap District line.
- Precinct # 7- Francis M. Harman, Overseer. Mentions Alexander Suiter's, Wm. Kidd's and
Hiram Robinett's.
- Precinct # 8- H.C. Newberry, Overseer. Mentions Grassy Branch, B.D. Graves, James M.
Stowers, hands at Solomon & Joseph Waddle's farm.
- Precinct # 9- Charles S. Grayson, Overseer. Mentions Randolph Grayson's Shop, Henry
Newberry and Solomon Waddle.
- Commonwealth VS James S. Wyrick. On indictment # 2. Jury cannot agree on a verdict,
adjourned until tomorrow at 9:0'clock AM
- Nancy Neel VS John Myers. On an appeal from the judgement of a Justice of The Peace.
  (Continued on page 414)

Page 414- July 6, 1875- The case of Neel VS Myers, continued until next term of Court.
- William Groseclose's Executors, VS John M. Hicks. On an appeal. A rule is awarded against
Eli F. Groseclose for failure to appear as a witness. Case continued.
- Court adjourned until tomorrow morning at 8:0'clock AM.
- Wednesday morning, July 7, 1875-
- Commonwealth VS Dow Davis. Defendant failed to appear. Had posted bond for $100.00,
with Sam'l. H. Newberry, Dunn Newberry, George W.K. Green and Wm. Hicks, his sureties.
Ordered that Davis and his sureties appear at next term of Court. (Part of item on page 415)

Page 415- July 7, 1875-
- Commonwealth VS James S. Wyrick. On indictment # 2. Jury could not agree on a verdict. A
new trial ordered. Wyrick with Acles Fanning his security posts bond for $50.00 each, to assure
his return to court.
- Following is a list of Petit Jurors and the amount paid to them for their services:-
 W.H. Hawkins, $1.00; Wm. Stowers, $1.00; A.W. Miller, $1.00; S.W. Bird, $1.00; J.A.L.
Groseclose, $1.00; W.G. Painter, $1.00; Jas. A. Repass, $1.00; A. Fry, $1.00; Jas. W. Thompson,
$1.00; Jos. A. Fanning, $1.00; G.N. Pegram, $1.00; J.H. Thompson, $1.00; John Havens, $3.00;
W.A. Bennett, $1.00; Wm. Kitts, $3.00; T.N. Finley, $3.00; Jacob Waggoner, $3.00; Wythe G.
Waddle, $3.00; Henry Repass, $3.00; John W. Harman, Sr. $3.00; B.D. Graves, $3.00; and
Robinett Waddle, $3.00. Certified to the auditors for payment.
- The following persons are allowed $2.00 each for their services on the Grand Jury- Paul James,
Ganam Kitts, J.S. French, A.G. Thompson, Jas. T. Taylor, Peter Kitts, H.C. Groseclose and
Henry Newberry. Ordered that same be certified to the County Treasurer for payment.

Page 416- July 7, 1875-
- Wm. Dillow, Collector and Constable, makes claim for $2.60 which was allowed.
- The Commissoner of this county being unable to make settlement of the Fiduciary account of Jacob Waggoner, administrator of Joseph L. Cooley, deceased, it is ordered that Wm. L. Yost, one of the Commissioners, settle same and make report to the court.
- Wythe C. Newberry & others made motion that the court appoint a curator to take charge of the personal estate of John Mustard, deceased, during the contest in regard to the will of John Mustard. Christian Bane Price, the principal devisee in said will appeared in person and the court was of the opinion that Price is entitled to the place of Curator of the estate. Price is given until the first day of next term of court to give such bond and security as may be required.
- On motion of John A. Barnitz, ordered that John Franklin, contractor to keep that portion of the Fancy Gap & Tazewell Turnpike from Walkers Mountain to Garden Mountain, with Jno. S. Mcutt, Commissioner, be summonsed to appear and show cause why contract should not be rescinded· and the toll gates to the said road thrown open.
- Commonwealth VS Charles Waddle. Felony. The court overruled the motion to quash the indictment. Waddle's bail is set at $400.00, which he could not post. He was remanded back to jail and the case continued until next term of court. (Part of item on page 417)

Page 417- July 7, 1875-
- Ordered that the court adjourn until tomorrow at 9:0'clock AM.
- Thursday morning, July 8, 1875- Geo. W. Easley, Judge.
- Commonwealth VS Charles Waddle. Indictment for a felony. Waddle together with, Joseph Waddle and Samuel H. Newberry, his securities, posted bond for $400.00 each, to assure the appearance of said Waddle at next term of court.
- K.C. Thornton, Jailor, presents claim for $5.30, which was allowed.
- Ordered that the court adjourn until first day of next term of court. G. W. Easley, Judge.

Page 418- Monday, August 2, 1875-
- Commonwealth VS M.S. Pool. Violation of Revenue laws. Case continued from last term. Pool admits owing %50.00 to be levied against his goods & chattels, to assure his appearance in next term of court to answer the charges against him.
- Austin French, Albert Linkous, Miles Roland and W.W. Ashworth, post bond for $50.00 each, to assure their appearing in next term of court as a witness on behalf of M.S. Pool.
- On motion of Albert Linkious, the rule against him for not appearing as a witness for M.S. Pool, was discharged.
- The last will and testament of Simon Foglesong, deceased, was presented and partly proven by the oaths of Jacob Waggoner, one of the witnesses. Continued for further proof.
- Commonwealth VS Charles Waddle. Indictment for felony. (Continued on page 419)

Page 419- August 2, 1875- Waddle set to the bar in custody of the jailor. Case was continued until next term with same bond and sureties as on page 418.
- Commonwealth VS Dow Davis & others. Davis failed to appear. His sureties, Sam'l. H. Newberry, D.B. Newberry, Wm. Hicks and G.W.K. Green, paid the $100.00 bond.
- Geo. W. Kinzer, late surveyor of this county, returned a plat and report of survey of several tracts of land, surveyed for A.J. Grayson. Since it conforms with title papers, ordered recorded.

- Jno. C. Hanshew & others VS James Bottomly. On suggestion. Thos. A. Snider, was summonsed to answer whether or not he had effects in his hands belonging to Bottomly. After interrogation, he says he is indebted to Bottomly for $75.00. Plaintiff to recover from Snider, garnishee, the sum of $52.25 plus costs. (Part of item on page 420)

Page 420- August 2, 1875-
- Commonwealth VS Fulton Rider. For lewd & lascivious cohabitation. The jury consisting of, A.B. Honaker, B.D. Graves, W.P. Hornbarger, Isaac Kegley, Elias Blankenship, R.W. Clark, J.A.T. Groseclose, James Clark, James H. Bruce, Wythe C. Newberry, Ganam Kitts and B.F. Petrie, heard evidence and adjourned until tomorrow.
- On motion of Geo. W. Kinzer, ordered that Jos. Kinder, Henry Kimberling and Elias Foglesong, be appointed Commissioners to go on and view the route and report on the expediency of establishing a new road from a point on Wyrick Branch near George Dilman's up the back valley by Harner's Mill to a point in the turnpike road near Sarah Groseclose's, and report back to the court with names of land owners who may require compensation.

Page 421- August 3, 1875- (Date in reality is August 2, 1875)
- The Court appoints C.B. Price as curator of the estate of John Mustard, deceased. Price, with Geo. P. Price, his security, posts bond for $500.00 and took the oath prescribed by law.
- Court is adjourned until tomorrow morning at 9: 0'clock.
- Pursuant to an act of the General Assembly of VA, approved March 31, 1875 in relation to Grand Juries. It is ordered that the September and February Terms of Court be and they are hereby designated as Grand Jury Terms.

- Tuesday Morning, August 3, 1875- Geo. W. Easley, Judge.
- Wm. Groseclose's Executors, VS Jno. M. Hicks, assignee of J.M. French. Case continued.
- On motion of A.W. Miller at a former term of court, I.K. Price, Pendleton Burton and Leonard Morehead were appointed to report on the expediency of changing the location of the road leading from east end of M.A. Robinett's land to a point west of A.W. Miller's. his day they returned the report. Ordered that Mary Ann Robinett, owner of the land through which the said road passes, be summoned here at the next term of Court and show cause if any why the road should not be made as set forth in the report.
- James Tolbert presents claim for $28.00, for caring for WM. F. Tolbert, a lunatic. Allowed.

Page 422- August 3, 1875-
- Commonwealth VS Fulton Rider. Verdict, "Guilty". Rider fined $50.00. The court took time to consider the motion of Rider to set aside the verdict.
- Commonwealth VS James S. Wyrick. Petit Larceny. The special jury heard part of the evidence and were adjourned until tomorrow.
- Commonwealth VS J. Wharton Repass. On an attachment for failing to appear as a witness. Repass did not appear. The attachment ordered to be enlarged and directed to the Sheriffs of Wythe, Bland and Lee Counties.
- Ordered that the Court adjourn until tomorrow at 8:0'clock AM.

Page 423- Wednesday Morning, August 4, 1875. Geo. W. Easley, Judge.

- Commonwealth VS Fulton Rider. On lewd and lascivious cohabitation. The court overruled the motion of Rider to have the jury's verdict set aside. Rider to pay the $50.00 fine plus costs. Rider took exceptions, 2, 2, 3, 4 & 5, which were made part of the record.
- A report of settlement by Geo. W. Robinett, guardian of the heirs of Jas. W. Grayson, deceased, ordered filed for exceptions.
- Commonwealth VS James S. Wyrick. Indictment for Petit Larceny. The jury which adjourned yesterday, fully heard the evidence today and adjourned until tomorrow.
- James H. Stowers, acknowledged himself indebted to the Commonwealth in the amount of $50.00, to be levied against his goods chattels and lands. (A bond to assure his appearance in court as a witness in a case "Commonwealth VS M.S. Pool "

Page 424- Thursday Morning, August 5, 1875- Geo. W. Easley, Judge.-
- Commonwealth VS Hannah Chandler. Misdemeanor. Chandler pleads "not guilty". Case continued on motion of Chandler.
- On motion of Sanders Wyrick, a rule is awarded against Henry and Wythe Newberry, to show cause why they have not complied with their agreement to open a new road leading down the hollow through the lands of James Thompson and Adam Waggoner to Walker's Creek, which was to be established as a public road at the last February term and which the said Henry and Wythe Newberry agreed to open.
- Commonwealth VS Fulton Rider. On motion of Rider the Court suspended the judgment against Rider which was rendered at last term of Court, for a period of 30 days from this date.

Page 425- August 5 1875-
- Commonwealth VS James S. Wyrick. Indictment for larceny. Jury unable to reach a verdict, were adjourned until tomorrow morning at 9:0'clock AM.
- Following, a list of jurors with the amount paid to them for their services as Petie Jurors:-
A.B. Honaker, $2.00; B.D. Graves, $2.00; W.P. Hornbarger, $2.00; Isaac Kegley, $2.00; Elias Blankenship, $2.00; R.W. Clark, $2.00; J.A.T. Groseclose, $2.00; James Clark, $2.00; James H. Bruce, $2.00; W.C. Newberry, $2.00; Ganam Kitts, $2.00; B.F. Petrie, $2.00; S.W. Bird, $4.00; H.G. Thompson, $4.00; Peter Kitts, $4.00; Geo. W. Bennett, $4.00; C.C. Bales, $4.00; A.R. Woodyard, $4.00; Hiram Rider, $4.00; James Rader, $4.00; J.W. Chandler, $4.00; S.M. Stuart, $4.00; G.N. Pegram, $4.00 and L.L. Quarles, $4.00. Certified for payment.
- Samuel W. Williams, presents claim for $5.00, which is allowed.
- Court adjourned until tomorrow morning at 9:0'clock AM.

Friday Morning, August 6, 1875- Court sat pursuant to adjournment.
- Commonwealth VS James S. Wyrick. Indictment for Petit Larceny. (Continued on page 426)

Page 426- The jury could not reach a verdict. A new trial ordered for Wyrick. He posted a bond for $50.00 with Acles Fannon and John F. Locke, his securities.
- Court adjourned until the first day of the next term. Signed by Geo. W. Easley, Judge.

Page 427- Monday September 6, 1875- Hon. Geo. W. Easley, Judge,
- Following is a list of deeds presented and recored at the Clerk's Office since last term of court-
- William Kitts & wife to T.N. Finley, trustee, 185 acres on Walker's Creek. August 7, 1875.

- Wm. A. Kidd & wife to Thomas G. Coburn, 5 acres on Hunting Camp Creek, for $40.00. Dated August 16, 1875.
- Wm. Umbarger & wife to Samuel Dilman, 28 acres on North Fork of the Holston, for $200.00. Dated Feb. 27, 1875.
- G.H.Morgan & wife to R.C. Kent, trustee, a deed of trust to secure Robert Raper the sum of $1,500.00. 25o acres on the waters of Kimberling. Dated aug. 14, 1875.
- The will of Simon Foglesong was presented in court and fully proven by the oath of John Repass, one of the witnesses. Henry and Joseph Foglesong named as executors, with Eli F. Groseclose and John Repass, their security, posted bond for $1,000.00 and took the oath prescribed by law. John Repass, Joel H. Spangler and Henry Foglesong, Sr. are appointed to appraise the personal property of Simon Foglesong, deceased, and report to the court.
- The will of James Wilson, deceased, presented and proven by oaths of Thomas O. Wilson and Geo. M. Tibbs, the witnesses thereto. Thomas O. Wilson the named executor, with Joseph and Henry Foglesong, his securities, posted bond for $600.00. (Part of item on page 428)

Page 428- September 1875-
- Jacob Waggoner, John Repass, and Joel H. Spangler, appointed to appraise the personal estate of James Wilson, deceased and make report thereof.
- Samuel H. Newberry, John Repass and Harman Tilson, appointed as commissioners to lay off and divide among the several heirs, the lands of James Wilson, deceased. They are authorized to employ a surveyor if necessary.
- Commonwealth VS James S. Wyrick. Indictment for Petit Larceny. The case is continued (again). A rule is awarded against James Robinett, Jr. a witness for the Commonwealth for failure to appear in court. John F. Locke and Acles Fannon were sureties for Wyricks bond in the amount of $50.00 each.

Page 429- Ordered that James A. Dillow who has proven that he is physically unable to work on the public roads, is exempt from same.
- Commonwealth VS M.S. Pool. Violation of Revenue Laws. Case continued again. A rule is awarded against Albert Linkious, W.W. Ashworth and Miles Roland, witnesses for the defendant, for failure to appear in Court. Pool posted bond for $50.00.
- Ordered that Simon Stowers and O.E. Wright be appointed as commissioners to view and report on the expediency of making changes in the road leading from Stowers' Shop to Rock Lick and return with their report a map or diagram of said road.
- A Grand Jury of Inquest was sworn in consisting of the following persons, B.F. Petrie, foreman; D.A. Walker; Levi S. Woodyard; Harvy Gross; Jno. W. Harman, Sr.; M.L Bumgardner; W.H. Groseclose; Jno. M. Cassell; Ganam Kitts; J.W. Thornburg; A.G. Thompson; W.N. Mustard; H.A. Pauley; W.A.B. Bird; B.P. Stafford; J.M. Stafford; A.G. Harman; M.B. Allen and R.W. Clark. (Continued on page 430)

Page 430- The Grand Jury of Inquest, found the following indictments,-
- Commonwealth VS Henry Hounshell. Indictment for misdemeanor. A true bill.
- Commonwealth VS G.F. Rider. Indictment for misdemeanor. A true bill.
- Commonwealth VS Julia A. Tolbert. Indictment for misdemeanor. A true bill.

- The Grand Jury of Inquest having nothing further before them were discharged.
- Ordered that answers to indictments be returnable at next term of Court.
- Ordered that members of the Grand Jury at this term be paid the sum of $1.00.
- Commonwealth VS Charles Waddle. Indictment for Felony. A rule is awarded against F.H. Johnston, a witness for the Commonwealth, for failure to appear in court. On motion of Waddle, a rule is awarded against ??? Neel, witness for Waddle for failure to appear. Bail was posted for Waddle with Joseph Waddle, his security, in the amount of $400.00 each.

Page 431- H.B. Groseclose and Eli Repass post bond for $50.00 to insure their presence in court to witness for Charles Waddle.
- John Crabtree has been dead for more that 3 months. On motion of C.C. Bailes, the Sheriff is ordered to take and administer the said estate of John Crabtree.
- Nancy Neel VS John Myers. Case dismissed. Myers to recover from Neel and her security, G.C. Thorn, his cost by him expended.
- Wm. N. Harman is hereby released from his position as Overseer of the Road in Mechanicsburg District. W.W. Blankenship appointed in place of said Harman.
- James Tolbert presents his claim for $34.00, for caring for Wm. F. Tolbert, a lunatic. Allowed.

Page 432- September 1875-
- James Tolbert is allowed an increase in his pay for keeping Wm. F. Tolbert, a lunatic, from $1.00 per day to $1.25 per day.
- Elizabeth Henderson VS B.P. Stafford. Defendant makes motion that the case be docketed.
- Wm. C. Williams & John Fanning VS Wm. N. Harman. On notice to quash an execution. Plaintiffs make motion that this notice be docketed.
- I.T. Gollehon appointed Justice of The Peace in place of --- Cox, who failed to qualify.
- On F.G. Helvey's application to discontinue the road known as the "Valley Road" from George Bogle's house to Point Pleasant Academy and from there to Walkers Creek & Holston Turnpike, it is ordered that John H. Hoge, James Robinett, Jr. and D.O. McNiel be appointed Commissioners to view said road and report in writing whether in their opinion if any inconveniences would result from discontinuing said road.

Page 433- September 1875-
- On motion of Isaac S. Harman, it appears that it is necessary to rearrange Road Precinct # 11 and # 12 in Mechanicsburg District. A.G. Harman, Jno. P. Roach and D.O. McNiel are appointed to lay off, alter or rearrange said precincts and allot the hands to work the public roads and to report to the Court at the next term.
- D.W. Dunn, County Treasurer, presented a list of delinquent license taxes in Mechanicsburg District. Assessor, Z.T. Weaver.
- On motion of I.M. Repass at the last July term of Court, F.F. Repass, H.H. Tilson and Henry Groseclose were appointed to view and report on the expediency of establishing a new road from the mountain road on the west end of Bland County, beginning at or near the gate of Jonas Groseclose through lands of Thos. A. Snidow and James M.C. Wilson to near the mouth of Daniel Hanshew's lane. Report returned this day and it is ordered that the land owners appear in next term of court and show cause why said road should not be established as a public road as set forth in the said report.

- On motion of H.C. Newberry, Overseer of the roads, precinct # 8, Seddon District, it appears that it is impractical to build a new bridge on Walkers Creek-Holston Turnpike near Leady's. Ordered that H.C. Newberry, A.J. Grayson and James A. Repass be appointed as commissioners to receive bids to repair or rebuild the bridge, and report to the Court.
- Ordered that Paul James, A.W. Kidd and Thomas G. Coburn, go on the rout and report on the expediency of establishing a new road from Alex. Suiter's down Hunting Camp Creek to the R.& G. Turnpike, and report to the court, (continued on page 434)

Page 434- September 1875- ---------whether or not any yard, orchard or garden will be taken and that land owners be named and what damages any party might claim.
- Court adjourned until tomorrow at 9: 0'Clock Am.

- Tuesday Morning, September 7, 1875- Ho. Geo. W. Easley, Judge.
- Thomas J. Muncy says he is aggrieved by an entry in the return of the list of persons assessed with a license, made by Z.T. Weaver, assessor in Mechanicsburg District, whereby he is charged with $10.00 license tax as an attorney at law. He moved the court to exonerate him from paying this tax. It appeared that Muncy had also been assessed in the Seddon District for the same amount. He was exempt from paying the tax levied in Mechanicsburg District.

Page 435- September 1875-
- A report of settlement by A.T. Suiter, guardian for the heirs of James T. Gills, deceased. No exceptions taken, it is ordered to be recorded.
- A report of settlement by F.I. Suiter, administrator of Stephen Gose, deceased. Ordered filed for exceptions.
- A report of settlement by Catherine C. Crockett, administratrix of C.G. Crockett, deceased. Ordered to be filed for exceptions.
- The sale and appraisement bill of the estate of William Crawford, deceased, ordered recorded.
- A report by A.G. Updike, administrator of B.F and Julia Corder, deceased, ordered to be filed for exceptions.
- A report of settlement by Geo. Robinett, guardian of the heirs of Jas. W. Grayson, deceased, ordered to be filed for exceptions.
- On motion of Joseph Wohlford and Catherine C. Crockett, J.H. Hoge, Z.T. Weaver and J.P. Roach were appointed commissioners to lay off and assign to the parties entitled thereto, the dower interest of Nancy Nicewander, deceased, in the lands of her deceased husband, Abraham Nicewander. Said report filed last July for exceptions and no exceptions taken was ordered to be recorded.
- H.G. Dennis VS K.C. Thornton. On an appeal. Case continued.

Page 436- September 1875-
- John Fanning & Wm. C. Williams VS Wm. N. Harman. Motion to quash an execution. The court takes time to consider.
- Elizabeth Henderson VS B.P. Stafford. Case dismissed without prejudice. Stafford to recover from Henderson his costs for his defense expended.
- It appearing that the public privy on the Courthouse square is in such a condition that it is necessary that something be done to prevent the same from becoming a nuisance. Ordered that

the Jailor be directed to keep the said privy in good condition for which he shall be paid a reasonable compensation.

- Wm. Groseclose's Executors VS Jno. M. Hicks assignee of J.M. French, appellees. On an appeal. The court finds no error in the judgment. Appellant to recover from H.C. and J.A.T. Groseclose (executors) and A.J. Muncy, their security, the sum of $30.00 and his costs. (Part of item on page 437)

Page 437- September 1875-
- Commonwealth VS Daniel and Rufus Robinett. The writs of "capias" having been returned "not found", the Commonwealth's Attorney orders new writs to be awarded against the defendants and directed to the Sheriff of this county, returnable at next term.
- Ordered that Court be adjourned until first day of next term. Signed, G.W. Easley, Judge.

Page 438- Monday October 4, 1875- Hon. Geo. W. Easley, Judge.
- Following is a list of deeds recorded in the Clerk's Office since last term of court-
- Elias Repass & wife to Archibald Peery, two tracts of land in Bland & Tazewell Counties, one for 40+ acres and one for 822 acres, for $400.00. Dated Sept. 1, 1875.
- An agreement between Betsy Henderson and Wm. N. Harman in regard to Dower in lands of John Henderson, deceased. Dated Dec. 10, 1874.
- Randolph Waddle to Ephraim Waddle, all his rights and title to the lands of Robinett Waddle, deceased, for $400.00. Dated Aug. 27, 1875.
- Jno. A. Kelly, commissioner & others, to the Board of Supervisors of Bland County, 3 tracts amounting to 204 acres on which the Poor House is situated, for $1,230.00. Dated Jan. 25, 1875.
- Andrew Hanshew & wife to Sarah Tibbs, 60 acres in Sharon Township for $200.00. Dated May 31, 1873.
- A.J. Grayson & wife to W.N. Mustard, a tract of land for $12.00. Dated July 20, 1875.
- C.H.C. Fulkerson to George N. Pegram for a house & lot in Seddon, for $400.00. Dated August 23, 1875.
- Commonwealth VS James S. Wyrick. Indictment for Petit Larceny. Case is continued until the next January term. Wyrick with James S. Robinett and Wm. H. Hoge, his securities, posted a bond for $100.00 each to assure his appearance in Court. (Part of item on page 439)

Page 439- October 1875-
- On motion of Joseph Gullion, it appearing that Susan Gullion has been dead for more than three months, ordered that the sheriff take her estate and administer it according to law.
- A special Grand Jury consisting of the following persons were summonsed- A.J. Muncy, foreman; A.G. Harman; Jas. T. Taylor; Paul James; Peter Kitts and Eli Steel were impaneled and went to their room and brought the following indictment-
- Commonwealth VS Adam. Lampert. Felony. A true Bill.
- Commonwealth VS Adam and James L. Lambert. Adam failed to appear. A warrant issued against him and James Lambert, his security.

Page 440- October 1875- The will of Alexander Suiter, deceased, with codicil attached was presented and proven by the oaths of A.W. Kidd and E.S. Kidd, the two witnesses. Ordered to be recorded. F.I. Suiter and A.L. Suiter, the named executors allowed to qualify without bond.

- On motion of F.I. and A.L. Suiter, executors of Alexander Suiter, deceased, A.J. Grayson, J.M. Stowers and W.T. Hamilton were appointed to appraise the personal estate of Alexander Suiter, deceased and make report to the court.

- A report of settlement by A.J. Grayson, administrator of Emily Grayson, deceased, ordered to be filed for exceptions.

- A report of settlement by A.J. Grayson, administrator of James W. Grayson, deceased, ordered to be filed for exceptions.

- A report of settlement by Geo. W. Robinett guardian of the heirs of James W. Grayson, deceased, and on motion of W.W. Grayson one of the heirs, confirmation of said report is continued until next term of court.

Page 441- October 1875-

- H.C. Newberry, A.J. Grayson and James A. Repass, who were appointed at last term, to receive bids for building a new bridge across Crab Orchard Creek. The lowest bid being for $273.50. Ordered that the Commissioners let the contract to said bidder.

- On motion of H.F. Bruce and Felix Buck, it is ordered that S.I. Patterson, M.L. Bumgardner and John F. Umbarger, go on the ground and and report on the expediency of establishing a new road from a gate near the north fork of Holston on the Black Lick and Plaster Bank Road, to Felix Buck's Potter Shop and to report back with a map or diagram.

- The rule against Albert Linkious and Miles Roland for failure to appear as witnesses for M.S. Pool, is hereby discharged.

- D.O. McNiel, A.G. Harman John P. Roach, who were appointed to rearrange and allot the hands to work the roads in precincts # 11 & 12, Mechanicsburg District, returned their reports which were ordered to be filed for exceptions.

- A.D. Lambert is appointed Overseer of the new road from near S.L. Gibson's to A.D. Lambert's and with the following hands, keep the road in good repair. Hands are, George and Samuel Gibson, J.G. French, P.W. Hanks, Jas. Songer and N.H. Ford. (Part on page 442)

Page 442- October 1875-

- On motion of Thos. G. Coburn, Paul James, T.G. Coburn and A.W. Kidd, were appointed at a former term to view and report on the expediency of establishing a new road from R&G Turnpike up Hunting Camp to Alex. Suiter's. This day they returned their report. Land owners claim no damages. Stipulated that should Paul James wish to erect a mill on his property, the said road is not to interfere with it. T.G. Coburn is appointed Overseer to allot the hands to work said road.

- Wohlford & Noble presented a claim against the County for $1.43, for aid given to Josephine Burgis, a pauper. Allowed and certified to Board of Supervisors.

- Commonwealth VS Charles Waddle. Indictment for felony. Case continued until tomorrow morning. Waddle together with Joseph Waddle, his security, posts bond for $400.00 each.

Page 443- October 1875-

- Randolph Grayson, Charles Grayson, Henry Newberry, Robinett Waddle, H. B. Groseclose, F.H. Johnston, Henry Repass and I.G. Pauley, acknowledge a bond for $50.00 each to assure their appearance in court to witness in the case of Commonwealth VS Charles Waddle, tomorrow morning at 9:0'clock AM.

- William Dillow appointed as Constable for Seddon District. Samuel H. Newberry and T. N.

Finley were his securities for a bond of $2,000.00.

- J. Henderson Bruce, appointed Supervisor for Seddon District. Bruce with J.G. Kegley and Henry Newberry, his securities, posted bond for $1,000.00 and took the prescribed oath of office.
- Samuel W. Young VS H.G. Thompson and Jno. R. Compton. Docketed and continued.
- Thos. J. Higgenbotham VS H.G. Thompson & Jno R. Compton. Docketed and continued.
- Young & Higgenbotham VS H.G. Thompson & Jno. R. Compton. Docketed and continued.

Page 444- October 1875-
- Dr. J.M. Hamilton presents a claim for $22.50. Allowed.
- Rees Crabtree, Constable in Sharon District, presents a claim for $11.50. Allowed.
- C.C. Banks, acting Constable, presents claim for $19.40. Allowed.
- At last term of Court, Simon Stowers and O.E. Wright were appointed commissioners to report on the expediency of changing the road from Stowers Shop to Rock Lick. They returned their report saying that the road should be changed. Ordered that land owners, John Wright, O.E. Wright, Jacob McNiel, Mrs. M.L. Wessendonck and Mrs. M.A. Buchanan, agent for Washington Wysor, through whose land the road will pass, be summonsed to appear and show cause if any why said road should not be changed.
- Ordered that the members of the Grand Jury be allowed $1.00 for their services.
- Commonwealth VS M.S. Pool. Violation of Revenue Laws. After much wrangling the jury found Pool guilty as charged and assessed his fine at $30.00. (Part of item on page 445)

Page 445- October 1875-
- Jurors who heard the above case were, S.W. Bird, B.D. Graves, E.M. Melvin, Henderson Moore, T.N. Finley, Wm. Dillow, Wm. E. Hoge, C.B. Price, Wm. Kitts, James Clark, D.L. Tickle and Addison Harman.
- Memorandum: The above defendnat took exceptions to the courts rulings and tendered his bill of exceptions which were signed, sealed and made a part of the record.
- Commonwealth VS Hannah Chandler. Misdemeanor. Continued until January term of court.
- Court adjourned until tomorrow morning at 9:0'clock AM.

Page 446- Tuesday Morning, October 5, 1875-
- Commonwealth VS Henry Hounshell. Misdemeanor. Continued until January Term.
- James Tolbert presented his claim for $7.50, for caring for Wm. Tolbert, a lunatic. Allowed.
- W.G. Painter presents a claim for $3.00 which is allowed.
- Robinett Waddle and Henry Repass presented a claim for $6.85 which was allowed.
- K.C. Thornton, jailor, presented a claim for $2.90 which was allowed.

Page 447- October 1875-
- Commonwealth VS G.F. Rider. Misdemeanor. Continued until January term 1876.
- Commonwealth VS Julia A. Tolbert. Misdemeanor. Continued until January term 1876.
- Jurors on page 445, and the amounts allowed them for servuce as Petit Jurors.
- Commonwealth VS M.S. Pool. The verdict rendered yesterday is upheld.
- Court adjourned until tomorrow morning at 9:)'clock AM.

Page 448- Wednesday October 6, 1875-

- The court designates that the January, April, July and October terms of court for the trials of misdemeanors.
- Commonwealth VS M.S. Pool. Violation of Revenue Laws. The execution of the judgment of yesterday is suspended for a period of 30 days to allow the defendant to apply to the circuit for an appeal.
- Commonwealth VS Charles Waddle. Indictment for felony. Continued until next November term. Waddle with Joseph Waddle his security posts bond for $400.00 each.
- F.H. Johnston, Henry Newberry, Robinett Waddle, Charles Grayson, Henry Repass, W.G. Waddle, I.G. Pauley, Randolph Grayson, Margaret Waddle, Charles Grayson, Ann Waddle and L.D. Bogle posted bond for $50.00 each to assure their appearance in court as witnesses, in the case of Commonwealth VS Charles Waddle at the December next term of court.

Page 449- October 1875- (Part of the above item on this page)
- H.B. Groseclose, Jas. McNeel, Eli Repass, Rhoda Waddle, Mary Waddle, Adaline Waddle and Jno. Lampert, post bond for $50.00 each to assure their appearance in the December next term of court as witnesses for Charles Waddle.
- The will of Kate C. Crockett, presented and proven by oaths of D.H. Muncy and Jno. R. Compton. John S. Crump, the named executor, qualified as such and with Sallie J. Crockett, his security posted bond for $1,000.00.
- On motion of John S. Crump, executor of Kate C. Crockett, deceased, D.H. Muncy, Jno. P. Roach, and A.G. Updike as appraisers of the personal estate of Kate C. Crockett, deceased.
- Ordered that all cases not otherwise disposed of, be continued until next term.
- Court adjourned until the first day of the next term. Signed, G.W. Easley.

Page 450- Monday November 1, 1875-
- Following is a list of deeds presented and recorded in the Clerk's office since last term of court-
- Stephen Repass & wife to James A. Repass, 10+ acres on Walker's Creek known as the Stephen Repass Mill property, for $1,000.00. Dated 2-19-1875.
- Alex Umbarger & wife and Stephen Repass & wife to James A. Repass, 159 acres on Walker's Creek, for $1,000.00. Dated 2-19-1875.
- A deed of trust from James Clark to J.M. French, trustee, to secure Eli Leady, a tract of land on Wolf Creek known as the Wm. L. Day land. Dated 10-4-1875.
- John H. Hoge, Special Commissioner, to John Havens, about 80 acres on south side of Brushy Mountain, for $32.16. Dated 11-17-1874.
- Richard Moore & wife to W.W. Hamilton, 3/4ths of an acre in Bland County, a deed of gift. Dated 9-27-1875.
- James H. Wilson & wife to A.B. Waggoner, 40 acres onWolf Creek, for &700.00.
Dated 2-2-1875.
- A deed of trust from Wm. N. Harman to James B. Miller, trustee, to secure S.H. Newberry, G.H. Morgan, Ira D. Hall, R.F. Watts, P.W. Strother and G.W. Easley, the sureties for said Harman on a bond in the penalty of $1,600.00, conveying 800 acres on the waters of Kimberling Creek. Dated 9-13-1875.
- A deed of trust from Franklin Grayson & wife to S.W. Williams, trustee, to secure Cynthia Grayson and the other heirs of John Grayson, deceased, in the amount of $8,400.00, 2,967 acres, being the same land conveyed to Franklin Grayson by John Grayson, decd. Dated 10-13-1875.

Page 451- November 1875-
- A special jury of inquest consisting of the following persons, Henry Newberry foreman, Jas. T. Taylor, T.N. Finley, Jno. M. Cassell, Elias Foglesong, J.N. Johnston and R.B. Repass, were impaneled and sworn in. They found the following indictment:
- Commonwealth VS Rufus Miller, Indictment for felony. A true bill.
- Commonwealth VS Rufus Miller. Case continued and prisoner remanded to jail.
- C.C. Banks, James H. Bruce and Turner Wheeler, posted bond for $50.00 each, to assure their appearance in court as witnesses for the Commonwealth VS Rufus Miller.
- A Power of Attorney from John G. Crockett to W.T. Hamilton, authorizing Hamilton to sign his name to the official bond of Robt. Wylie, administrator of C.G. Crockett, deceased, which was proven to be in the hand writing of the said John G. Crockett by the testimony and oath of S.W.Williams and Robt. Wylie which said power of attorney is ordered to be filed.
- On motion of John G. Crockett by attorney. Robert Wylie is appointed administrator with the will annexed of Calvin G. Crockett, deceased. Wylie, with John G. Crockett, by his attorney in fact, W.T. Hamilton, his security, posts bond for $1,000.00.

Page 452- November 1875-
- Commonwealth VS Adam & James L. Lambert. Dismissed.
- C.C. Banks, acting Constable, presents claim for &4.30. Allowed.
- Turner B. Wheeler, presents claim for $5.25. Allowed.
- Newton Waddle presents claim for $1.50. Allowed.
- C.W. Grayson presents claim for $1.50. Allowed.
- P.P. Hayes presents claim for $2.00. Allowed.
- J.A.T. Groseclose presents claim for $.75. Allowed. (Yes seventy five cents)

Page 453- November 1875-
- Rufus Miller VS Commonwealth. An appeal from a judgment of a Justice of the Peace. The attorney for the Commonwealth says he will not prosecute further. Miller is acquitted.
- George W. Suiter appointed as Overseer of the Poor for Seddon District. He with W.C. Williams, his security posts bond for $500.00 and takes oaths of office.
- On motion of H.F. Bruce & Felix Buck at a former term of court, S.I. Patterson, M.L. Bumgardner and John F. Umbarger who were appointed to report on the expediency of establishing a new road from a gate on the Black Lick and Plaster Bank Road to Felix Buck's potter's shop, returned their report today. Land owners claim no damage, except Catherine Spangler who is summonsed to next term of court to show why said road should not be establshed as set forth in the report.
- Jno. Fanning & Wm. C. Williams VS William N. Harman. On motion to quash a writ. Plaintiff's motion is overruled and defendant to recover from the Plaintiffs, his costs. Plaintiffs file a bill of exceptions. (Part of item on page 454)

Page 454- November 1875-
- F.M. Brandon VS Malvina Cubine. Continued until December term of court.
- Bland County VS Henry & Wythe C. Newberry. Continued until December term of court.
- H.G. Dennis VS K.C. Thornton. Case continued until December term of court.
- Samuel W. Young VS H.G. Thompson & others. Continued until December term of court.

- Young & Higginbotham VS H.G. Thompson & others. Continued as above.
- Thomas G. Higginbotham VS H.G. Thompson & others. Continued as above.
- Court adjourned until the first day of next term. Signed by G.W. Easley, Judge.

Page 455- Monday December 1875- HOn. Geo. W. Easley, Judge.
- Following, a list of deeds presented and recorded in the Clerk's Office since last term of court-
- Francis Wright & wife to D.F. Morehead, 100 acres+- on Kimberling Creek, for $250.00. Dated 10-9-1875.
- Ellen J. Suiter to John H. Bird, conveying her dower interest in the "Old William Suiter Tract". Dated 10-7-1875.
- H.R. Mustard & wife to B.P. Stafford, 2 tracts of land (34 & 1//2 acres) for $300.00. Dated 11-5-1875.
- B.P Stafford & wife to W.S. Mustard, conveying dower interest in the lands of John Henderson, deceased, for $300.00. Dated 11-5-1875.
-Wm. Kelly to E.G. Booth, a deed of release. Dated 11-13-1875.
A.J. Nye to Elizabeth Nye, a tract of land on Brushy Mountain for $350.00. Dated 11-17-1875..
- H.M. Kitts presented a claim for $1.12 & ½ cts. .Examined and allowed.
- J.C. Painter presented a claim for $12.00. Allowed.
- John A. Barnett, produced a certificate of his appointment as a Justice of The Peace and together with T.G. Hudson his security posts bond for $500.00 and took prescribed oaths.

Page 456- December 1875- On motion of Joseph Wohlford & I.S. Harmen, ordered that Z.T. Weaver, Jno. P. Roach and Dr. Wm. E. Hoge be appointed Commissioners to report on the expediency of establishing a new road from the end of the public road at Point Pleasant to Henry Harman's old homestead through the lands of James Robinett, Joseph Wohlford and Sallie J. Crockett, widow of the late John C. Crockett, deceased, to the road leading from the residence of the late John C. Crockett, to the Turnpike road near Harvey Nicewandre's, and report if any yard, orchard or garden will be damaged.
- On motion of George W. Kinzer, ordered that Henry Foglesong, Jr. and Peter Spangler are appointed to report on the expediency of establishing a new road from west of Peter Spangler's up Harner's Creek near Peter Umbarger's and from there to new route by Red Oak Grove Church to Walkers Creek & Holston Turnpike to near Sallie Groseclose's and also the route by Jonas Umbarger's to intersect with the Walker's Creek & Holston Turnpike at or near the Indian graves east of Sharon Springs.

Page 457- December 1875-
- Z.T. Weaver presents a claim against the Commonwealth for $291.00. Allowed.
- On motion of James A. Hancock, Alex Umbarger, Thos. F. Crutchfield, James P. Crutchfield, Wm. A. Monday, Margaret Crutchfield and Samuel Puckett, heirs and distributees of Wm. J. Crutchfield, deceased, T.J.Hudson is appointed administrator of Wm. J. Crutchfield. Hudson, with Elias Repass, his security posts bond for $1,200.00 and is granted letters of administration.
- James A. Hancock appointed guardian for Wm. Kelley Hancock (Son of the said Jjames A. and Harriet L. Hancock), an infant under the age of 14. Hancock, with T.G. Hudson, his security, posts bond for $200.00.
- Ordered that the Overseers of the Poor bind out Doc Melvin(colored), infant son of Emma

Melvin, (colored) deceased, until he attains the age of 21.
- Peter Spangler, John Repass and Thos. A. Wilson, appointed and sworn as appraisers of the personal estate of Wm. J. Crutchfield, deceased and make report of same.
- Hiram Pauley VS I.S. Harman. Harman refused to give security asked for by Pauley. The defendant's power and authority as Trustee is revoked and annulled.

Page 458- December 1875-
- H.C. Newberry, A.J. Grayson and James A. Repass, Commissioners, appointed to superintend the building of the new bridge across Crab Orchard Creek under contract with James C. Painter and C.C. Banks, this day returned their report that the said bridge has been built according to said specifications. The same is accepted by the court.
- Commonwealth VS Charles Waddle. Indictment for felony. Out of 16 persons examined, 12 were picked as jurors, namely: Thos. O. Wilson, J.T. Burton, B.L. Bird, J.T. Myers, A.B. Pauley, N.H. Ford, A.D. Lambert, D.G. Bird, Alex Nicewander, Joseph A. Fanning, John Cooper and John F. Strock. Case continued until tomorrow morning at 9 0'clock AM
- Court adjourned until tomorrow morning at 9:0'clock AM.

Page 459- Tuesday Morning Decamber 7, 1875-
- Simon Stowers and O.E. Wright appointed at an earlier term of court to report on the expediency of changing the road leading from Stowers Shop to Rock Lick. Ordered that the road be changed according to said report, there being no objections by the land owners.
- I.K. Price, Pendleton Burton and Leonard Muirhead, appointed at an earlier term on motion of A.W. Miller, to report on the expediency of changing the road from a point east of the lands of Mary A. Roberts to a point west of A.W. Miller's. There being no objections by the land owners, it is ordered that the changes be made.
- Commonwealth VS Charles Waddle. Indictment for felony. Jury after hearing part of the evidence adjourned until tomorrow morning.
- Ordered that the Sheriff summons from the bystanders, 24 persons, legal jurors to appear here tomorrow morning to serve as jurors in the trial of Rufus Miller, on an indictment for felony.

Page 460- Wednesday Morning December 8, 1875-
- Commonwealth VS Charles Waddle. The jury heard more evidence in this case and were adjourned until tomorrow.

-Thursday Morning December 9, 1875-
- Commonwealth VS Charles Waddle. Jurors heard remainder of evidence and part of the arguments of Counsel, adjourned until tomorrow morning at 9:0;clock Am.

Friday Morning December 10, 1875-

Page 461- Friday Morning December 10, 1875-
- Commonwealth VS Charles Waddle. On indictment for felony. Jurors fully heard arguments by counsel and not being able to reach a verdict were adjourned over until tomorrow at 9 AM.
- Court adjourned until tomorrow.

Still on page 461- Saturday Morning December 11, 1875-
-Commonwealth VS Charles Waddle. Indictment for felony. Jury renders verdict of "Not Guilty" and the prisoner is acquitted and discharged.
- Memorandum: On trial of this cause the counsel for the prisoner took exceptions to the ruling of the court and tendered bills of exceptions Nos. 1,2 & 3, which were made part of the record.
- On application of I.M. Repass to establish a new road from the gate near Jonas Umbarger's to James McWilson's. Road shall be established pursuant to their report, except it is agreed by plaintiff and defendant to this cause, that H.H. Tilson, Henry Groseclose and F.F. Repass, commissioners sent to view said road----- report if any yard, orchard or garden will be taken.
(Part of this item on page 462)

Page 462- December 1875-
- J.G. Kegley, Sheriff, presented claim for $146.00 which was examined and allowed.
- K.C. Thornton, Jailor, presented claim for $54.95, which was examined and allowed.
- Commonwealth VS Rufus Miller. Indictment for felony. From a panel of 24 persons, the following 12 were picked to serve on this jury, namely: Eli Repass, Hiram Hall, J.S. French, Wm.itts, J.M. Stowers, I.G. Pauley, Geo. Bogle, Jr., W.A. Bennett, D.D. Graves, H.A. Pauley, G.C. Pauley and Henry Dowling. They returned the following verdict " We the jury find the defendant guilty of house breaking in manner and form as charged in within indictment with intent to commit larceny as therein charged and fix his imprisonment in the Penitentiary House of this Commonwealth at one year" (Continued on page 463)

Page 463- December 1875-
Prisoner, (Rufus Miller) had nothing to say. Ordered that the sheriff remove and convey said Miller to the penitentiary as soon as possible.
- J.G. Kegley, Sheriff, presents claim for $17.50. Examined and allowed.
- Samuel W. Williams, Attorney for the Commonwealth, presents claim for $20.00. Allowed.
- Commonwealth VS Rufus Miller. Counsels argue over evidence produced at former court. Trial is continued and Miller remanded back to jail.

Page 464- December 1875-
- Nancy Kitts presented a claim for $24.00 which was examined and allowed.
- William T. Hamilton, Clerk of this Court, presented claim for $10.00 for defending Rufus Miller, charged with a felony. Certified to the Board of Supervisors for payment.
- Ordered that the terms of this court be hereafter commenced and held on the Tuesday after the first Monday in each month, instead of in the first Monday as at present.
- Samuel W. Williams, James M. Stowers and D.W. Dunn, Commissioners appointed at a former term, to let to contract the keeping in repair the abandoned Turnpike roads, are authorized to accept the proposition of ---- Orey, to keep the road from Sharon Springs to the Smyth County line in good repair for 5 years.
- Ordered that all causes not otherwise disposed of be continued until next term.
- Court adjourned until first day of next term. Signed G. W. Easley, Judge.

Page 465- Tuesday January 4, 1876- Ho. Geo. W. Easley, Judge.
- Following is a list of deeds presented and recorded since the last term of court-

- E.M. Melvin & wife to J.M. Hamilton, a house and lot in Mechanicsburg, lying on Water Street, for $350.00. Dated 3-6-1875.
- Jacob Waggoner & wife to C.C. Bailes, 100 acres on north fork of the Hoslton, for $400.00. Dated 3-19-1873.
- Elias Repass & wife to Elias Foglesong, 35 & 1//2 acres on north fork of the Holston, for $385.00. Dated 3-15-1875.
- A Deed of Trust on personal property from T.J. Munsey to S.W. Williams, to secure John M. Hicks. Dated 12-11-1875.
- Partition of the dower of Nancy Nicewander, deceased, in the lands of Abraham Nicewander, deceased, as made by Commissioners J.H. Hoge, Z.T. Weaver and J.P. Roach, are confirmed and ordered to be recorded.
- J-nus (Jonas?) Huddle, Henry Foglesong and Elias Foglesong, appointed at a former term, to assign to the parties entitled thereto, the Real Estate of Joseph Kimberling, deceased, returned their report which was ordered to be filed for exceptions.
- Samuel H Newberry, John Repass and H.H. Tilson, appointed at a former term, Commissioners to laty off and assign to the parties entitled thereto, the Real Estate of James Wilson, deceased. This day returned their report which was ordered filed for exceptions.
- A report of settlement by F.I. Suiter, administrator of Stephen Gose, deceased, having been filed for exceptions and none being taken, ordered to be recorded. (Part of item on page 466)

Page 466- January 1876-
- A report of settlement by A.G. Updike, administrator of B.F. & Julia Corder, deceased, having been filed for exceptions and none taken, ordered to be recorded.
- A report of settlement by Catherine C. Crockett, administrator of Calvin G. Crockett, deceased, having been presented at a former term of court and filed for exceptions and none being taken was confirmed and ordered to be recorded.
- Commonwealth VS James S. Wyrick. Indictment for Petit Larceny. The prisoner appeared in court according to the condition of his Recognizance entered into at the October term of court. The jurors, James Lambert, Jno. M. Cassell, H.H. Groseclose, Thos. P. Umbarger, M.L. Bumgardner, James M. Kidd, Felix Buck, H.M. Pruett, S.H. Harden, Wm. Umbarger, Stephen Kimberling and Wesley Lambert after hearing part of the evidence were adjourned until tomorrow at 9 0'clock AM.
- Ordered that Samuel W. Williams, James M. Stowers and D.W. Dunn, appointed Commissioners at a former term of court, to let the contract for keeping in repair the abandoned turnpike roads, are hereby authorized to accept the proposition of Monroe Kirby to keep the road from Bland C.H. to Sharon Springs in repair for 5 years.
- K.C. Thornton, jailor, makes claim for $50.00 for caring for James Hughes (colored), a lunatic in the County Jail. Allowed. (Part of item on page 467)

Page 467- January 1876-
- John M. Hicks presents claim for $35.85, as a guard for Sheriff J.G. Kegley, for conveying Rufus Miller to the Penitentiary in Richmond. Allowed.
- Commonwealth VS G.F. Rider. Indictment for misdemeanor. Commonwealth's Attorney declines to prosecute further. Defendant is acquitted and discharged.
_ Commonwealth VS Julia Tolbert. Indictment for a misdemeanor. Acquitted & discharged.

- Ordered that Court adjourn until tomorrow at 9:0'clock AM.

Page 468- Wednesday Morning January 1876-
- Commonwealth VS James S. Wyrick. Indictment for Petit Larceny. The jury having been adjourned yesterday, heard more evidence and was again adjourned until tomorrow morning.
- Court adjourned until tomorrow morning at 9 0'clock AM.

Thursday Morning January 6, 1876-
- Commonwealth VS James S. Wyrick. Petie Larceny. The jury came again and heard more evidence and part of the arguments by the attorneys, and adjourned until tomorrow morning.
- Court is adjourned until tomorrow morning at 9: 0'clock AM.

Friday Morning, January 7, 1876-
- Whereas during the term of this Court, Mr. H.H. Tilson met with an accident while attending Court, yesterday the 6th of January 1876, at Fannon's Hotel and whereas the Court, members of the Bar and officers of the Court are desirous of expressing our sincere regret at the unfortunate accident which deprives us of a good and worthy citizen and also of expressing our sympathy for the family of the deceased. Resolved that these resolutions be spread upon the records and a copy sent to the family of the deceased. (Part of item continued on page 469)

Page 469- January 1876-
- Commonwealth VS James S. Wyrick. Petit Larceny. All parties again appeared and the jury found the defendant "Guilty". His sentence was set at 30 days in jail and to pay the costs for this prosecution. Objections by the defense were overruled. Wyrick, remanded to jail.
- Commonwealth VS Hannah Chandler. Misdemeanor. A rule is awarded against Joseph Moore for failure to appear in Court as a witness for the Commonwealth. (Part of item on page 470)

Page 470- January 1876-
- Commonwealth VS Henry Hounshell. Misdemeanor. Hounshell confesses to a judgment of $1.00 and the cost of this prosecution. Agreed by both parties.
- On motion of T.N. Finley, it is ordered that J. Calvin Smith, H. Bruce and John Wilkenson, report on the expediency of establishing a new road from the south-east end of Main Street in the Town of Seddon, through the lands of J.M. French, to as near as possible to the line between said French and said Finley, thence eastward to the Isaiah Bruce's line. French's Mill mentioned. Viewers are to return with a map or diagram of proposed road.
- Upon motion of John S. Crump, A.G. Updike and John R. Compton, it is ordered that James S. Robinett, John J. Mustard and Davis MUnsey, be appointed viewers, to go on and report on the expediency of establishing a new road from D.O. McNeil's Mill to the Mill of John R. Compton, via the residence of A.G. Updike and determine what damages might be done and if any yard, garden or orchard would be taken. (Part of item on page 471)

Page 471- January 1876-
- Ordered that the report of Wm. E. Hoge, Z.T. Weaver and J.P. Roach, viewers appointed to locate a new road from Henry Harman's old homestead to Nicewander's, be recommitted to the viewers with instructions that thay report the names of landowners on said route.

116

- Samuel W. Williams, Attorney for the Commonwealth, presents claim for $10.00. Allowed.
- Sheriff, J.G. Kegley, makes claim for $7.10. Allowed.
- The Inventory of the personal estate of Kate C. Crockett, decd. presented in court and recorded.
- The Inventory & sale bill of the personal estate of James Wilson, decd. presented and recorded.
- The Inventory and sale bill of personal estate of Wm. J. Crutchfield, decd, ordered recorded.
- List of Petit Jurors for trial of misdemeanors, James Lambert, Jno. M. Cassell, W.H. Groseclose, Thos. P. Umbarger, M.L. Bumgardner, James M. Kidd, Felix Buck, H.M. Pruett, S.H. Harden, Wm. Umbarger, Stephen Kimberling and Wesley Lambert.
- Court adjourned until the first day of next term.

Page 472- February 8, 1876-
- Following, a list of deeds presented and recorded since the last term of Court-
- A deed of trust form John H. Hoback to Thos. J. Muncy, trustee, to secure J.M. French, for $100.00. Dated 12-24-1875.
- Deed of Trust on both Real & Personal property, from John S. Hoback to Thos. J. Muncy, trustee, to secure, S.M. Yost and J.M. French, sureties on the said Hancock,s bail bond for the sum of $500.00. Dated 1-1-1876.
- John Burton & wife to Giles French, 467 acres on Wolf Creek for $1,500.00. Land is partly in Bland and partly in Giles County. Dated 2-22-1873.
- Newton M. Kitts & wife to Wm. H. Groseclose, 441 acres on head waters of the Holston, for $200.00. Dated 5-25-1875.
- Elias Repass & wife to Elizabeth Patterson, 4&1/2 + acres, for $45.00. Dated 11-15-1875.
- James M. French, Commissoner, to William N. Harman, (no quantity given) land on Kimberling, for $150.00. Dated 11-5-1875.
- Elizabeth Mustard to James H. and John J. Mustard, conveying her dower interest in the lands of her deceased husband, Joshua Mustard, lying on the waters of Walkers Little Creek, for (no consideration given) Dated 6-26-1875.
- A report of Commissioners appointed to divide the Real Estate of Hiram Robinett.

Page 473- February 1876-
- Henry Newberry, foreman, Moses Akers, B.P. Stafford, M.B. Allen, S.M. Hamilton, W.P. Bruce, Allen Mustard, T.N. Finley, W.A.B. Bird, R.W. Clark, J.S. French, Peter Kitts, Joseph Foglesong, Elias Foglesong, Newton Shufflebarger, M.A. Fox, T.J. Neel and A.J. Honaker, were empanneled and sworn as a Grand Jury, came into court having found the following indictmentand - Commonwealth VS Charles Rider and George Minnix (colored), alias George Morton(colored) on a charge of felony, a true bill. The jury adjourned until tomorrow.
- W.V.B Tilson appointed administrator of the estate of H.H. Tilson, deceased. (The widow having refused to act) Tilson, with George W Robinett, his security posted bond for $4,000.00.
- Appraisement and sale bills of personal estate of Hiram Robinett, deceased, presented in court and ordered to be recorded.
- A report of settlement by I.S. Harman, trustee for Polly Parsons, ordered to be filed for exceptions. (J.H. Hoge, Commissioner of Accounts)

Page 474- February 1876-
- Wm. N. Harman VS Wm. C. Williams & John Fanning. Docketed and continued.

- Commonwealth VS Adam Lambert. Indictment for Felony. Lambert in custody of the Sheriff, pled "Not Guilty". Prisoner could not raise bail for $200.00 and was remanded back to jail. Case continued.
- Thomas Collins VS Sarah Swader. Indictment for felony. Dismissed by consent of parties.
- Commonwealth VS George Minnix. Indictment for felony. Case continued. Minnix with James H. and Henry P. Mustard, his securities, posted bond for $200.00. (Part of item on page 475)

Page 475- February 1876-
- W.H. Hawkins & Jacob Trinkle post bond for $50.00 each, to assure their appearance in court as witnesses for the Commonwealth VS George Minnix.
- Wm. E. Hoge, John P. Roach, and Z.T. Weaver, who were appointed at a former term to locate a new road from Henry Harman,s old Homestead to the house of the late John C. Crockett, returned their amended report. On motion of Joseph Wohlford and I.S. Harman, it is ordered that James Robinett, Joseph Wohlford and SallieCrockett, the land owners, be summonsed to appear and show cause if any why the road should not be established as a public road.

Page 476- February 1876-
- Catherine Spangler, land owner, claims damages of $40.00, due to the new road which will pass through her property, which is allowed. (from the Black Lick & Plaster Bank Road to Felix Buck's Potters Shop) Viewers were, M.L. Bumgardner, John F. Umbarger and S.I. Patterson who were appointed at a former term of court.
- Sheriff J.G. Kegley presents claim for $5.50 for clothing furnished to James Hughes, colored. Allowed.
- Deputy Sheriff Gordon Wohlford presents claim for $4.25. Allowed.
- K.C. Thornton, jailor, presents claim for $12.50. Allowed.
- K.C. Thornton, jailor, presents claim for $25.10 for care & maintenance of James Hughes a colored lunatic confined in jail. Allowed.

Page 477- February 1876-
- George W. Wysor is aggrieved by an entry in the Land Book, concerning 1075 acres on Kimberling Creek. Assessed at $1.00 per acre, changed to .75cents per acre. (Z.T. Weaver, assessor) First assessed in the name of James V. Pendleton.
- Pendleton Burton makes claim for $1.00. Allowed.
- Settlement by Acles Fannon, administrator of Tunis Muncy, deceased, with J.H. Hoge, assistant Commissioner of Accounts and filed for exceptions.
- The several parties who were appointed to lay off the several districts of the County into Road Precincts, are allowed $1.00 for their work.
- F.M. Brandon VS Melvina Cubine. Case dismissed on motion of the Plaintiff.
- Court adjourned until tomorrow morning at 10:O'clock AM.

Page 478- Wednesday Morning February 9, 1876-
- On motion of Robt. H. Bailey, ordered that J.D. Honaker, W.A. Linkious and A.B. Honaker, report on the expediency of changing the location of the road from the ford on Laurel Creek at Rocky Gap to a point below Honaker's Mill. These viewers will report on damages done to land owners and return with a map or diagram of said road..

- The Grand Jury returned an indictment against Wm. Cubine, for misdemeanor. True Bill.
- Ordered that members of the Grand Jury be paid the sum of $2.00 each for their services.
- On motion of John S. Crump, ordered that M.B. Allen, Jno. R. Compton and A.G. Updike, be appointed to view and report on the expediency of locating a new road form Henry Harman's Old Homestead to the house of the late John C. Crockett.

Page 479- February 1876-
- B.F. Petrie, former Road Commissioner, appointed to locate a route for a new road from O.E. Wright's to the Giles County line, returned his report. Ordered that Mrs. M.L Weisendonct, James Burton and John Wilkenson appear and show cause if any why road should not be established as a public road.
- Samuel W. Young VS H.G. Thompson & others.
- Thomas J. Higgenbotham VS H.G. Thompson & others.
- Young & Higgenbotham VS H.G. Thompson & others.
{ The above defendants suggest that Young is not a resident of Virginia and suggest that he be bonded for the costs of trial(s). S.S. Dinwiddie in open court signed and acknowledged a bond for $25.00 and these 3 cases are consolidated. Plaintiffs to recover from the defendant Harvey G. Thompson, late Constable of Bland County, the sum of $38.84 plus interest and costs. Memo:- The defendants tendered 2 bills of exceptions to the ruling, which wer signed sealed and made a part of the record. (Part of item on page 480)

Page 480- February 1876-
- All causes not otherwise disposed of are continued until next term
- The following persons are appointed as Registrars for the County of Bland for the next two years- Viz- Hiram Rider for Mechanicsburg District; Wm. Kitts for Seddon District; John Deavor for Sharon District; A.B. Honaker for Rocky Gap District and Joseph Cameron for Cameron's District.
- Ordered that Court be adjourned until the first day of the next term.

Page 481- Tuesday March 7, 1876- George W. Easley, Judge.
- Following is a list of deeds presented and recorded in the Clerk's Office since last term of Court-
- Thomas A. Snider & wife to H.H. Tilson, 162 ½ acres in Rich Valley, North Fork of the Holston, for $2,700.00. Dated 12-15-1875.
- John M. Cassell & others to George R. Hufford, 42+ acres in west end of Bland for $423.50. Dated 10-17-1875.
- Elias Repass & wife to R.C. Kent, trustee, to secure I. M. Repass the sum of $380.00, conveying 200 acres +- in Rich Valley. Dated 1-10-1876.
- A deed of release from John H. Reed, J. Avery Richards and John P. Putnam, trustees under the will of B.F. Reed, deceased, Mary S.C. Reed, John H. Reed & Sarah P., his wife and the trustees of the Episcopal Theological School to Giles County Iron Company, conveying 40,000 acres of land lying in Bland and Giles Counties known as the "Angel's Rest Tract". Dated 7-1-1875.
- Commonwealth VS George Minnix. Indictment for felony. A rule is awarded the defendant against Jane Wohlford, Fulton Rider, James Sheppard and Sallie Minnix, that they appear and show cause why they did not appear as witnesses for the defendant. J.H. Mustard posted Minnix's bond for $200.00. Case continued until next term. (Part of item on page 482)

Page 482- March 1876-

- W.H. Hawkins and Jacob Trinkle post bond for $50.00 each to assure their appearance in court as witnesses for the Commonwealth VS George Minnix.
- A.J. HIcks, N.B. Dodson
- and P.P. Hays, appeared in court and were discharged of their recognizance of appearing as witnesses in Commowealth VS Adam Lambert.
- On motion of James Tolbert, it appearing the William F. Tolbert has been dead for more that 3 months, ordered that the Sheriff of the County take the estae and administer it according to law.
- Laura A Tilson, Ransom E. Tilson and James P. Tilson, infants over 14 years of age, selected Mary J. Tilson as their guardian. The Court also appoints Mary J. Tilson (the mother) as guardian for her other children who are all under the age of 14, namely, Unice V. Tilson, Charles C. Tilson, George F. Tilson and Rachel G. Tilson. Mary J. Tilson with W.T. Hamilton & H.C. Groseclose, her securities, posts bond for $5,000.00 as the law requires. (Part of item on page 483)

Page 483- March 1876-

- K.C. Thornton, jailor, presents claim for $18.20, for maintaining and caring for James Hughes (colored), a lunatic confined in the jail. Claim is allowed. Admission to the asylum has been requested but refused for lack of room.
- K.C. Thornton, jailor, makes claim for $8.40 which is allowed.
- On motion of H.G. Kitts, it is ordered that J. Henderson Bruce, Wm Wilkinson and Andrew Kitts, are appointed Commissioners to allot the hands to work the public roads from J.M. French's Mill down the Creek and report at next term.
- Ordered that all persons who have acted as Commissioners or viewers on Public roads are allowed the sum of $1.00. (Under orders of an act of the Assembly approved March 20, 1875)
- J.B. Helvey VS Ida Neidermaier. James Kidd says he is indebted to the defendant in the amount sufficient to pay the plaintiff's demand. Ordered that Helvey recover from the defendant the sum of $9.62. (Paid by Kidd) (Part of item on page 484)

Page 484- March 1876-

- Samuel H. Newberry, John Repass and H.H. Tilson, appointed Commissioners to divide the Real Estate of James Wilson, deceased, among his heirs entitled thereto under the will of said Wilson, having returned their report and the same being filed at the January term of court and filed for exceptions, and none being taken, the said report is confirmed and ordered to be recorded..
- Jonas Huddle, Henry Foglesong and Elias Foglesong, Commissioners appointed to divide the lands of Joseph Kimberling, deceased, among his heirs, the report having been filed for exceptions and none being taken is confirmed and ordered to be recorded
- A report of settlement by I.S, Harman, Trustee for Polly Parsons, having been filed for exceptions and none being taken is confirmed and ordered to be recorded.
- A report of settlement by Acles Fannon, administrator of Tunis Muncy, deceased, having been filed for exceptions and none being taken is confirmed and ordered to be recorded.
- A report of settlement by Adam Waggoner, Guardian for Margaret and Foster Waggoner, infant children of George E. Waggoner, deceased, ordered filed for exceptions.
- D.O. McNiel, A.G. Harman and Jno. P. Roach, having been appointed Commissioners to rearrange the Road Precincts # 11 & # 12 in Mechanicsburg District. A new Road Precinct is to

be formed out of # 11 & 12 to be known as Precinct # 14, with A.G. Harman as Overseer, form the W.& H. Turnpike north of Point Pleasant Academy to Gordon Saunders' via A.Q. Harman's. Lands of Isaac S. Harman and Wm. E. Hoge also mentioned. (Part of item on page 485)

Page 485- March 1876-
- The following Overseers of the Roads were allowed certain amounts for their work, their names are, S.L. Gibson, Geo. W. Fanning, W.W. Blankenship, John Deavor, J.M. Fanning, A.F. Harman, I.P. Lambert, John W. Harman, H.F. Bruce, A.G. Harman, Henry G. HIcks, George Walters, D.G. Bird, James T. Burton, D.O. McNiel and W.W. Grayson as surveyor. Certified.
- On motion of F.G. Helvey, J.H. Hoge, D.O. McNiel and J.S. Robinett at the September term of court, were appointed Commissioners to view the public road from George Bogle's to Point Pleasant Academy and the part between the Academy and W.&H. Turnpike and report their opinion. Their opinion was that the road should be discontinued. Orederd that said road be discontinued. (Part of item on page 486)

Page 486- March 1876-
- Joseph Wohlford and Isaac S. Harman had applied for a new road to run from the Homestead of the late Henry Harman to the residence of the late John C. Crockett. Sally J. Crockett who held a dower interest in said Crockett land and John S. Crump also an heir, voiced objections against the said road.

Page 487- March 1786-
- On motion of James S. Wyrick, ordered that J. Henderson Bruce, Wm. Wilkenson and James H. Muncy, appointed Commissioners to report on what hands will work the road leading from J.S. Wyrick's via James Thompson's, and how much it will cost to open the said road.
- On motion of Gordon Wohlford, I.K. Price, Overseer of Precinct # 6 in Mechanicsburg District, with his hands, work the road between W.&.H. Turnpike near Harvey Nicewander's. to the residence of Gordon Wohlford.
- S.S. Reeder, appointed Commissioner in Chancery as one of the Commissioners to settle accounts of fiduciaries, whereupon Reeder took the prescribed oaths of office.
- On motion of Joseph Wohlford, it is ordered that A.J. Grayson, A.J. Muncy and James M. Fanning appointed Commissioners to go on the road from the late John C. Crockett's residence to to the house of Gordon Wohlford and report at next term.
- On motion of John S. Crump, it is ordered that A.G. Updike, J.J. Mustard and Sam'l. P. Mustard, be appointed as Commissioners to report on the expediency of changing the location of the road from the north side of Walkers Creek to the house of Gordon Wohlford so as to put it on the line between Jno. S. Crump and T.E. Mitchell's share of the Wohlford land, change to be on Crump's land.
- On motion of George W. Kinzer at the last term of court, Jno. Repass, Henry Foglesong and Peter Spangler, to report on the expediency of establishing a new road from west of Peter Spangler's up Harner's Creek near Peter Umbarger's. Red Oak Grove Church is mentioned. (Part of this item listed on page 488)

Page 488- March 1876-
- Mentions a new road from John P. Roach's to Compton's Mill.

- Court adjourned until next term.

Page 489- Tuesday April 4, 1876-
- Following is a list of deeds presented and recorded in the Clerk's Office since last term of court-
- A Power of Attorney from Wayman A. Harman to Wm. N. Harman. Dated 4-1-1875.
- E.A. Davis & wife to James R. Hager, a tract of land on Laurel Fork formerly owned by Joshua Pruett, for $600.00. Dated 9-2-1875.
- James R. Hager & wife to Squire Hager, conveying a life's interest in a tract of land on Laurel Fork.(Joshua Pruett tract) Dated 2-22-1876. (No cnsideration stated)
- Adam Waggoner & wife to David W. Waggoner, 100 acres+- on Walkers Creek. Dated 2-18-1876. (Probably a deed of gift)
- Deed of release from George W. Brown to Henry M. Pruett, conveying rights and title and interest in certain lands on Wolf Creek for $100.00. Dated 3-14-1876.
- John M. Cassell & others to P.P. Hays, a 5 acre tract of a 128 acre tract sold by Elias Foglesong, commissioner. For $250.00. Dated 11-6-1875.
- Solomon Waddle & others to Wm. G. Waddle, 1 acre+ a deed of gift. Dated 2-12-1876.
- Catherine Akers & others to Moses Akers, 60 acres off the land of Moses Akers, Sr. deceased. For $200.00. Dated 2-12-1876.
- Power of Attorney from Mary J. Tilson to W.T. Hamilton. Dated 2-24-1876.
- Deed of Trust from James Jones to Eli F. Groseclose, trustee to secure Crockett & Blair the sum of $75.00, conveying 60 acres on Walkers Little Creek, dated 5-10-1872.

Page 490- April 1876-
- Wm. L. Yost, Commissioner, to George W. Robinett, 66 ½ acres of the lands of Hiram Robinett, deceased. Dated 2-17-1876.
- A report of Commissioners, of the of the division of the lands of Joseph Kimberling, deceased, among his heirs.
- Report of Commissioners dividing lands of James Wilson, deceased, among the heirs entitled under the will of the said Wilson.
- Frank S. Blair, Commissioner, to Millard C. Dills, 350 acres of the land of P.H. Dills, deceased. Dated 1-4-1872.
- Frank S. Blair, Commissioner, to Edward V. Dills, 345 acres of the land of P.H. Dills, deceased. Dated 1-4-1872.
- A paper purporting tro be the will of Andrew Hanshew, deceased, was presented and partly proven by the oath of J.M. Kinder, one of the witnesses. Continued for further proof.
- Commonwealth VS Perry Day. Misdemeanor. Day pleads "not guilty" and case is continued.
- J. Newton Johnston, is appointed Justice of the Peace for Rocky Gap District.

Page 491- April 1876-
- Peter G. Snavely VS Sarah Groseclose. On an appeal from a Justice of the Peace. Continued.
- P.P. Hays, produced evidence of his ordination and regular communication with the Methodist Church. Hays with Elias Foglesng, his security, posts bond for $1,500.00 and is granted permission to celebrate the rites of matrimony.
- Wm. N. Harman VS Wm. C. Williams & John Fanning. Case continued.
- On motion of D.W. Dunn, Rees Crabtree, qualified as a deputy and took the oath.

- The widow of James M. C. Wilson, deceased, relinquishes her right to administer her deceased husband's estate. John M. Wilson is appointed and with Joseph Ewald, Felix Buck & Jno. S. McNutt, his securities, posted bond for $500.00. and was granted certificate to obtain letters of administration.
- The widow of Samuel Hanshew, deceased, relinquishes right to administer her deceased husband's estate. John M. Wilson with Joseph Ewald, Felix Buck & John S. McNutt, his securities, posts bond for &100.00 and obtains certificate for obtaining letters of administration.

Page 492- April 1876-
- Felix Buck, Henry Groseclose, Isaac Repass & I.T. Gollehon, appraisers of the personal estate of James M.C. Wilson, deceased.
- Same men as above to appraise the personal estate of Samuel Henshew, deceased.
- Margaret Susannah and Sarah Elizabeth Bogle, infants over the age of 14, select Juliaan S. Bogle as their guardian, which is approved by the Court. Court also appoints Juliaan S. Bogle as guardian for Luemma Isabell, Lucinda Catherine, Joseph Longstreet, George William, James Harvey, Genoa Ann and John Lockhart Bogle, infants under the age of 14, all children of John Bogle, deceased. Julian Bogle, with Jas. M. Fanning, J.H. Mustard &Hugh C. Fanning, her securities, posts bond for $200.00 conditioned as the law requires.
- On motion of George Walters, Overseer, Seddon Precinct, C.C. Banks, Paul James & W.W. Compton appointed Road Commissioners to allot the hands in the precincts of George Walters, Henry Hicks, Thos. Coburn and Wm. C. Williams and make report at next term of court.
- A report of settlement by D.F. Thompson, guardian of Marietta E. Waggoner, ordered filed for exceptions.
- Commonwealth VS Adam Lambert. Indictment for felony. (Continued on page 493)

Page 493- April 1876- Lambert led to the Bar in custody of Sheriff. Noted that the prisoner had escaped from jail between February and March and was at large at the March term of court. The jurors, W.P. Hornbarger, W.H. Hawkins, S.A. Melvin, Elisha Bond, Alex. Niswander, Newton Waddle, J.N. Fannon, Wm. Kitts, James Kidd, Isaac Kegley, Paul James and John Chandler, after hearing the evidence and returned a verdict of "Guilty of Felony" and fixed his sentence at 18 months in the peneteniary. Defendant moved the court to set aside the verdict and the argument is continued until tomorrow.
- Commonwealth VS George Minnix. Indictment for felony. Jury was sequestered and case continued tomorrow.

Page 494- Guggenheimer & Cone & Co. VS Ida Neidermaier. James Jidd appeared in court and says he is indebted to the defendant for $60.00 less $9.62, awarded to J.B. Helvey at last term of court. Case continued until next term of court.
- A report of settlement by Allen T. Suiter, guardian for the infant children of Jas. T. Gills, deceased. Ordered filed for exceptions.
- Presented in Court, the appraisement bill, list of property taken by the widow and the sale bill of the personal property of H.H. Tilson, deceased. Ordered to be recorded.
- Court adjourned until tomorrow morning at 9 0'clock AM.

Page 495- Wednesday Morning April 6, 1876-

- Expediency of establishing a new road from near Jonas Groseclose's to James M.C. Wilson's. F.F. Repass' Mill mentioned.
- The following are appointed Judges of Election for the ensuing year and their precincts-
Seddon Precinct - Henry Newberry, Isaac Kegley & A.N. Thompson.
Sharon Precinct- W.T. McNutt, Elias Foglesong & A.W. Shewey.
Mechanicsburg Precinct- Robt. C. Green, Isaac J. Davis & Hiram Rider.
Cameron's Precinct- A.R. Bogle, John A. Smith &F.C. Bogle.
Rocky Gap Precinct- W.W. Compton, Geo. W. Brown & A.D. Lambert.
The following are designated as Commissioners, A.W. Shewey, Robt. C. Green, A.R. Bogle, George W. Brown and Henry Newberry.
- In compliance with Sec. 16, Chap. 54 of Code 1873- J.N. Fannon is appointed Registrar for Town of Seddon and W.G. Painter, S.S. Reeder and John Wilkinson appointed Judges of Election for said town.
- Hiram Rider appointed Registrar for Town of Mechanicsburg and John H. Hoilman, W.P. Mustard and S.H. Bernard appointed as Judges of Election for said town.

Page 496- April 1876-
- J.H. Thompson permitted to qualify as deputy Treasurer.
- Sallie J. Crockett and John S. Crump, take the $60.00 offered them at a prior term of court, for damages sustained by the new road, asked for by Joseph Wohlford and Isaac S. Harman.
- Ordered that the new road be established leading from D.O. McNiel's Mill to to Compton's Mill. Viewers were Jas. S. Robinett & others. On motion of John S. Crump, A.G. Updike and John R. Compton at a former term of court.
- Commonwealth VS Adam Lambert. Court refused to set aside the verdict of yesterday and Lambert is remanded to jail. (Part of item on page 497)

Page 497- April 1876-
- Memorandum- The counsel for the defendant (Adam Lambert) took exceptions to the Court's ruling and tendered his bill of exceptions which were made a part of the record.
- Commonwealth VS George Minnix. Jury heard further evidence and adjourned until tomorrow.
- K.C. Thornton, jailor, makes claim for $19.50 for maintaining James Hughes, colored, a lunatic in the County jail. Allowed
- K.C. Thornton, jailor, makes claim for $2.50 for clothing for James Hughes, a lunatic, confined in the County jail. Allowed.
- Dr. A.J. Nye, John F. Locke and Thos. J. MUncy, appointed to inspect the county jail.

Page 498- April 1876- Ordered that the Court be adjourned until tomorrow.

Page 498- Thursday Morning April 6, 1876- Geo. W. Easley, Judge.
- Commonwealth VS Hannah Chandler. A rule awarded against Giles B.Thomas, a witness for the Plaintiff, for failure to appear in court. Case continued until next term of court.
- George W. Fanning, D.F. Muirhead and Gordon Wohlford, appointed Commissioners to report on changes to be made in the road from Mechanicsburg via the Brick Church east of the house of John P. and Miller B. Allen, to the Giles County.
- Samuel W. Williams, Commonwealth's Attorney, makes claim for $20.00. Allowed

- W.T. Hamilton, County Clerk, Makes claim for $5.00. Allowed.

Page 499- April 1876-
- The following persons are allowed the sum of $1.00 for services as jurors in the trial of Adam Lambert indicted for felony. Viz. W.P. Hornbarger, W.H. Hawkins, S.A. Melvin, Elisha Bond, Alex. Niswander, Newton Waddle, J.N. Fannen, Wm. Kitts, James Kidd, Isaac Kegley, Paul James and Paul Chandler.
- The following persons are allowed the sum of $3.00 for their services as jurors in the trial of George Minnix indicted for felony. Viz.- F.P. Crigger, Hiram Hounshell, Wm. Dillow, Newton Shrader, B.D. Graves, S.L. Kitts, Wm. H. Lambert, A.J. Kitts, Geo. W. Kidd, Chas. A. Repass, J.W. Thompson and Pendleton Burton.
- Commonwealth VS Adam Lambert. Indictment for felony. The sentence which was imposed at an earlier term to be carried out. However sentence was suspended until May 8th to allow the prisoner to appeal to the Circuit Court.

Page 500- April 1876-
- Commonwealth VS George Minnix. Indictment for felony. The jury found George Minnix (alias George Morton) guilty in the second count of the indictment and fixed his sentence at 130 days in the County jail. Minnix, remanded to jail.
- J.G. Kegley, Sheriff, makes claim for $27.60. Examined and allowed.
- J.G. Kegley, Sheriff, makes claim for $5.00. Examined and allowed.
- J.G. Kegley, Sheriff, makes claim for $36.00. Examined and allowed.
- Ordered that Wm. C. Williams, Overseer of Mechanicsburg Precinct, awarded $4.00 for warning hands to work on the public road. Allowed.

Page 500- April 1876-
- All causes not otherwise disposed of be continued until next regular term.

Page 501- Tuesday June 6, 1870 - Geo. W. Easley, Judge.
- Following is a list of deeds presented and recorded in the Clerk's Office since last term of Court.
- Wm. C. Miller & wife to Henry Newberry, their interest and rights in the lands of Wm. Hearn, deceased, for $20.00. Dated 2-25-1875.
- K.C. Thornton to W.T. Thornton, a quit claim deed conveying his interest in the lands of Hiram Thornton, deceased. Dated 4-3-1876.
- John Akers & others to Wm. S. King, 40 acres on Walkers Creek, for $100.00. 2-11-1876.
- F.S. Blair, Commissioner, to Nancy J. Martin, conveying dower interest in lands of P.H. Davis, deceased. Dated 1-4-1872.
- Power of Attorney from Peter Baily, Henderson Baily, Elizabeth Blankenship and Naoma Su, to Cloyd Adkins. Dated 2-21-1875.
- Marcellus Baugh, guardian of infant heirs of Nichotia, his wife, to James W. Thompson, 21 acres on Walkers Creek, for $112.00. Dated 1-1-1876.
- John J. Mustard & wfe to Samuel P. Mustard, releasing their moity in 480 acres on Walkers Creek , for (no consideration given). Dated 5-13-1874.
- Wm. McNeil & wife and Obediah Smith & wife to B.H. Oxley, conveying two undivided shares in the estate of Henry W.? Helvey, deceased, for $50.00. Dated 4-29-1872.

- Report of Commissioners assigning Sallie F. Crockett her dower in trust in the lands of her late husband, Jno. C. Crockett, deceased. Report confirmed in August term of 1875.
- James Jones to Sarah C. Srader, 47 ½ acers on Walkers Little Creek, for $47.50. Dated 6-14-1875.

Page 503- June 1876-
- Gleaves Thompson to Sam'l. H. Newberry, conveying his interest in the lands of his father, Isaiah? H. Thompson, deceased, now in possession of S.H. Newberry, for $250.00. Dated 5-13-1875.
- A patent from Commonwealth of Virginia to Harman Newberry, for a survey of 1579 ¼ acres in Bland County, dated 11-15-1875.
- A report of settlement by D.F. Thompson, guardian of Marietta E. Waggoner, infant of F.P. Waggoner, deceased, having been filed for exceptions and none being taken is certified and ordered to be recorded.
- A report of settlement by A.T. Suiter, guardian of infant heirs of James Gills, deceased, filed for exceptions and none being taken is certified and ordered to be recorded.
- A report of settlemant by Adam Waggoner, guardian of Margaret & Foster Waggoner, infant heirs of George Waggoner, deceased, having been filed in March for exceptions and none being taken was ordered to be recorded.
- The appraisement and sale bill of the Samuel Hanshew, deceased, approved and recorded.
- The appraisement and sale bill of James M.C. Wilson, deceased, approved and recorded.
- The will of Sophronia Robinett, deceased, presented and proven by oaths of A.J. Nye and Elias Repass, witnesses thereto. On motion of George Robinett, James M. Stowers appointed administrator and with will annexed and with D.W. Dunn & George Robinett, his securities posted bond for $1,000.00 and received certificate for obtaining letters of administration.

Page 504- June 1876-
- The will of Andrew Hanshew, presented and fully proven by testimony of James Cox. Amassa Tibbs one of the heirs is appointed administrator of said will. Jonas H. Groseclose & Jno. M. Cassell surities on bond for $400.00. Jonas H. Groseclose and Henry Groseclose appointed to appraise the personal estate of Andrew Hanshew, deceased.
- Application of F.F. Repass to establish a new road. Jonas H. Groseclose opposes same.
- O.C. Harman appointed Overseer of Road precinct # 14 in plave of A.G. Harman.
- Dr. A.J. Nye presented a claim for $7.75. Allowed.

Page 505- June 1876-
- On motion of George Walters, L.D. Bogle, W.N. Mustard & W.P. Hornbarger appointed as Commissioners to rearrange the road precincts and allot the hand to work same on Little Creek and Hunting Camp Creek.
- Newton M. Havens presented his petition saying he was illegally detained in custody by the Sheriff. John F. Locke, S.S. Reeder and Paul James had obtained said warrant for his arrest saying that Havens was a lunatic. Upon examination it was determined that Havens since April 26, 1876, had been returned to sanity and is now of sound mind was illegally imprisoned. Havens was discharged from custody.
- On motion of Henry Foglesong, Overseer of Road Precinct # ? in Sharon District, it is ordered

that Elias Foglesong, James A. Repass and I.T. Gollehon be appointed Commissioners to rearrange road precincts and allot the hands. Road up Harner's Branch is mentioned.
- K.C. Thornton, jailor, presents a claim for $30.80, for care & Manitenance of James Hughes, (colored) a lunatic. Examined and allowed.

Page 506- June 1876-
- K.C. Thornton, jailor, presents claim for $9.60. Allowed.
- K.C. Thornton, jailor, presents a claim for $28.85, for keeping N.M. Havens, a lunatic. It appearing that application for admission of said lunatic into the Lunatic Asylum was refused for lack of room.
- On motion of N.B. Stimson,- Isaac Stowers, Thomas F. Walker and John H. Bird are appointed viewers to review proposed road changes on the Wolf Creek & Clear Fork Turnpike. Peter Adkins' house is mentioned.
- On motion of David Waddle, ordered that Joel H. Spangler, James E. Wilson and John S. Wilson be appointed viewers to report on the expediency of establishing a new road from David Waddle's house to WC & H. Turnpike. George Groseclose's house is mentioned.

Page 507- June 1876-
- J.G. Kegley, Sheriff, makes claim for $2.30. Allowed.
- Commonwealth VS Adam Lambert. Larceny. Commonwealth's Attorney says he will not further prosecute. Lambert pleads guilty to petit larceny. Prisoner is to spend one month in jail and is remanded to jail.
- Young & Higginbotham VS H.G. Thompson. Case continued.
- Samuel W. Young VS H.G. Thompson. Case continued.
- T.J. Higginbotham VS H.G. Thompson. Case continued.
- Bland County VS Henry and W.C. Newberry. Case about opening a new road from A.J. Wyrick's via James Thompson's to Walkers Creek.
- Wm. N. Harman VS Jno. Fanning & Wm. C. Williams. George Wohlford is indebted to the defendants for $90.00. Harman denied Fanning's claim of said debt. Court orders Fanning to render an inventory of his real and personal property. A.W. Miller, John J. Mustard and Isaiah K. Price to appraise said property. Case continued. (Part of item on page 508)

Page 508- June 1876-
- A report of settlemant by J.H. Hoge, of the estate of John Bogle, deceased, presented in court and filed for exceptions.
- H.G. Dennis VS K.C. Thornton. On appeal. Case continued.
- Peter G. Snavely VS Sarah Groseclose. On appeal. Case continued.
- Court adjourned until first day of next term.

Page 509- Tuesday July 4, 1876- George W. Easley, Judge.
- Following is a list of deeds presented and recorded in the Clerk's Office since last term of court-
- Wm. A. Kidd & wife to Thomas G. Coburn, 2 ¾ acres on Hunting Camp Creek, for $21.25. Dated 3-20-1876.
- Wm. T. Hamilton, Special Commissioner, to the heirs of Peter C. Honaker, deceased, conveying 600 acres on Buck Horn Mountain. Dated 3-17-1876.

- Boston & Allen Wilburn to John Wolf & Wm. L. White, two tracts (260 acres) for $1,000.00. Dated 11-13-1875.
- Wm. N. Harman to John Wolf & Wm. L. White, 240 acres on Kimberling Creek for $600.00. Dated 3-13-1875.
- Hiram Hall & wife to Pheba E. Cooper, a tract north of town of Seddon, for $125.00. Dated 4-27-1876.
- A Power of Attorney from Jubal Scarberry wife, Rhoda P., and Dicy Lambert to George W. Lambert. Dated 5-20-1876.
- Wm. L. Yost Cmmissioner, to Victoria R. Crigger, 120 acres of the lands of Hiram Robinett, deceased. Dated 2-17-1876.
- Wm. L. Yost, Commissioner, to F.M. Robinett, 63 ½ acres of the lands of Hiram Robinett, deceased. Dated 2-17-1876.

Page 510- July 1876-
- Wm. L. Yost, commissioner, to Arbana Robinett, 59 acres of the lands of Hiram Robinett, deceased. Dated 2-17-1876.
- Wm. L. Yost, Commissioner, to Virginia Stowers, 65 acres of the lands of Hiram Robinett, deceased. Dated 2-17-1876.
- Wm. L. Yost, Commissioner, to Arminta Stowers, 75 acres of the lands of Hiram Robinett, deceased. Dated 2-17-1876.
- Wm. L. Yost, Commissioner, to Geneva A.E.C. and F.S. Stowers, 103 acres of the lands of Hiram Robinett, deceased. Dated 2-17-1876.
- Wm. L. Yost, Commissioner, to Amanda Waddle, 80 acres of the lands of Hiram Robinett, deceased. Dated 2-17-1876.
- A lease from Michael Waddle to Wm. L. Yost, John D. Peery and Charles R. Boyd, for 350 acres in Bland County. Dated 6-12-1876.
- John H. Hoge, appointed as administrator of Ralph Bogle, deceased with will annexed. Hoge with Gordon Wohlford, his security posts bond for $2,000.00.
- Dr. J.M. Hamilton, presents claim for $1.00, for medicine and visit provided for Adam Lambert, a convicted felon held in the County jail. Allowed.

Page 511- July 1876-
- Commonwealth VS James Jones & Mary Colbret. Indictment for misdemeanor. Ordered that this indictment be dismissed. Defendants to pay costs.
- Cloyd Adkins VS A.D. Lambert. On an appeal from a Judgment. Motion by defendant to dismiss was overruled. Cause is continued until next term.
- W.N. Mustard, L.D. Bogle & W.P. Hornbarger were appointed to rearrange road precincts in Seddon District. James & T.G. Coburn made exceptions.
- Wm. N. Harman VS John Fanning & W.C. Williams. The order entered at last term appointing appraisers to value the homestead of John Fanning is enlarged so that appraisers be required to report at the next term.
- Commonwealth VS Hannah Chandler. Defendant admits guilt. Fined $1.00 plus costs.
(Part of item on page 512)

Page 512- July 1876-

Members of a special Grand Jury of Inquest, viz:- Wm. E. Hoge, foreman; A. A Ashworth, Daniel Waddle, F.M. Robinett, E.S. Kidd, Wmm. Kitts and Isaac Kegley. They found the following indictments-
- Commonwealth VS Newton M. Havens, Indictment for felony. A treu bill.
- Commonwealth VS Commonwealth VS John Collins & Ro. King. Misdemeanor. A true bill.
- Peter G. Snavely VS Sarah Groseclose, admr. of Peter Groseclose, deceased. Case continued at cost of the defendant.
- On motion of Thos. Wohlford, it appearing that Hiram Muncy has been dead more than 3 months. Ordered that the sheriff take said estate and administer it according to law.

Page 513- July 1876-
- J.G. Kegley, Sheriff, makes claim for $2.00, for clothing furnished to James Hughs, (colored) a lunatic held in the County jail. Allowed.
- K.C. Thornton, jailor, makes claim for $11.85. Allowed.
- The sale and appraisement bill of the estate of Andrew Hanshew, deceased, ordered recorded.
- C.B. Price, curator of estate of John Mustard, deceased, returned inventory report. Recorded.
- A report of settlement by L.J. Miller, executor of Charles Miller, deceased. Filed for exceptions.
- Ordered that members of the Grand Jury be allowed the sum of $1.00.

Page 514- July 1876-
- Commonwealth VS Rufus Robinett. Robinett agrees to pay $1.00 fine plus costs. Dismissed.
- Names of Petit Jurors- James C. Painter, Geo. D. Painter, L.L. Quarles, Charles A. Repass, J.N. Fannon, T.N. Finley, Harvy G. Thompson, W.G. Waddle, Wm. A. Thomas, J.H. Thompson, Acles Fannon and John Deavor.
- Samuel W. Williams presents claim for $20.00. Allowed.
- John Havens appointed committee for Newton M. Havens, a lunatic. He posted bond for $100.00 with Thomas J. Muncy & James M. French, his securities.
- T.J. Higginbotham VS H.G. Thompson.
- Sam'l. W. Young VS H.G. Thompson.
- Young & Higgenbotham VS H.G. Thompson. (Continued on page 515)

Page 515- July 1876-
- The three above cases are to be consolidated. Ordered that the plaintiffs recover from Thompson, the sum of $22.13 plus interest and costs. Credits noted.
- Samuel W.Williams is allowed $5.00 for prosecuting Adam Lambert.
- The Town of Seddon failed to elect officers at last May election. Ordered that George W. Bennett, K.C. Thornton, Peter Kitts, J.C. Painter, A.J. Nye and Hiram Hall, be appointed trustees for the Town Corporation, to serve as such until the next election.
- Commonwealth VS Newton M. Havens. Indictment for felony. The court having reasonable doubt of the defendants sanity orders the trial be suspended. A jury found Havens to be insane. Case was dismissed. Havens ordered to be sent to an asylum as soon as there is room.
-(Part of item on page 516)

Page 516- July 1876-

- Rees Crabtree, Deputy for D.W. Dunn, Treasurer, presents list of insolvents in the capitation and property taxes for 1875.
- D.W. Dunn, Treasurer, presents a list of delinquent real estate taxes in the district of G.M. Tibbs, assessor, for the year 1875.

Page 517, July 1876-
- J.H. Thompson, Deputy for D.W. Dunn, Treasurer, presents a list of insolvents in the capitation and property taxes in James D. Honaker's district of Rocky Gap. For 1875.
- J.H. Thompson, Deputy for D.W. Dunn, Treasurer, presents list of delinquent Real Estate taxes in James D. Honaker's Rocky Gap District.
- D.W. Dunn, Treasurer, presents a list of delinquent Real Estate taxes in Seddon District.
- D.W. Dunn, presents list of insolvents for capitation & personal property taxes for 1875.

Page 518- July 1876-
- Two items of delinquency on taxes for 1875 presented by D.W. Dunn.
- H.G. Dennis VS K.C. Thornton. On an appeal. Dismissed by agreement.
- H.G. Dennis VS K.C. Thornton. Dennis to recover from Thornton $17.35. Credit noted.
- Wm. Dillow, Constable & Giles B. Thomas, presents claim for $3.30. Allowed.
- Court adjourned until first day of next term.

Page 519- Tuesday August 7, 1876- Geo. W. Easley, Judge.
- Following is a list of deeds presented and recorded in the Clerk's Office since last term of court-
- Charles Edwards & Margaret A., his wife to Elizabeth & Kissiah Wilson, conveying their interest in the real estate of James Wilson, deceased, for $300.00. Dated 5-15-1876.
- An agreement between Jonas H. Groseclose & Susannah Groseclose, regarding real estate and personal property. Dated 10-26-1875.
- Julia A. Tolbert, Melvina Cubine to E.M. Melvin, conveying their interest in the real estate of George & John Melvin. Dated 8-30-1875.
- Nancy M. Niswander to Julia E. Bradham, 20 acres of the land of Jacob Niswander, deceased. For $300.00. Dated 5-6-1876.
- Deed of Trust on real estate from Franklin Grayson to H.C. Newberry, trustee, conveying 2967 acres, being land Grayson now lives on, to secure debt to F.I. Suiter $675.00. Dated 7-6-1876.
- William S. Mustard VS Elizabeth Henderson. Unlawful Detainer. Court overruled defendants motion to quash. She pleads "not guilty". Case continued at cost of defendant.

Page 520- August 1876-
- Guggenheimer, Cone & Co. VS Ida Neidermaier. Case continued.
- Cloyd Adkins VS A.D. Lambert. On an appeal from a judgment of a Justice of the Peace. On evidence produced, the court decided that the judgment was in error. Lambert to recover from Adkins and his security, Samuel Stimson, the sum of $52.00 plus interest & costs.
- Geo. W. Kinzer presented 2 claims against the county for work done as surveyor on roads, for $21.00. Allowed.
- On motion of William Helvey & Joseph Shrader, ordered that A.B. Waggoner, P.W. Rice and G.P. French, report on the expediency of establishing a new road from near Brown's Ford through the lands of Henry Pruett, Jno. Shrader & Wm. Helvey, to the house of said Helvey.

- Page 521- August 1876-
- At a meeting held at Seddon, the Board of Supervisors ordered that $150.00 be added to the salaries of the supervisors.
- Matter of rearranging Road Precincts. Parker Hornbarger, James Starks, George Starks, F.I. Suiter, T.G. Coburn, W.P. Hornbarger, and Randall Grayson, George Walters were mentioned.

Page 522- August 1876-
- Road Precinct # 6 to include Hunting Camp Road. ----
- On motion of Daniel Waddle, at the June term, Joel H. Spangler, James Wilson & Jno. L. Wilson appointed as viewers of the road.
- T.J. Higginbotham VS H.G. Thompson & others.
- Young & Higginbotham VS H.G. Thompson.
- Sam'l. W. Young VS H.G. Thompson.
(In these 3 causes there was a judgment in favor of the plaintiffs, and the Clerk allowed an attorney's fee in each case. Ordered that only one be taxed.
- H.C. Newberry, Overseer of Road Precinct # 8, resigns.. F.M. Robinett replaces him.
- Court adjourned until tomorrow morning at 9 0'Clock AM.

Page 523- Wednesday Morning August 9, 1876-
- In the matter of the settlement by George Robinett, guardian of the heirs of James W. and Emily Grayson, made by J.H. Hoge, considering the exceptions of the heirs, it is ordered that the settlement be restated.
- In matter of settlement of the accounts of A.J. Grayson, administrator of James W. Grayson, deceased, with J.H. Hoge, commissioner. An item of $17.90, interest was omitted in the year of 1867, by Commissioner Hoge. Ordered that said report be amended.
- A report of settlement by A.J. Grayson, administrator of Emily Grayson, deceased, having been presented at a former court and filed for exceptions and none being taken, is ordered to be recorded.
- A report of settlement by L.J. Miller, executor of Joseph T. Hicks, deceased, having been filed in the July term for exceptions and none being taken, is ordered to be recorded.

Page 524- August 1876-
- A report of settlement by L.J. Miller, administrator of Charles Miller, deceased, having been filed in July for exceptions and none being taken is ordered to be recorded.
- Wm. N. Harman VS Jno. Fanning. On suggestion to George Wohlford. A.W. Miller, I.K. Price and J.J. Mustard, having been appointed at a former term to appraise the property of John Fanning, returned a report showing property valued at $1,715.00, all of which said Jno. Fanning claims as a Homestead. Harman moves the court to render a judgment against the garnishee, George Wohlford on the following grounds, 1st- That Fanning had filed his Homestead deed before the service of the garnishee on George Wohlford., which did not embrace debt on Wohlford. Case is finally dismissed.
- The sale bill of personal property of the estate of P.C. Honaker, deceased, ordered recorded.
- Drs. J.M. Lovell and F.P. Dunn, presents claim of $5.00, for examination of Newton M. Havens.

Page 525- August 1876-
- F.I. Suiter VS Bland County Board of Supervisors. Court takes until next term to consider.
- Bland County VS Dr. J.M. Lovell. Court takes until next term to consider.
- Bland County VS Dr. L.J. Miller. Court takes until next term to consider.
- Bland County VS D.A. Miller. Court tales until next term to consider.
{ These last three items concern decisions made by the Board in allowing certain accounts.}
- K.C. Thornton makes claim for $40.25, for keeping and boarding Newton M. Havens, a lunatic, confined in the County jail. Allowed.

Page 526- August 1876-
- Peter G. Snavely VS Sarah Groseclose, administrator of Peter Groseclose, deceased. On an appeal of a judgment. Court says judgment is in error and is reversed. Snavely to recover from Groseclose the sam of $30.13 with interest from May 27, 1849 to April 16, 1861 then from April 10, 1865 till paid. Snavely also to recover his costs.
- Court adjourned until first day of next term.

Page 527- Tuesday September 5, 1876-
- Following is a list of deeds presented and recorded in the Clerk's Office since last term of Court-
- Charles P. Wheeler to Henry P. Wheeler, conveying his interest in a tract of land on Kimberling, for 200.00. Dated 4-12-1876.
- S.W. Williams, Commissioner, to John H. Pegram, 300 acres on Walkers Little Creek. No consideration given. Dated 6-4-1876.
- W.P. Cecil to W.E. Peery and Charles R. Boyd, conveying to each an undivided one third interest in 2,000 acres on Round Mountain of Wolf Creek, for $1.00. Dated 7-15-1876.
- The will of Stephen Repass presented and proven by oaths of W.T. Hamilton and D.W. Dunn was ordered to be recorded. The executors, Wm. G. Repass, James A. Repass and R.B. Repass, qualified and with J.G. Kegley & D.W. Dunn their securities posted bond for $800.00.
- W.T. Hamilton, D.W. Dunn and G.W. K. Green are appointed to appraise the personal property and Real Estate of Stephen Repass, deceased.

Page 528- September 1876-
- On motion of James Franklin one of the heirs of Rachel Harman, James Franklin and Wayman A. Harman, appointed administrators of the estate of Rachel Harman, deceased. James Franklin, with Henry Newberry, H.C. Newberry &J.M. Stowers, his securities, posted bond for $1,500.00 and took oath. Liberty given to Wayman Harman the other administrator, to appear and give bond in the same amount within 90 days.
- On motion of James Frnklin, administrator of Rachel Harman, deceased, H.C. Newberry, W.N. Mustard and S.H. Newberry, appointed appraisers of of the personal property of Rachel Harman, deceased.
- On motion of John F. Locke and J. Henderson Bruce, A.J. Grayson is appointed a committee for the property of Josiah Bruce, a lunatic. Grayson with Locke and J.H. Bruce, his securities, posts bond for $500.00.
- In the matter of the application of Wm. Helvey and Joseph Shrader to establish a new road- the report of viewers, P.W. Price, A.B. Waggoner and G.P. French, was presented. Ordered that the road leading from Wolf Creek & Clear Fork known as Brown's Ford, through lands of Henry

Pruett, John Shrader and Wm. Helvey to the house of said Wm. Helvey, be established as a public highway with leave to any parties whose lands the road passes through to erect gates across said highway.

- On motion of T.G. Hudson, Overseer of road precinct # 4 in Sharon District, said Hudson is unable with the means at his disposal to repair or build a new bridge on the W & H. Turnpike near Joseph Groseclose's. Ordered that James A. Repass be appointed to accept bids and report at next term of court. (Part of item on page 529)

Page 529- September 1876-
- Names of those sworn toa Grand Jury of Inquest, A.N. Thompson, foreman; F.M. Compton, P.R. Suiter, James Thompson, R.C. Green, J.M. Pruett, Timothy Hamilton, C.A. Seagle, I.N. Umbarger, I.T. Gollehon, A. Fry, Wm. M. Bird, I.G. Pauley, C.S. Grayson, Edward Bruce and Samuel Damewood. These jurors having not finished their business are adjourned until tomorrow.
- Commonwealth VS Perry Day. Indictment for Larceny. Jurors, W.P. Hornbarger, Henry Newberry, Newton Waddle, Wm. Kitts, F.P. Crigger, James Clark, S.S, Melvin, Luther Moore, S.C. Davis, D.A. Miller, A.J. Thompson and J.N. Fannon could not agree on a verdict and they adjourned until tomorrow morning at 9'O'Clock AM.
- Ordered a rule against J.D. Honaker, A.B. Pauley, I.M. Repass and George Walters for failure to appear after being summonsed to appear in court.
- On application of Daniel Waddle for a new road from his house to the Walkers Creek & Holston Turnpike- Thomas G. Hudson filed exceptions to the report of the viewers. Ordered that viewers go on ad find another route for said road. (Part of item on page 530)

Page 530- September a876-
- On application of I.M. Repass on establishing a new road or an extension of the application to the mill of F.F. Repass. Jonas Umbarger contested and was awarded $35.00 damages. Road to be established.
- Court adjourned until tomorrow morning at 9 O' Clock AM.

Wednesday Morning September 6, 1876-
- K.C. Thornton, Jailor, makes claim for $28.00 for (said lunatic). (not named).

Page 531- September 1876-
- A report of settlement by Thos. F. Walker, administrator of John W. Hatch, deceased, was presented and filed for exceptions.
- A report of settlement by F.I. Suiter, late sheriff of Bland County, and as such administrator of E.A. Sheppard, deceased, was filed for exceptions.
- A report of settlement by John H. Hoge, administrator of John Bogle, deceased, having been filed at a former term of court and filed for exceptions and none being taken, is confirmed and ordered to be recorded.
- The will of John Kinsel presented and proven by oaths of Jno. S. McNutt, W.T. McNutt and W.L. Yost. Eldred M. Scott, the named executor, posted bond for $1,200.00 with Jno. S. McNutt and D.W. Dunn, his securities.
- On motion of Elderd Scott, executor of John Kinsel, deceased, Jno. S. McNutt, Elias Foglesong and John Repass, appointed appraisers of the personal property of John Kinsel, deceased.

133

- Dr. J.L. Lovell presents a claim for $10.00. Allowed.
- The Grand Jury aworn yesterday, returned the following,
- Commonwealth VS Elisha Blankenship, indictment for Felony. A true Bill.

Page 532- September 1876-
- Commonwealth VS Millard King. Indictment for Felony. A true Bill.
- Commonwealth VS James M. Spencer. Indictment for misdemeanor. A true Bill.
- Commonwealth VS Sarah Pauley. Misdemeanor. A true Bill (2 charges)
- Commonwealth VS George Hancock. Misdemeanor. A true Bill. (2 charges)
- Commonwealth VS John Collins. Assault & Battery. A true Bill.
- Commonwealth VS James D. Honaker. Assault & Battery. A true Bill.
- Commonwealth VS George Wohlford. Misdemeaner. A true Bill.
- Commonwealth VS Giles Linkious. Assault & Battery. A true Bill.
- Commonwealth VS Joseph Hearn. Larceny. A true Bill.
- Commonwealth VS Millard King. Misdemeanor. A true Bill.
- We the Grand Jury present Almarine Woodyard, Road Commissioner for the Corporation of the Town of Mechanicsburg, for not keeping the roads under his control in such condition as the law directs, on the evidence of R.C. Green and Timothy Hamilton, members of the Grand Jury.
- Having nothing further before them, the Grand Jury was discharged.

Page 533-September 1876-
- William S. Mustard VS Elizabeth Henderson. Unlawful detainer. Mustard to recover from Henderson the said premises in dispute and his cost by him expended in this case.
- The above plaintiff prays for a writ to the Sheriff to be directed to cause him to have possession of his land. Writ was granted.
- Names of Petit Jurors for this term of court for trials of misdemeanors are- S.S. Melvin, Luther Moore, Henry Newberry, S.C. Davis, A.G. Thompson, Wm. Kitts, D.A. Miller, Newton Waddle, F.P. Crigger, W.P. Hornbarger, J.N. Fannen and James Clark.
- Ordered that members of the Grand Jury be awarded the sum of $2.00 each for their services.

Page 534- September 1876-
- Petit Jurors awarded the sum of $1.00 each,for their services.
- A rule against Almarine Woodyard for not keeping the road in good repair as the law requires.
- F.I. Suiter VS Bland County Board of Supervisors. For disallowing an account for $55.00 for caringfor Sarah Suiter, a pauper. Ordered that the decision of the Board was in error. Suiter to recover his $55.00 plus his costs expended in this suit.
- Bland County VS J.M. Lovell. Decided that the Board was not in error. Claim refused.

Page 535- September 1876-
- Bland County VS L.J. Miller. Decided that the Board was not in error for refusing the claim. Claim is dismissed at cost of Miller.
- Bland County VS D.A. Miller. Miller had made and been paid a claim for $57.50. Board was not in error in allowing claim. Appeal is dismissed and Miller to get his costs for this suit.
- Commonwealth VS Jack Carr. Larceny. A writ of capias awarded against Carr directed to the Sheriff of Tazewell County, returnable at next term of Court.

K.C. Thornton, Jailor, presents claim for $6.50, for clothing bought for N.M. Havens, a lunatic, confined in the County Jail. Allowed.

Commonwealth VS Joseph Hearn. Larceny. A writ of capias awarded against Hearn, directed to the Sheriff of Bland County, returnable at next term of Court.

- Commonwealth VS Perry Day. Petit Larceny. A new trial is awarded to the defendant.

- Court adjourned until first day of next term of Court.

Page 537- October 3, 1876-

- A list of deeds presented and recorded in the Clerk's Office since last term of Court.-

- Dills Adkins to Sarah Adkins, his interest in the lands of Isaac Adkins, deceased, for $150.00. Dated 7-1-1876.

- Wm. A Hearn to Henry Newberry, his interest in the lands of Wm. Hearn, deceased, for $21.42. Dated 9-5-1876.

- Wm. Umbarger & wife and Jas. A. Repass to Isaac G. Pauley, 53 acres in Bland County, for $500.00 in money and $300.00 in land. (No date given)

- Wm. Umbarger & wife and Jas. A. Repass, Trustee, conveying the John H. Lindamood tract of land to secure Alex. Umbarger the sum of $598.84. Dated 9-2-1876.

- Isaac G. Pauley & wife to Wm. Umbarger, 77 acres on south side of Brushy Mountain, for $300.00. Dated 9-2-1876.

- Boyd Thompson to Samuel H. Newberry, his interest in the Josiah M. Thompson tract of land, for $225.00. Dated 8-25-1876.

- G.S. Smith, assignee in Bakkruptcy of Ballard P. Stafford to Wm. G. Stafford conveying 86 acres on Walkers Creek for $400.00. Dated 4-28-1876.

- John G. Crockett to Joseph Wohlford, 767 acres+-, being the same land devised to Crockett by his father, for $7,000.00. Dated 11-28-1874.

- Jno. S. Hoback to F.S. Blair, Trustee, conveying a tract of land with (saw & grist) mill on it. Land was purchased by Hoback from Jas. D. Honaker, to secure Crockett & Blair the sum of $50.00. Dated 9-12-1876.

- James M. French, Special Commissioner, to James D. Honaker, a share in the Real Estate of P.C. Honaker, deceased. Dated 3-29-1876. (No consideration given)

- James M. French, Special Commissioner to Robt. H. Bailey & wife, their share in the lands of P.C. Honaker, deceased. Dated 3-29-1876.

Page 538- October 1876-

- James M. French, Special Commissioner, to James Bailey & wife, conveying Bailey & wife's share of the lands of P.C. Honaker, deceased. Dated 3-29-1876.

- James M. French, Special Commissioner, to John Honaker, Honakers share of the lands of P.C. Honaker, deceased. Dated 3-29-1876.

- James M. French, Special Commissioner, to W.B. Honaker, Honalker's share of the lands of P.C. Honaker, deceased. Dated 3-29-1876.

- James M. French, Special Commissioner, to Matilda J. Honaker. Matilda's share of the lands of P.C. Honaker, deceased. Dated 3-29-1876.

- James M. French, Special Commissioner, to Mary C. Honaker, Mary's share of the lands of P.C. Honaker, deceased. Dated 3-29-1876.

On motion of A.J. Grayson, Trustee in a deed of trust executed by Uriah Bean to secure Eli

Leady. Said trustee is hereby ordered to make settlement and report to court the statement of liens against the fund in the hands of the trustee.
- Wm. P. Bogle, for benefit of Wm. Kitts (now for benefit of Wythe G. Waddle VS Wm. Deavor, George W. Suiter & F.F. Repass. Wm. P. Bruce owes Suiter $102.00 and Wm. W. Fanning owes Suiter $20.00. Plaintiffs to recover from defendants the amount of garnishees plus costs.

Page 539- October 1876-
- Ordered that the report of F. I. Suiter, administrator, with J.H. Hoge, Commissioner, of the estate of E.A. Sheppard, deceased, be returned to Hoge to determine what amount will go to the widow and heirs.
- K.C. Thornton, Jailor, makes claim for $2.10. Allowed.
- K.C. Thornton, Jailor, makes claim for $ 27.00. for keping and boarding N.M. Havens, a lunatic, in the county jail. Allowed.
- D.O. McNiel VS Wm. N. Harman. On a warrant by a Justice. McNiel to recover from Harman, the sum of $64.00, with credits amounting to $14.00. Harman to pay costs.
- In the matter of Daniel Waddle's application for a new road from his house to the W&H. Turnpike- Ordered that T.G. & Hannah C. Hudson the owners of land through which road will pass, be summonsed to appear at next term and show cause if any why road should not be established as a public highway.
- A report of settlement by Thos. F. Walker, administrator of John W. Hatch, deceased, with J.H. Hoge, Commissioner of accounts, having beed filed for exceptions and none being taken is ordered to be recorded.
- Gordon Wohlford, Deputy for J.G. Kegley, Sheriff, presents claim for $3.50. Allowed.
- Ordered that F.G. Helvey, Overseer of the Poor, bind out the following named children, Victoria Harman, (colored), age (no age given), Geo. W. Chandler age 8 and Henry Chandler, age 7.
- Court adjourned until first day of next term.

Page 541- Tuesday November 5, 1876-
- Following is a list of deeds presented and recorded in the Clerk's Office since last term of Court-
- David Schindell, Trustee, and Samuel Emmert to E.G. Booth. Deed of release. Dated 9-19-1876
- W.L. Yost, Commissioner, to Jno. Kinzer, 50 acres of land for $100.00. Dated 4-26-1876.
- R. Hall & wife to Wm. M. Bird, 11 acres East of Mechanicsburg, for $900.00.
Dated 12-13-1875.
- A deed of Homestead made by James Tolbert, dated 10-16-1876.
- A deed of Homestead made by John B. King, dated 10-25-1876.
- H.C. Groseclose appointed a Commissioner in Chancery and took necessary oaths.
- The rule against George Walters for not appearing in court as a juror is hereby discharged.
- A.D. Lambert VS Cloyd Adkins & Wm. M. Bishop. Defendants failed to appear. Ordered that Lambert recover from defendants the sum of $37.10, plus interest & costs.
(Part of item on page 542)

Page 542- November 1876-
- Commonwealth VS Wm. Cubine. Cubine in custody of the jailor was brought to the Bar and moved the court to quash the indictment in this case, which the court overruled. Cubine pleads "not guilty". From a panel of 24 persons, the following were picked as jurors to hear this case-

Joel Spangler, Geo. Walters, James Kidd, J.C. Painter, R.G. Thomas, W.C. Williams, E.S. Kidd, Wm. Kitts, Wm. Hederick, J.L. Wilson, Pendleton Burton and L.D. Helvey. They, after hearing part of the evidence were sequestered until tomorrow.

Page 543- Commonwealth VS Wm. Cubine. Mentions a bond executed to Malvina Cubine by Jno. R. Compton and G.C. Thorn. Mentions Gordon Wohlford and Robert Wylie. Case continued until tomorrow morning.
- Court adjourned until tomorrow at 9'O'Clock AM.

Page 544- Wednesday Morning November 6, 1876 (Old Book says December, which is in error)
- Commonwealth VS Wm. Cubine. The prisoner, Wm. Cubine with Malvina Cubine, his security, posted a bond for $500.00 each, to assure his appearnace in court tomorrow morning.
- T.G. Hudson VS Daniel Waddle. On application to establish a new road. Case continued.
- On motion of Acles Fannon, ordered that Wm. Kitts, Wm. M. Bird and Mitchell Kegley, view and report on the expediency of establishing a new road from near the house of B.H. Penley to the line between said Fannon and report at next term of court. (Part of item on page 545)

Page 545- November 1876-
- Elias Harman in an execution against Wm. N. Harmen, moved the court to appoint three disinterested Free Holders to assess the value of the Real & Personal property of Wm. N. Harm Harman. Ordered that A.G. Updike, John J. Mustard and Jno. P. Roach, after first being sworn, do assess the value of the property of Wm. N. Harman, set apart and designated in his Homestead Deed, and report to the court.
- K.C. Thornton, Jailor, makes claim for $64.00 for keeping N.M. Havens, a lunatic confined in the County Jail. Allowed.
- Ordered that Court stand adjourned until tomorrow morning.

Page 546- Thursday Morning November 7, 1876. (This date on page 545)
- Commonwealth VS Wm. Cubine. Petit Larceny. Jury finds Cubine "not guilty".
- The road from the Brick Church and Jno. P. and Miller B. Allen is very much out of repair. It is impossible for Geo. W. Fanning to repair same with the means under his control, and also that the road bed must be moved out of the Kimberling Creek and put on the banks of the land owned by said Jno. P. and Miller B. Allen, who have offered to give sufficient quantity for said road. James M. Hamilton is appointed as Commissioner to make suitable contract for someone to protect said road and make report at next term of court.
- J.G. Kegley, Sheriff, makes claim for $69.75. Allowed.
- Wm. T. Hamilton, County Clerk, makes claim for $2.50. Allowed.
- Samuel W. Williams Prosecuting Attorney, makes claim for $10.00. Allowed.

Page 547- A.D. Lambert VS D.A. Miller & L.D. Helvey. Pendleton Burton says he is indebted to L.D. Helvey for &20.00. Lambert to recover from the said garnishee, Burton $15.50 with interest and costs.
- A report of settlement by Thos. F. Walker, administrator of John W. Hatch, deceased, filed for exceptions at a former term and none being taken, is ordered to be recorded.
- A report of settlement by J.H. Hoge, administrator of John Bogle, deceased, presented at a

former term of court for exceptions and none being taken is ordered to be recorded.
- A report of a settlement by Jas. H. Muncey, guardian of Wm. A. and Lucinda Hearn, presented and ordered to be filed for exceptions.
- The former report of settlement by J.H. Hoge, having been recommitted, F.I. Suiter, late Sheriff and as such, administrator of E.A. Sheppard, deceased. Ordered that the report by Hoge be confirmed and Suiter is ordered to distribute the funds to the parties entitled.
-

Page 548- Novenber 1876-
- William C. Williams, Surveyor of roads in Mechanicsburg District, from Widow Neel's to mouth of Buck Lick Branch, stated that he was unable with the hand & means under his control, to open and keep in repair the said road. James M. Hamilton is appointed a Special Commissioner to determine if this is a case for County funding.
- Court adjourned until first day of next term.

{ There is a gap of two months before the next term of Court}

Page 549- Tuesday, February 6, 1877- Geo. W. Easley, Judge.
- Following is a list of deeds presented and recorded in the Clerk's Office since last term of Court.
- John Deavor & wife to Elias Foglesong, 78 acres for $527.00. Dated 1-12-1876.
- Robt. Doak & wife to F. G. Huddle, conveying Doak's interest in a certain tract of land. Consideration, $1.00. Dated 11-7-1876.
- J.M.C. Wilson & wife and Jno. M. Wilson, to Thos. A. Snider, for 61 acres for $205.00. Dated ?-26-1876.
- Harvey K. Niswander & wife and J.R. Patton & wife to T.E. Mitchell, for $230.00 Dated 10-13-1876. (Number of acres not given)
- James M. Sheppard & wife to Harriet A. Weaver, 72 acres, for $1,000.00. Dated 1-13-1877.
- J.M. Hamilton & wife to Cosby Sheppard, a house & lot in Mechanicsburg, for $900.00. Dated 1-11-1877.
- A Deed of Trust from Henry Davis to Samuel C. Davis, conveying a tract of land on Walker's Little Creek known as the Joshua Mustard Tract. No monetary amount mentioned. Dated 4-4-1876.
- J.H. Hoge, Trustee, to F.M. Gordon, a house & lot in Mechanicsburg. Dated (not given)
- W.P. Bruce & wife to J.H. Hoge, 250 acres, for $2,750.00. Dated 11-13-1876.

Page 550- February 1877-
- A report of settlement by A.J. Grayson in a Deed of Trust executed to said Grayson to secure Eli Leady, made before Wm. L. Yost, Commissioner in Chancery. Report was earlier filed for exceptions. Mentioned also are, Hezekiah Harman, Thomas Shannon, Eli F. Groseclose, Robert Doak, Harvey Kitts, Young & Higginbotham and Wm. Groseclose's Executors.
- On motion of S.T. Gibson, Overseer of Road district in Rocky Gap, leading from Deer Hollowto the top of East River Mountain, he is hereby released and removed from his position and W.A. Linkious to take his place.

Page 551- February 1877-
- J.M. Pruett, appointed Overseer in 4th Mechanicsburg precinct in place of W.W. Blankenship,

deceased. L.F. Morehead, appointed overseer of Kimberling, in place of Isaac Lambert who has moved from the area.

- W.A. Lincious, (Linkous) overseer in Rocky Gap, stated that he was unable to put the road in good repair with the hands and means under his control. Thos. J. Kinzer to report the facts as to whether or not County funds can be used.

- O.E. Wright is relieved from working on the public road.

- Jno. R Compton desires an alteration in the road from the Brick Church to the mouth of the lane leading to his house. Geo. W. Fanning, M.B. Allen and G.C. Thorn to examine said proposed alteration and report to the court.

- On motion of L.J. Miller, Assessor, Daniel A. Miller is permitted to qualify as his assistant. He took the oath of office as prescribed by law.

Page 552- February 1877-

- On motion of Isaac Bland, it appearing that Lee A. Kitts has been dead for more than three months, it is ordered that the Sheriff take and administer the estate according to law.

- Members of a Grand Jury of Inquest are- A.J. Grayson, foreman; Felix Buck, Joseph Thomasson, J.C. Painter, Ephriam Waddle, Jessie Justice, James Thompson, P.R. Suiter, Stephen Fox, I.G. Pauley, Joel Spangler, Jas. H. Bruce, I.S. Harman, B.P. Brown, Wm. Kitts, Stephen Lambert, Wm. H. Hawkins, Jas. S. Robinett and A.D. Groseclose. They found the following indictments,

- Commonwealth VS Sam'l. Collins. Indictment for misdemeanor, a true Bill.

- Commonweal;th VS Andrew Dillman. Indictment for misdemeanor, a true Bill.

- J.C. Thornton, Jailor, makes claim for $65.00 for keeping N.M. Havens, a lunatic in the County Jail. Allowed.

- K.C. Thornton, Jailer, makes claim for $4.50, for clothing for N.M Havens, a lunatic. Allowed.

Page 553- February 1877-

- K.C. Thornton, Deputy for Sheriff J.G. Kegley, makes claim for $.50 cents. Allowed.

- James Robinett and H.R. Mustard, Executors of Samuel Wohlford, deceased, VS H.A. Pauley and Wm. Wilkerson. Plaintiffs to recover from defendants, the sum of $162.60, plus interest and costs.

- Guggenheimer Cone & Co. VS Ida Neidermaier. Case continued.

- Geo. Robinett, guardian, VS F.M. Harman, Adam Waggoner & A.W. Shewey, sureties in the official bond of A.C. Waggoner, late Sheriff of Bland County. Plaintiff to recover from the defendants the sum of $108.50 plus interest from Oct. 1869 till paid. Credits noted.

Page 554- February 1877-

- Commonwealth VS Jack Carr. Indictment for Larceny. Trial continued and Carr posts bond for $50.00 to assure his appearance in Court.

- Wm. N. Harman VS James B. Singer (Songer?) & D.A. Miller. Case continued.

- The Court appoints H.C. Groseclose a Commissioner of Chancery, to settle the accounts of all fiduciaries which may be laid before him.

- James D. Honaker moved the Court to appoint a committee to take charge of the estate of John S. Hoback, a convict now confined in the penitentiary. Joel H. Spangler was appointed as his Cmmittee. He refused to act. J.G.Kegley, Sheriff, was appointed totake and care for Hoback's estate as prescribed by law.

Page 555- February 1877-
- Daniel Waddle VS T.G. Hudson. On an appeal to have a new road established. Case continued.
- Court adjourned until tomorrow.

Wednesday Morning February 7, 1877-
- Frederick Cook appointed Overseer of the road in Rocky Gap District, in place of Archibald Barnitz, who has removed from this county.
- Isaac S. Harman, appointed Supervisor of Mechanicsburg District, in place of J.M. Hamilton who has resigned. Harman with A.J. Grayson, Gordon Wohlford and J. Gord. Kegley, his securities, posted bond for $1,000.00 and took oath of office.
- I.K. Price, Overseer for Mechanicsburg District, makes claim for $10.00. Allowed.

Page 556- February 1877-
- Archibald Barnett, Road Overseer for Rocky Gap District, makes claim for $3.00. Allowed.
- Wm. H. Hanshew, presents claim for $156.00, for taking care of Louisa Hanshew, a lunatic.
- Martin L. Perry, orphan of Jessie Perry, deceased, makes choice of H.C. Groseclose as his guardian. Groseclose with John Repass, hhis security, posts bond for $600.00.
- William C. Williams, Surveyor of the road for Mechanicsburg District, says he cannot, with the hands and means available, keep the road in good repair. Isaac S. Harman appointed to examine and make report on whether or not this is a case for county funds.
- Daniel Waddle VS T.G. Hudson. On application for a new road. Dismissed. (Part of item on page 557)

Page 557- February 1877-
- Commonwealth VS Rufus Miller. Indictment for Larceny. A writ of capias ordered for the defendant who failed to appear in Court. Directed to the Sheriffs of Bland & Wythe Counties.
- John P. & Miller B. Allen agree to having the road properly repaired from the Brick Church to their property. Isaac S. Harman is appointed to make contract with said Allens. it must be stipulated that the coast to the county not exceed $75.00.
- (Part of item on page 558)
- Court adjourned until the first day of next term.

Page 559- Tuesday March 6, 1877- Geo. W. Easley, Judge.
- Following is a list of deeds presented and recorded in the Clerk's Office since last term of court-
- W.L. Yost, Commissioner, to Matilda Kitts, 24 acres. (No consideration or date given)
- P.R. Spracher, Commissioner, and John D. Perry & wife to James Honaker. Real Estate.
- Henry Felty & wife to Stephen S. Kitts, 37 acres+ for $300.00.
- Allen T. Suiter to Franklin I. Suiter, 300 acres for $5,000.00.
- Samuel W. Williams appointed Trustee in place of S.S. Dinwiddie who has relinquished said trust, from Geo. R.C. Floyd to secure W.P. Floyd and Cecil & Dinwiddie, bearing date of May 7, 1871 and recorded in Bland County July 11, 1871.
- On motion of Wm. P. Mustard- I.K. Price, John P. Roach and A.B. Pauley, are appointed

viewers to go on and report on the expediency of making changes in the road from J.M. Fanning's to the old house of Harvey Niswander's, and report the names of the land owners through whose lands the roas will pass.

- On motion of Henry Foglesong, Surveyor of Sharon Road Precinct, James A. Repass is appointed Special Commissioner to determine if the surveyor is able, with the means at hand and f it will require Connty funds. (Part of item on page 560)

Page 560- March 1877-
- Commonwealth VS Sarah Pauley. Indictment for fornication, # 1. Pauley did not appear. The jury, namely, J. W. Hicks, H.F. Bruce, R.B. Repass, Stephen Kimberling, Chas. B. Ramsey, Thompson Gregory, W.J. Bean, T.N. Finley, A.F. Miller, Elias Blankenship, I.S. Harman and Alex. Niswander, returned "guilty" Verdict and set her fine at $20.00 plus costs.
Commonwealth VS Sarah Pauley. Indictment for fornication # 2. Commonwealth's Attorney says he will not prosecute further. Pauley is acquitted and discharged.
Commonwealth VS George Hancock. Indictment for fornication, # 1. Hancock confesses a judgment for $20.00. He is fined $20.00 and costs.

Page 561- March 1877-
- Commonwealth VS George Hancock. Indictment for fornication, # 2. Commonwealth's Attorney refuses to prosecute further. Hancock is acquitted and discharged.
- Commonwealth VS Jack Carr. Indictment for Larceny. The jury found Carr "not guilty".
- Commonwealth VS George Wohlford. Indictment for Assault & Battery. Wohlford confesses guilt and is fined $5.00 and costs.
- Commonwealth VS James D. Honaker, for Assault & Battery.
- Commonwealth VS Giles Linkous, for Assault & Battery. (Commonwealth's Attorney says he will not prosecute further on these last two cases because of former trial and conviction.).

Page 562- March 1877-
- Commonwealth VS John Collins. Assault & Battery. Collins pleads "not guilty" and the case is continued.
- Commonwealth VS Andrew Dillman. Assault & Battery. Case dismissed.
- Commonwealth VS William Cubine. Indictment for Larceny. Case continued at next term of court. Alex. Niswander gives bond for $25.00, to assure the appearance of his sons, W.H. and James Niswander to witness for the Commonwealth in this case.
- Commonwealth VS Perry Day. Indictment for Larceny. Acquitted and discharged.

Page 563- March 1877-
- Harriet A. Weaver VS G.H. Morgan. Unlawful detainer. Case docketed and continued.
- Commonwealth VS Wesley Jones. Assault & Battery. Capias against Jones directed to the Pulaski and Bland Counties, returnable at next term of court. Case continued.
- Commonwealth VS William King. Assault & Battery. Capias against King directed to the Balnd County Sheriff, returnable at next term of Court. Case continued.
- Commonwealth VS Joseph Hearn. Indictment for Larceny. Capias against Hearn directed to the Bland County Sheriff, returnable at next term of Court. Case continued.
- On motion of S.C. Davis, J.H. Pegram, S.C. Davis & Moses Akers appointed Commissioners to

allot and work the hands in Mechanicsburg road precinct and report to the Court.

Page 564- March 1877-
- A report of settlement by Thos. O. Wilson, executor of James Wilson, deceased, with H.C. Groseclose, Commissioner, was this day presented and filed for exceptions.
- A report of settlement by Jas. H. Muncy, guardian for W.A. & L. Hearn, with J.H. Hoge, Commissioner of accounts, having been filed at a former term for exceptions, and none being taken is ordered to be recorded.
- A report of settlement by L.J. Miller, executor of Wm. Crawford, deceased, with J.H. Hoge, Assistant Commissioner of Accounts, presented and ordered filed for exceptions
- Ordered that Court stand adjourned until tomorrow at 9: O'Clock AM.

Wednesday morning March 7, 1877-
- Commonwealth VS Daniel Robinett. Violation of Revenue Laws. Capias awarded against Robinett and case docketed, returnable to next term of court.
- C.C. Banks for benefit of Jno. M. Hicks VS G.S. Ritter. On motion of Ritter, a rule is awarded against W.M. Adkins, for failure to appear as a witness for the defendant.

Page 565- March 1877-
- K.C. Thornton, Jailor, presents claim for $29.00 for keeping N.M. Havens, a lunatic, housed in the County Jail. Claim is allowed.
- On motion of Joseph Wohlford, ordered that John P. Roach, I.S. Harman and Jas. S. Robinett, be appointed Commissioners to allot the hands to work the road from the house of the late Henry Harman by way of Sally J. Crockett's residence to near Harvey Niswander's, & make report.
- Isaac S. Harman, appointed special commissioner to let contract for some person to work and keep in repair, the road from Widow Neel's to Buck Lick Branch. Cost of same not to exceed $45.00 that the commissioner said is essential for work to be done.
- Dr. A.J. Nye, makes claim for $2.50. Allowed.
- R.B. Repass, Surveyor of Sharon District, tendered his resignation which was accepted. John C. Stowers appointed to take his place.
- H.F. Bruce, Surveyor of the road leading from Rock Lick Turnpike to Felix Buck's potter shop, tendered his resignationwhich was accepted and Felix Buck appointed in his place.

Page 566- March 1877-
- M.L. Bumgardner, appointed Road Surveyor in Sharon District leading from Joseph Groseclose's to F.F. Repasses.
- N.B. Stimpson, Road Surveyor in Rocky Gap District, tendered his resignation, and E.A. Davis appointed in his place.
- Ordered that the following claims of Surveyors of the several Road Precincts for summoning hands to work on theirrespective roads be allowed, viz:
N.B. Stimpson, for 2 days summoning hands----------------------------------$2.00.
R.B. Repass,   "   "   "   "   "   ----------------------------------$2.00
H.F. Bruce,   " 1 day   "   "   ----------------------------------$1.00
Henry G. Hicks, " 2 days   "   "   ----------------------------------$2.00
I.G. Hudson,   " 2   "   "   "   ----------------------------------$2.00

John W. Harman,	for	2 days summoning hands	---------------------------------$2.00
D.G. Bird,	"	1 day " "	----------------------------$1.00
Jacob Kitts,	"	3 days " "	----------------------------$3.00
Newton Waddle,	"	1 day " "	----------------------------$1.00
O.C. Harman,	"	1 days " "	----------------------------$2.00
E.E. Epperson,	"	2 days " "	----------------------------$2.00
A.F. Harman,	"	3 days " "	----------------------------$3.00
J.M. Fanning,	"	3 days " "	----------------------------$3.00
Henry Foglesong,	"	3 days " "	----------------------------$3.00
W.T. McNutt,	"	2 days " "	----------------------------$2.00
S.C. Davis,	"	2 days " "	----------------------------$2.00
I.G. Coburn,	"	4 days " "	----------------------------$4.00.

The above amounts certified to the Board of Supervisors to be paid.

- Thomas H. Kinser, who was directed to go on the road of W.A. Linkious, Surveyor, and report whether or not it was necessary to appropriate County Funds to aid in putting the said road in good repair, having returned his report, the court directs Kinser to contract for four, four foot logs or bridges, not to exceed the cost of $20.00

Page 567- March 1877-

- Contract by Isaac S. Harman with John P. & Miller B. Allen in regard to the road near the Brick Church, ordered to be filed.
- Ordered that the Giles County Iron Company, through whose lands the road from the Brick Church to near John Compton's, be summoned to appear at next term and show cause if any why why said road should not be made.
- Commonwealth VS Charles Rider. Indictment on Felony. Case redocketed and continued.
- Commonwealth VS Rufus Miller. Indictment for Felony. Continued.
- Commonwealth VS Elisha Blankenship. Indictment for Felony. Continued.
- Commonwealth VS Millard King. Indictment for Felony. Continued.
- Commonwealth VS Jas. S. Wyrick. Indictment for Felony. Continued.
- Commonwealth VS Jas, M. Spencer. Indictment for misdemeanor. Continued.
- Commonwealth VS Almarine Woodyard. For Information.
- Commonwealth VS Samuel Collins. Indictment for misdemeanor.
- Guggenheim Cone & Co. VS Ida Neidermiah. Summons on suggestion. Continued.
- James B. Songer VS D.A. Miller. Summons on suggestion. Continued.
- The following Petir Jurors are allowed the sums opposite their names for theie services in trials of misdemeanors Viz: J.W. Hicks, $2.00; H.F. Bruce, $2.00; R.B. Repass, $2.00; Stephen Kimberling, $2.00; Charles B. Ramsey, $2.00; Thompson Gregory, $2.00; W.J. Blair, $2.00; T.N. Finley, $2.00; A.F. Miller, #1.00; Elias Blankenship, $2.00; I.S. Harman, $2.00; Alex. Niswander, $2.00 and J.C. Painter, $2.00. Certified to the Auditor for payment.

Page 568- March 1877-

- Harriet H. Weaver, wife of Z.T. Weaver, who sues by Z.T. Weaver, her next friend, against G.H. Morgan. Unlawful detainer. Ordered that the plaintiffs recover form Morgan, the possession of a tract of land with it's appurtenances in the writ of summons. A writ to the sheriff directing them to receive their said property, is granted.

Commonwealth VS Rufus Miller. Indictment for Larceny. Case continued until next term and Miller is remanded to jail.
- Ordered that J. Henderson Bruce & Jas. A. Repass be appointed Commissioners to examine the bridge on the W.& H. Turnpike on the east side of Seddon, and report if county funds will be needed to repair or build the bridge.
- Court adjourned until first day of next term. G.W. Easley, Judge.

Page 569- Tuesday April 3, 1877- Hon. Geo. W. Easley, Judge.
- Following is a list of deeds presented and recorded in the Clerk's Office since last term of court-
- Ro. Wylie, Commissioner, to C.C. Tilson, 55 acres of land.
- Ro. Wylie, Commissioner, to L.A. Tilson, 71 acres of land.
- Ro. Wylie, Commissioner, to Geo. F. Tilson. 56 acres of land.
- Ro. Wylie, Commissioner, to J.P. Tilson, 50 acres of land.
- Ro. Wylie, Commissioner, to R.E. Tilson, 135 acres of land.
- Ro. Wylie, Commissioner to W.H. Tilson, 72 acres of land.
- Ro. Wylie, Commissioner, to E.V. Tilson, 76 acres of land.
- Ro. Wylie, Commissioner, to R.G. Tilson, 100 acres of land.
- Ro. Wylie, Commissioner, to ? ?   Tilson, 77 acres of land.
- Ro. Wylie, Commissioner, to M.V. Gollehon, 93 acres of land.
- Thos. A. Snider & wife to W.V. B. Tilson, 61 acres of land for $305.00.
- Joseph Brown & wife to G.W. Groseclose, 56 acres, for $800.00. (Part of item on page 570)

Page 570- April 1877-
- James M. Stafford & wife; Robt. Woolridge & wife and Orrel Dunnagun & wife to S.A. Melvin, conveying their interest in 271 acres of land for $350.00.
- R.B. Wyrick to Asa Wyrick, conveying Real Estate for 200.00.
- Sallie Jones to Geo. W. Fanning, conveying sixty ?? acres for $700.00.
- Mark R. Bogle to School Trustees of Rocky Gap Township, conveying Real Estate for $10.00.
- On motion of Robt. C. Green, one of the creditors of the estate of Allen Fizer, deceased, Wm. Dillow is appointed as administrator of said Fizer's estate. Dillow, with A.J. Grayson, his security, posted bond for $200.00. Wm. Kitts, A.J. Grayson and C.M. Rudder were appointed to appraise the personal estate of Allen Fizer and make report as the law requires.
- John S. Wilson, James E. Wilson and Joel H. Spangler presents claim for $2.00 each. Allowed.
- Commonwealth VS James M. Spencer. Indictment for disturbing religious worship. Spencer did not appear and a second warrant was issued directed to the Seageant of the City of Richmond.

Page 571- April 1877-
- Commonwealth VS William Cubine. Indictment for Petit Larceny. Continued until next term and the defendant posts bond for $50.00, to assure his appearance in Court, and not to leave the county without permission of the Court.
- Alex. Niswander posted bond for his two minor sons, James & Harrison for $50.00, to assure their appearance as witnessses in behalf of the Commonwealth VS. William Cubine.
- John M. Cassell VS C.A. Seagle. Unlawful detainer. Continued at cost of the defendant.
- James A. Repass presented a claim for $14.00 which was allowed.
- B.H. Penley, Surveyor of roads in Seddon District, presents claim for $2.00. Allowed.

- Page 572- April 1877-
- K.C. Thornton, Jailor, makes claim for $27.00, for caring for N.M. Havens, a lunatic, confined in the County Jail.
- K.C. Thornton, makes claim for $12.25. Examined and allowed.
- On motion of J.M. Pruett, it is ordered that B.F. Petrie, I.K. Price & Wm. P. Mustard, be appointed viewers of changes to be made in the road leading from near Rail Hollow on Wm. N. Harman's land via the Hector road to the division line between Muirheads and E. Blankenship's.
- I.S. Harman who was appointed a Commissioner to go on the public road leading from Widow Neel's to Buck Lick Branch and determine how much county funds will be needed. He returned his report from which it appears that $40.00 will be needed and that he has contracted with A.W. Miller to do the work. Ordered that Harman's report be confirmed.
- Commonwealth VS John Collins. Assault & Battery. Jury could not agree on a verdict, and case is continued until tomorrow. (Part of item on page 573)

Page 573- April 1877-
- On motion of Wm. Helvey, ordered that Jno. Shrader, P.W. Rice and Wm. Helvey, be appointed Commissioners to allot the hands to open and keep in repair, the road on the Wolf Creek - Clear Fork Turnpike near the ford known as Brown's Ford through lands of Henry Pruett, John Shrader, Wm. Helvey to the house of Wm. Helvey.
- Commonwealth VS Rufus Miller. On Indictment for Larceny. Miller moved the court to discharge him because more than 3 terms have passed since he was brought to the bar to answer charges against him. Court overruled his motion. Case continued until next term and the prisoner was remanded to jail.
- Guggenheimer Cone & Co. VS Ida Neidermaier. On suggestion to James Kidd. It is agreed that the note of James M. Kidd of $60.00, except $20.00 on suggestion by Helvey, be paid to Plaintiffs. Otto Neidermaier appeared for the defendant.

Page 574- Ordered that Court adjourn until tomorrow at 9: O'clock AM.

Wednesday Morning April 4, 1877-
- William H. Hanshew presents claim for $43.00 for keeping Louisa Hanshew, an adjudged lunatic. Allowed.
- A report of settlement by T.G. Hudson, administrator of Wm. J. Crutchfield, deceased. Ordered to be filed for exceptions.
- A report of settlement by W.V.B. Tilson, administrator of H.H. Tilson, deceased. Ordered to be filed for exceptions.
- A report of settlement by A.J. Muncy, administrator of Wm. Hearn, deceased. Was filed at a former term of court and filed for exceptions and none being taken was ordered to be recorded.
- A report of settlement by Thos. O. Wilson, executor of James Wilson, deceased, filed at a former term of court and filed for exceptions and none being taken was ordered to be recorded.
- A report of settlement by L.J. Miller, administrator of Wm. Crawford, deceased, filed at a former term of court and filed for exceptions and none being taken was ordered to be recorded.
- A settlement by A.T. Suiter, Guardian for the infant heirs of James T. Gills, ordered filed for exceptions.

Page 575- April 1877-
- A settlement by Adam Waggoner, Guardian for Margaret & Foster Waggoner, which is ordered to be filed for exceptions.
- Saml. C. Davis, John H. Pegram & M. (Moses) Akers, appointed at a former term to reallot the hands in Road Precinct # 13, Mechanicsburg District, this day returned their report. It is ordered that another precinct be formed to embrace the following boundry. Viz: Beginning on the top of Walkers Little Mountain at the Cove Turnpike running west to the magisterial line thence north with the said line to the top of the big Mountain, thence east to the head of the long spur, thence with the top of the long spur to the west corner of S.C. Davis' land, thence south with Davis' land crossing the creek to the mouth of the hollow at the old Patterson path, thence with said hollow to the top of the mountain to the beginning. James W. Davis is appointed as surveyor of the new precinct and the following named hands are to work the road as required by law, Robt. King, Ephraim Wampler, James Collins, John Collins, Wm. L. Collins, Sam'l. Collins, Thos. J. Collins, Moses Akers, Wm. D. Akers, Isaac Lefler, Wm. T. King, Josephus King and James W. Davis.
- Commonwealth VS John Collins. Assault & Battery. Jury could not agree. New trial ordered.
- On motion of Jas. P. Tilson, ordered that I.M. Repass, Elias Repass and Eli F. Groseclose be appointed to report on the expediency of changing the location of the road from Jonas Groseclose's to F.F. Repass' Mill.

Page 576- April 1877-
- Superintendent of The Poor VS George W. Suiter & others. Suiter moved the court to quash, because he had not had ten days notice. It was sustained and Suiter to recover his costs.
- Jas. A. Repass & J. Henderson Bruce who were appointed at last term of court to examine and report on the bridge east of Seddon, returned their report. Said bridge ought to be rebuilt.
Ordered that W.L. Yost & J. Henderson Bruce advertise & receive bids for building said bridge.
- Ordered that James A. Repass, is hereby authorized to contract some person to work the road on which Henry Foglesong is surveyor. Costs not to exceed $50.00.
- C.C. Banks for benefit of John M. Hicks VS George S. Ritter. The plaintiff to take nothing and the defendant to recover form Banks, his costs expended.

Page 577- April 1877-
- The following persons, allowed $2.00 for their service as jurors in the trials for misdemeanors-
James H. Bruce, James C. Painter, Paul James, Jacob S. Pauley, Wm. H. Hoge, A.G. Thompson, Jno. H. Bird, Wm. H. Hawkins, E.G. Thompson, James Tolbert, Newton Waddle & N. B. Stimpson.
- Ordered that causes not otherwise disposed of be continued until the next regular term.

- Tuesday May 8, 1877- George W. Easley, Judge.
- Following is a list of deeds presented and recorded in the Clerk's Office since last term of court-
- A Power of Attorney from John W. Franklin, James N. Taylor & Esther A. Taylor to James Franklin.
- A Power of Attorney from W.A. Harman to James Franklin.
- A Power of Attorney from C.C. Duff & Sarah Duff to James Franklin.
- E.A. Burgess and David Burgess to G.W. Lamb, 135 acres of land for $265.00.

- J.W. Bruce assigns one half of his interest in the estate of James P. Holms, deceased, to William Neel Harman, for (no consideration given).
- A deed of trust from Ann Wimmer to Sam'l. W. Williams, trustee, 60 acres of land to secure J.W. Brown for the sum of $60.00.

Page 578- May 1877-
- The following persons appointed as Judges of Election, in their respective precincts,-
Seddon Precinct- Henry Newberry, Issac Kegley and A.N. Thompson.
Sharon Precinct- W.T. McNutt, Elias Foglesong and A.W. Shewey.
Mechanicsburg Precinct- Robt. C. Green, Jas. T. Taylor and S.H. Bernard.
Cameron's Precinct- A.R. Bogle, Jno. A. Smith and F.C. Bogle.
Rocky Gap Precinct- W.W. Comptn, W.W. Ashworth and Wm. Lambert.
The following are designated as Commissioners, A.W. Shewey, Robt. C. Green, A.R. Bogle, W.W. Ashworth and Henry Newberry, to canvass the vote as required by law.
- J.N. Fannen is appointed as registrar in the Town of Seddon and J.M. Hamilton, R.L. Newberry and George Painter appointed Judges and also as Commissioners to count the votes.
- Hiram Rider appointed as Registrar for Mechanicsburg and James Sheppard, Allen Mustard and J.H. Hoilman, appointed as judges to act as Commissioners to count the votes.
- On motion of James H. Mustard, Jos. A. Fanning & Timothy Hamilton, it is ordered that Isaac S. Harman, John P. Roach and B.F. Petrie, be appointed as viewers to report on the expediency of changing the location of the road from Compton's Mill down Walkers Creek at points between the Mill and Ralph A. Stafford's house.

Page 579- May 1877-
- H.C. Fanning, Constable, presents clain for $3.40, which is allowed.
- K.C. Thornton, Jailor, presents claim for $14.25 which is allowed.
- E.H. Umbarger, Sheriff of Wythe County, presents claim for $8.40, which is allowed.
- K.C. Thornton, Jailor, presents claim for $35.00 for keeping N.M. Havens, a lunatic who is confined in the County jail.
- A sale bill of the personal estate of Rachel Harman, deceased, presented & ordered recorded.
- A report of settlement by F. I. Suiter, late Sheriff, and administrator of E.A. Sheppard, deceased, having been filed for exceptions and none being taken is ordered to be recorded.
- A report of settlement by A. T. Suiter, guardian for the heirs of James T. Gills, deceased, having been filed for exceptions and none being taken, is ordered to be recorded.
- A report of settlement by A.J. Muncy, administrator of Wm. Hearn, deceased, having been filed for exceptions and none being taken, is ordered to be recorded.
- A report of settlement by W.V. B. Tilson, administrator of H.H. Tilson, deceased, having been filed for exceptions and none being taken is ordered to be recorded.

Page 580- May 1877-
- A report of settlement by T.G. Hudson, administrator of W.J. Crutchfield, deceased, filed at a former term and filed for exceptions and none being taken, was ordered to be recorded.
- Wm. H. Hanshew presented a claim for $25.50 for keeping Louisa Hanshew, a lunatic. Application of said lunatic to the asylums, having been refused for lack of room. Claim Allowed.
- On the application of Joseph Wohlford, for allotment of hands on the road leading from the

Henry Harman homestead by way of Sallie J. Crockett's house to near Harvey Nicewander's. It is ordered that James M. Fanning and John P. Roach, overseers, work the said road with the hands belonging to each precinct.

- It is recommended that the road be changed from Jonas Groseclose's to F.F. Repasses Mill. Motion had been made by James P. Tilson at a former term and Elias Repass, I.M. Repass and Eli F. Groseclose viewed the road and made the report.

- On motion of Isaac Bland, ordered that James A. Repass, R.B. Repass and S.H. Newberry be appointed viewers to go on and report the expediency of establishing a new road from Daniel Perkey's by Isaac Bland's and back to the W & H. Turnpike near the barn of E.M. Scott. They, to report back to court any inconveniences which will result from said road establishment.

Page 581- May 1877-
- On motion of John L. Wilson, it is ordered that Joel H Spangler, H.C. Groseclose and Geo. W. Kinser be appointed as viewers to determine the expediency of establishing a new road from Joseph Groseclose's via John L. Wilson's across Brushy Mountain by Eiz. (Eliz) Deaver's and Henry Lambert's to the Poor Valley, and report back to the court.
- John M. Cassell VS C.A. Seagle. Unlawful detainer. Plaintiff to recover from defendant, the lands mentioned in the plaintiff's summons, plus costs. The defendant took exceptions to the ruling and tendered his bill of exceptions which was signed, sealed and made a part of the record.

Page 582- May 1877-
- Commonwealth VS Rufus Miller. On Indictment for Larceny. Miller moved the court to discharge him on the grounds that more than three terms of Court had passed since the indictment. The court sustained his motion and he was acqui tted and discharged.
- Evidence has been produced that Henry H. Foglesong is a citizen of this state and that he was wounded in the left hand in the military service during the late War. The nature of his wound is such that he is unable to preform manual labor and that he has never received anything from the State of Virginia, either an artificial limb or money in lieu thereof under the laws of the State of V VA
- The same as above for P.H.M. Bird, who was wounded in the right eye.
- On application E.D. Ludwig, one of the owners of the Kimberling Springs watering place, the court appoints him as Conservator of the Peace with jurisdiction over the grounds attached to said watering place, within the following bounds, Viz- with the space of one mile square immediately surrounding said spring with the power and authority as defined in Chapter 196 of the Code of 1873 and thereupon said Ludwig took the oath required by law.
- Ordered that W.L. Yost one of the Commissioners of this court take and settle the Fiduciary account of H.C. & J.A. Groseclose, executors of the estate of William Groseclose, deceased. (Part of item on page 583)

Page 583- May 1877-
- W.P. Hornbarger allowed the sum of $3.00 for summoning hands to work the road.
- Simms Stowers allowed the sum of &10.00 for summoning hands to work the road.
- W.L. Yost and J. Henderson Bruce, appointed Commissioners at last term of court, to get specifications and proposals for building a bridge on the W&H Turnpike on the ease side of the Town of Seddon. Their report stated the the lowest bid was for $293.00 which was accepted.

- Court adjourned until first day of next term.

Tuesday June 5, 1877- Geo. W. Easley, Judge.
- Following, is a list of deeds recorded in The Clerk's Office since last term of Court---
- Geo. W. Dillman & wife to Henry Newberry, conveying real estate, for $19.17.
- Eliz. Wilson to K.M. Wilson, conveying real & personal property for $1.00.

Page 584- June 1877-
- J.M. Starke & wife to Pendleton Burton, 100 acres of land for $500.00.
- Nancy Hounshell to Martin F. Hill, 100 acres of land for 300.00.
- J.H. Mustard to James S. Robinett, Trustee, a deed of trust conveying certain personal property, to secure Hiram Stinson & others.
- A Homestead Deed made by G.W. Hancock, May 15, 1877.
- Eliz, Deavor & others to Daniel Waddle, trustee, conveying 246 ½ acres of land and other property, in trust to secure W.T. Walker.
- Henry Lampert & wife and others to H. Newberry, conveying real estate for $217.35.
- Henry Lampert & wife and others to A.W. Shewey. Conveying 200 acres of land for $281.65.
- W.P. Cecil & wife to A.W. Shewey, 200 acres of land for 200.00.
- J.F. Furgusson & others to T.J.B. Spangler, real estate for $45.00.
- Wm. P. Bruce & wife to Henry Newberry 1 ½ acres of land for $18.00.
- S.H. Williams & wife to T.J.B. Spangler Spangler, real estate for $50.00.
- A report of settlement by F.I. Suiter, late sheriff, administrator of the estate of Stephen Gose, deceased, was presented and ordered filed for exceptions.
- A report of settlement by Thos. F. Walker, administrator for estate of John W. Hatch, deceased, presented and filed for exceptions.
- George W. Miller is appointed overseer of Road Precinct in Mechanicsburg in place of Wm. C. Williams, who has moved from the county.

Page 585- June 1877-
- There being satisfactory proof that Alexander F. Miller, was wounded in the left hip and leg in the late War, and that he is deprived of doing manual labor and that he has never received anything from the State of Virginia.
- Same as above for A.J. Songer who was wounded in the right arm.
- James D. Honaker, was elected Supervisor of Rocky Gap District. Wm. M. Bishop & John A. Davidson were his security for a bond of $1,000.00.
- James H. Muncy was elected Justice of the Peace for Mechanicsburg District.
- Isaac S. Harman was elected Supervisor for Mechanicsburg District. Gordon Wohlford, R.L. Newberry and J.G. Kegley were his security for a bond of $1,000.00.

Page 586- June 1877-
- Paul James was elected Justice of The Peace for Seddon District and took oath of office.
- Elias Blankenship was elected Justice of The Peace for Mechanicsburg District. Took the oath.
- P.W. Rice, was elected Justice of the Peace for Rocky Gap District. Took oath of office.
- E.A. Davis, elected Justice of The Peace for Rocky Gap District. Took oath of office.
- J.F. Locke, elected Justice of The Peace for Seddon District. Took oath of office.

- W.W. Ashworth, elected Justice of The Peace for Rocky Gap District. Took oath of office.

Page 587- June 1877-
- H.C. Fanning was elected Constable of Mechanicsburg District. J.M. Fanning & Jmaes M. Pruett were security for a bond of $2,000.00.
- Reece Crabtree was elected Constable of Sharon District. Stephen Lambert & Eli F. Groseclose were his security for a bond of $2,000.00
- Stephen Lampert was elected Justice of the Peace for Sharon District & took the oath of office.
- Jacob Waggoner was elected Justice of The Peace for Sharon Districe. Took oath of office.
- Elias Foglesong was elected Overseer of The Poor for Sharon District. He, with Reece Crabtree & W.L. Yost, his securities, posted bond for $500.00.

Page 588- Jine 1877-
- Colby Stowers was elected Overseer of The Poor for Rocky Gap District. Posted bond for &500.00 with Isaac Stowers, his security.
- J.H. Bruce was elected Supervisor of Seddon District. He posted bond for $1,000.00, with J.H. Hoge and Sam'l. H. Newberry, his securities.
- John A. Bennett was elected Overseer of The Poor for Seddon District. He posted bond for $500.00 with W.N. Mustard & J.G. Kegley, his securities.
- James A. Repass, elected Supervisor for Sharon District , posted bond for $1,000.00 with J.G. Kegley his security.
- A.L. Walker, elected Justice of The Peace for Seddon District, took the oath of office.

Page 589- June 1877-
- W.H. Hanshew makes claim for $21.00 for keeping Louisa Hanshew, a lunatic. Allowed.
- John Repass makes claim for $5.50 for services as a viewer of roads. Claim is allowed.
- Lydia Suiter, widow of Alexander Suiter, deceased, relinquishes her right to administer the estate of her deceased husband. On motion L.T. Stinson, one of the heirs, it is ordered that W.W. Ashworth administer the said estate with the will annexed. Ashworth posted a bond for $400.00, with A.A. Ashworth & Wm. M. Bird, his securities.
- George W. Robinett, one of the heirs of George Robinett, deceased is appointed administrator of the estate of the said George Robinett. He posted bond for $6,000.00 with A.J. Grayson and James M. Stowers, his securities and was granted the letters of administration.
- K.C. Thornton, jailor, makes claim for $28.00 for acring for N.M. Havens, a lunatic, confined in the County Jail. Claim is allowed.

Page 590- June 1877-
- S.C. Davis, Wm. T. King and Wm. E. Hoge, appointed viewers to determine the expediency of establishing a new road, four feet wide, from Walker's Little Creek across Walkers Big Mountain to intersect with some point on Walker's Creek Road. (On motion of H.H. Croy)
- On motion of W.W. Ashworth, administrator of Alex. T. Suiter, deceased, E.A. Davis, Robt. W.Harman & Jno. H. Bird are appointed to appraise the personal estate of Alex. Suiter, deceased.
- On motion of George W. Robinett, administrator of George Robinett, deceased, Charles S. Grayson, R.K. Kelley & James M. Stowers & John F. Locke, are appointed to appraise the personal estate of George Robinett, deceased.

- James M. Fanning, Road Overseer for Mechanicsburg District, tenders his resignation which is accepted and A.G. Updike is appointed to replace him and keep the road in good repair.
- On motion of W.A. Linkious, Road Overseer in Rocky Gap District, ordered that James D. Honaker be directed to purchase one "crow-bar", one stone hammer, two dirt shovels and one road pick to assist him in his work.
- Samuel W. Williams VS Austin French. On Judgment Appeal. Case is docketed and continued.

Page 591- June 1877-
- On the matter of the application of J.H. Mustard, Timothy Hamilton & Jos. A. Fanning for changing the road leading down Walker's Creek. The viewers appointed at last term of court, report that the changes are necessary. Ordered that A.G. Updike, John J. Mustard, Samuel P. Mustard, Harvey R. Mustard, Wm. S. Mustard, the heirs of Wm. Crawford, deceased, John F. Fletcher, M.A. Fletcher, Wm. G. Stafford and James M. Stafford, through whose lands the road will pass, be summoned to appear in court and show cause why the road should not be changed.
- G.C. Bailey, J.W. Compton and R.W. Harman are appointed viewers to report the expediency of of changing the road near the house of Sam'l. L. Gibson and report other pertinent facts.
- H.C. Groseclose, elected Justice of The Peace for Sharon District, took the oath of office.
- Samuel W. Williams presented a claim for $10.00 which was allowed.
- Wm. T. Hamilton presented a claim for $2.50 which was allowed.
- G.J. Holbrook an attorney is allowed the sum of $10.00 for defending Rufus Miller.

Page 592- June 1877-
- John W. Harman, surveyor of Road Precinct #12 in Mechanicsburg Precinct, tenders his resignation which the court accepts and W.R. Kitts is appointed in his place.
- T.E. Mitchell VS C.B. Price. Unlawful Detainer. Plaintiff to recover from the defendant the lands described in his summons. Plaintiff asks for a writ to the sheriff to cause him to have his land back. Writ was ordered.
- A report of settlement by H.C. & J.A.T. Groseclose, executors of William Groseclose, deceased, was presented and ordered filed for exceptions.
- The heirs of Peter H. Dills say that James D. Honaker, assessor for Rocky Gap, has charged them with taxes which are excessive. { There are 2 whole pages of the description of these lands and the amounts charged for taxes. Page 593 is completely filled with the charges.}

Page 594- June 1877-
- T.E. Mitchell VS C.B. Price. Unlawful Detainer. Price makes motion that he be granted 30 days suspension of the judgment against him upon condition that he make bond with good security for $100.00. Price, with B.D. Graves and J.H. Thompson, his securities, posts said bond. On motion of Mitchell, leave is granted him to withdraw the title bond executed by C.B, and Sarah Price.
- The heirs of Peter Dills on their charges of excessive taxes. The court deceded that the charges were in error and that they be exonerated from such charges. The heirs and their land laid off to them were, Viz- John H. Bird & wife, 242 acres; E.A. Davis & wife, 242 acres; E.W. Davis & wife, 308 acres; M.C Dills, 348 acres; to the widow of Peter H. Dills, 240 acres. 200 acres having been sold to the County for the County Poor Farm not liable for taxation. { Half of page 595 contains details of Peter Dills' land holdings.}(Court is adjourned until next term)

Page 595- County Court in Vacation at Mechanicsburg, June 7, 1877-
- Isaac J. Davis, elected Justice of The Peace in Mechanivsburg District, appeared and took oath.
Witnessed by Wm. T. Hamilton and signed by Judge G.W. Easley

Page 596- Tuesday July 3, 1877- Hon. Geo. W. Easley, Judge.
- Following is a list of deeds recorded in the Clerk's Office since last term of Court-
-F. Grayson to R.K. Kelley & wife. A title Bond dated 5-28-1877.
- Samuel W. Williams, Special Commissioner, to David G. Hamblin, conveying a portion of the
lands of A. Bralley, deceased, lying on Walkers Little Creek. Dated 6-4-1876.
- Wm. Umbarger & wife to S.W. Williams, a tract of land on Brushy Mountain. Dated 6-6-1877.
- Jacob Groseclose & wife to Henry Groseclose, conveying their right, interest and title in the
lands of Jacob Groseclose, deceased, for &200.00. Dated 5-3-1877.
- Eli F. Groseclose & wife to James P. Heneger, a tract of land on the Holston, for $980.00.
Dated 5-23-1877.
- Wm. M. Stafford to Hugh P. Johnston, conveying his right & title to the lands granted to Joseph
Stafford, deceased. Dated 6-15-1877.
- A Deed of Trust from Thomas J. Munsey to Samuel Bernard, Trustee, conveying the lands of
Hiram Munsey died seized & possessed, to secure Timothy Mitchell the sum of $200.00. Dated
6-9-1877.
- Leonora Robinett to Henry Groseclose, Trustee, for benefit of Daniel Waddle & wife,
conveying all her lands in Bland County, for the Waddles to care for her during her natural life.
Dated 6-20-1877.
- A Special Grand Jury of Inquest composed of, John H. Hoge, foremen; Jno. Repass; Paul James;
J.W. Compton and Newton Shufflebarger,   returned the following indictments- Commonwealth
VS Russell Carter, for Felony, a true Bill. (Part of item on page 597)

Page 597- July 1877-
- Ordered that the members of the Grand Jury be awarded the sum of &1.00 each.
- Several persons who were elected to various Municipal offices in Seddon have failed to qualify
as such in the time allotted them. Ordered that W.L. Yost, A.N. Thompson, John M. Hicks,
W.C.Hatcher, B. Dodd, W.T. Hamilton and J.M. Hamilton be appointed Trustees and Joseph
Thomas, Seargent and Acles Fannon as Overseer of The Roads in Seddon District. They will
serve until the next general election.
- John P. Roach makes claim for $4.00 as viewer of roads. Allowed.
- On motionof Ephraim Wampler, it appears that he is physically unable to work on the public
roads. Ordered that he be exempt from such labor.
- Commonwealth VS Wm. Cubine. Petit Larceny. Continued until term of court designated for
misdemeanors.
- Thomas F. Walker, appointed and commissioned a Notary Public for the County of Bland,
appeared and with James M. Stowers, his security posted bond for $500.00 and took oaths of
office as required by law. (Part of item on page 598)

Page 598- July 1877-
- F.G. Helvey appointed Overseer of The Poor, in Mechanicsburg District, with A.G. Thompson
his security posted bond for 500.00 and took oaths prescribed by law.

- W.H. Hanshew, presents claim for $22.00 for caring for Louisa Hanshew, a lunatic. Allowed.
- K.C. Thornton, Jailor, makes claim for $2.00 which was allowed.
- A report of settlement by the executors of the estate of Wm. Groseclose, deceased, having been filed for exceptions and none being taken, is ordered to be recorded.
- A report of settlement by Adam Waggoner, guardian of Margaret and Foster Wagner, having been filed for exceptions and none being taken is ordered to be recorded.
- A report of settlement by F.I. Suiter, late sheriff and administrator of the estate of E.A. Sheppard, deceased, having been filed for exceptions and none being taken, is confirmed and ordered to be recorded. (Partof item on page 599)

Page 599- July 1877-
- An application by various citizens of Seddon asking for the appointment of a Special Police for Seddon District. The following men were appointed as such, A.L. Walker, as Captain; B.H. Penley; A.N. Thompson; Joseph French and Dunn B. Newberry.
- Evidence produced which showed that Officers of this county do not have copies of The Code of Virginia, 1873, to which they are entitled. Ordered that copies be sent to them.
- Commonwealth VS John Collins. Assault & Battery. The jury consisting of W.P. Hornbarger, James Kidd, Simms Stowers, F.G. Helvey, J. Havens, Isaac Kegley, Jno. W. Havens, John C. Stowers, Wm. Kitts, John R. Bird, E.S. Kidd and H.G. Hicks, returned a guilty verdict whereupon the defendant moved the court to grant him a new trial, to which the court took time to consider.
- Court adjourned until tomorrwo morning at 9: O'Clock AM.

Page 600- Wednesday Morning July 4, 1877-
- For satisfactory reasons, the appointment of A.G. Uodike as Overseer of Roads in Mechanicsburg District, is hereby set aside and Isaac P. Lambert is hereby appointed to same.
- In the matter of the application of Jas. H. Mustard, Timothy Hamilton and Jos. A. Fanning, to change the road from Compton's Mill down Walkers Creek, all the owners of said land appeared and accepted the said changes except A.G. Updike. Ordered that the necessary cahnges be made but with leave for A.G. Updike to come to court and have the same set aside as far as his interest is effected.
- A list of Jurors who are each awarded the sum of $2.00 for their services in trials for misdemeanors - W.P. Hornbarger, James Kidd, Sims Stowers, F.G. Helvey, J. Havens, Isaac Kegley, Jno. W. Havens, John C. Stowers, Wm. Kitts, John R. Bird, E.S. Kidd and H.G. Hicks.
- In the matter of the application of J.M. Pruett for changes in the location of the Tazewell Road- J.W. Finley, the only land owner on whose land the changes are proposed, has consented in writing. (Slaty Bank is mentioned) Ordered that changes be made as set forth in said report. (Part of item on page 601)

- K.C. Thornton, Jailor, makes claim for $29.00 for taking care of N.M. Havens, a lunatic, confined in the County Jail.
- Commonwealth VS Wm. N. Harman and Orlenia Farmer. For lewd and lascivious cohabitation. Came the attorneys for both defendant and the Commonwealth. Defendants tendered several pleas in writing to which the Commonwealth objected, which objection the court took time to consider.
- John Havens, father of Newton M. Havens, a lunatic, now confined to jail, made application to

the court for permission to take said lunatic to his home and care for him. The court decedes that said lunatic will receive better care in his father's home. John Havens agrees to keep said lunatic for $.75 cents a day and posts bond for $500.00 with D.W. Dunn, J.M. Lovell, Wm. Hederick and J.M. French, his securities. Newton M. Havens to be delivered to his father in custody of the sheriff, and restrained.

Page 602- July 1877-
- The court being informed that Newton M. Havens owns or has an interest in some real estate in Mercer County, WVA, the value not known, The Commonwealth's Attorney for Bland County is instructed to ascertain the value of said property and take action to subject same to the payment of charges in keeping and providing for the said Newton Havens.
- D.W. Dunn, County Treasurer, presents a list of delinquent real estate taxes.
- D.W. Dunn, Treasurer, presents list of delinquent Capitation & Personal Property Taxes.
- Commonwealth VS John Collins. Assault & Battery. Collins is fined $1.00 to which he objected. He filed a bill of exceptions which were signed, sealed and made a part of the record.

Page 603- July 1877-
- Samuel W. Williams presents claim for $5.00, for prosecuting John Collins, charged for misdemeanor. Allowed.
- Samuel W. Williams VS Austin French, J.E. French & Jacob J. Hager. On an appeal from a judgmebt by a Justice of the Peace. Case was dismissed on March 24, 1877 in favor of the defendant. ($3.90 amount of bond). This day came Williams, it appearing that said judgment was in error and is reversed. Williams to recover from defendants the sum of &25.00, the amount of the debt in the warrant plus interest and costs.
- Commonwealth VS Russell Carter. Indictment fro Felony. Carter pled "not guilty" and moved the court to continue his trial until next term. Carter did not post bail and was remanded to jail.
- Margaret E. Patterson, W.A. Burnett, Jessie Robinson and Margaret Robinson, post bond for $50.00 each to assure their presence in court at the next term to witness for the Commonwealth against Russell Carter. (Part of item on page 604)

Page 604- July 1877-
- K.C. Thornton, Jailor, makes claim for $5.85 which was allowed.
- Ordered that all cases on the docket not otherwise disposed of be continued.
- Court adjourned until first day of next term. Signed by Judge G.W. Easley.

Page 605- Tuesday August 7, 1877-
- Following is a list of deeds recorded in the Clerk's Office since last term of Court-
- A deed of trust from Russell Carter, Alfred Carter and Richard Shields to J.M. Hamilton, trustee, both real & personal property to secure James M. French and Thomas J. Munsey. Dated 7-4-1877.
- P.H. Roar (Rorrer?) & wife to A.T. Newberry, 227 acres on Walkers creek, for $5,500.00. Dated 4-6-1877.
- James Hoge to Martha L. Miller, 300 acres on Kimberling Creek for $300.00. Dated 10-2-1870.
- Joseph Waddle & wife to Adeline Waddle, their interest in a tract of land on Laurel Fork Creek. Dated 4-14-1877.

- Jonas Umbarger & Wife to David Umbarger 30 acres in Rich Valley. Dated 5-9-1877.
- M.F. Hill to Luemma Fortner, 2 acres on Walker's Little Creek for $7.50. Dated 3-12-1877.
- A report os settlement by F.I. Suiter, administrator Stephen Gose, deceased, having been filed for exceptions and none being taken, is ordered to be recorded.
- A report of settlement by Thos. F. Walker, administrator of John W. Hatch, deceased, having been filed for exceptions and none being taken was ordered to be recorded.
- A report of settlement by G.W. Robinett, administrator of Hiram Robinett, deceased, presented and filed for exceptions.

Page 606- August 1877-
- A report of settlement by Richard Moore, surviving administrator of S.P. McGuire, deceased, was presented and ordered filed for exceptions.
- Commonwealth VS Russell Carter. Felony. Attorney for the Commonwealth says he will not prosecute further and the defendant id acquitted and discharged.
- Hawkins & Wohlford VS W.N. Martin. Case docketed and continued.
- It appearing that James A. Cameron, Esther Cameron and Gordon Cameron havebeen dead for more than three months and no person has applied for letters of administration. On motion of Joseph Meek, one of the creditors of the Camerons, it is ordered that the Sheriff take the estate of the said Camerons and administer it according to law.
- An order to obtain copies of the Code of Virginis to be furnished to officers of the Town of Seddon. W.D. Yost was mayor of said town of Seddon.
- K.C. Thornton, Jailor, makes claim for $16.80, which was allowed.
- I.P. Lambert tendered his resignation as Overseer of the Roads in Mechanicsburg District, which was accepted and Wm. P. Mustard took his place. (Part of item on page 607)

- Page 607- August 1877-
- D.W. Dunn, Treasurer, presented a list of property on the Commissioners Land Book, improperly placed there for the year of 1876 in the district of L.J. Miller, Commissioner of Revenue. The list when corrected was ordered to be certified to the Auditor of Public Accounts.
- William Dillow, this day appointed Constable in Seddon District. He posted bond for $2,000.00 with S.H. Newberry and T.N. Finley his securities and took the oath of office.
- George W. Kinzer presented a claim for &3.50 for services as surveyor of roads. Allowed.
- The appraisement and sale bill for the estate of Geo. Robinett, deceased, was presented and ordered to be recorded.
- The appraisement and sale bill for the estate of A.T. Suiter, deceased, ordered to be recorded.
- Court adjourned until first day of next term. Signed by Judge Geo. W. Easley.

Page 608- Monday September 4, 1877-
- Following is a list of deeds recorded in the Clark's Office since last term of Court-
- A Deed of Trust from Wilkerson to S.W. Williams, Trustee, conveying Real Estate, to secure D.W. Dunn and Harman Newberry. Dated July 21, 1876.
- J.L. Wilson & wife to Wm. Umbarger, 100 acres for $500.00. Dated (No date given)
- A Deed of Trust from W.H. Hawkins to Ro. (Robert) Wylie, Trustee, Real Estate and Personal Property to secure various creditors. Dated 8-2-1877.
- A Deed of Trust from W.H. Hawkins & wife to Ro. Wylie, Trustee, Real Estate to secure

Elizabeth M. Hawkins. Dated 8-2-1877.

- A Deed of Homestead made by James S. Wyrick, dated 8-2-1877.
- A.F. Harman, Overseer of Roads in Mechanicsburg District, tendered his resignation which was accepted. Obediah Smith appointed in his place.
- Samuel W. Williams presents claim for $10.00 which was allowed.
- Wm. T. Hamilton, Clerk, presented claim for $2.50 which was allowed.
- I.S. Harman presented a claim for $6.00 which was allowed.

Page 609- September 1877-
- On motion of Jacob E. Miller and Pendleton Burton, B.F. Petrie, J.M. Fanning and J.W. Finley are appointed viewers to report on the expediency of establishing a new road from the house of Jacob Miller to the Kimberling Road near Salem Church through the lands of Miller, Burton & Helvey and report to the court.
- On motion of A.B. Waggoner,- Jno. Shrader, Dr. J.W. Brown and J.G. French appointed to report on the expediency of establishing a new road to intersect with the new road established near the house of Henry M. Pruett and make report at next term.
- Wm. H. Hanshew presented a claim for $47.25, for caring for Louisa Hanshew a lunatic. Allowed.
- It appearing that there are no objections to the new road being established leading from the house of Joseph Groseclose via John L. Wilsons, across Brushy Mountain by Eliz. Devors & Henry Lamberts to the Poor Valley. John L. Wilson is appointed surveyor of said road and with the following hands to work it, Viz:- Thomas O. Wilson, Henry L. Lambert, James E. Wilson, John S. Wilson, James Spangler and Matthew Kitts. (Part of item on page 610)

Page 610- September 1877-
- Joseph Thomas presents claim for .75 cents, which is allowed.
- A Grand Jury of Inquest was sworn consisting of the following persons, Viz:- L.D. Bogle, foreman; Paul James, Jacob Muncy, Mitchell Kegley, F.P. Crigger, A.G. Thompson, H.C. Newberry, S.P. Mustard, Allen Mustard, B.F. Petrie, S.H. Bernard, J.M. Stafford, Wm. Stowers, C.J. Hudson, J.H. Lindamood, J.H. Crabtree, W.W. Ashworth and Newton Shufflebarger. They received their charge and returned the following indictment-
- Commonwealth VS John W. McGinnis. Indictment for Felony, a true Bill.
- John T. Cooley VS Jacob Waggoner. Warrant for debt. Plaintiff to recover form the defendant, the sum of $20.00 with interest and costs.
- Eli F. Groseclose VS James Cox. Unlawful Detainer. The plaintiff to recover from the defendant the Mill Property land as described in the summons, plus costs.

Page 611- September 1877-
- John H. Lindamood, appointed registrar for Sharon Precinct in place of John Deavor who has moved from said district. He took the prescribed oaths.
- Commonwealth VS Wm. N. Harmen. On indictment. Continued.
- Court adjourned until tomorrow morning at 9: O'Clock AM.

Wednesday Morning September 5, 1877-
- Hawkins & Wohlford VS W.H. Martin. On suggestion to John S. Crump. John S. Crump says

he is indebted to Martin in a sum sufficient to satisfy plaintiffs demand. Ordered that plaintiffs recover form John S. Crump, garnishee, the sum of $17.30 with interset and costs.

Page 612- September 1877-
- Armstead Cloud (colored) exempt from working on the public road because he is unable.
- Members of the Grand Jury are allowed the sum of $2.00 for their services..
- K.C. Thornton is allowed the sum of $1.00 for cutting the weeds on the public square.
- The grand jury returned the following indictments-
- Commonwealth VS John Waddle, for misdemeanor, a true Bill.
- Commonwealth VS Lewis Hobbs. For Felony, a true Bill.
- Having nothing further before them the jury was discharged.
Commonwealth VS John W. McGinnis. Indictment for Felony. McGinnis pled "not guilty". Trial is continued until next term. McGinnis with Dr. J.M. Lovell. his security posted bond for $50.00 each to assure hi appearance in court.

Page 613- September 1877-
- A report of settlement by Richard Moore, surviving administrator of himself and Elias Harman, deceased, administrators of Samuel P. McGuire, deceased, having been filed for exceptions and none being taken, is ordered to be recorded.
- A report of settlement by George W. Robinett, administrator of Hiram Robinett, deceased, having been filed for exceptions and none being taken was ordered to be recorded.
- A report os settlement by L.J. Miller, administrator of Wm. Crawford, deceased, was ordered filed for exceptions.
- Appraisment & sale bill of personla property of H.H. Tilson, deceased. Ordered recorded.
- Appraisement & sale bill of personal property of Allen Fizer, deceased, ordered recorded.
- Isaac G. Pauley appointed Surveyor of the road in Sharon District in place of John DeDeavor, who has moved from the district.
- Court adjourned until the first day of next term. Signed by Judge G.W. Easley.

INDEX

ADKINS, Cloyd- 108-118-125-158-159-170-176-186-203-204-208-218-265-511-520-541-
AKERS (ACERS), Moses- 111-371-401- ALLEN, Madison- 88- ASHWORTH, A.A.- 293- W.W.- 305-
385-391-586-589-

BAILEY, R.P & Co.- 134- BAILS- William R. (Wm. R.)- 79- BANE (Bean)- Uriah- 70-182-292- BANKS, C.C.- 444-
-452-576- BARCROFT & CO.- 43- BARNETT, Archibald- 556- BAUGH, David M.- 339- BENNETT, John A.- 15-145-
172-455-588- BENNETT, William A.- 28-33-40-41- BIRD, John R.- 15-111-148-150- BIRD, P.H.M.- 60-582-
BIRD,William M.- 133-136-139- BISHOP, William (Wm.)- 16-28-33-41-133-136-139-141-170- BLAIR, F. S.- 214-
-285- BLANKENSHIP, Berry- 115- BLANKENSHIP, Elias- 115-151-176-204-215-229-586- BLANKENSHIP, Elisha-
531-567- BLANKENSHIP, W.W.- 431- BOGLE, A.R. (Absolum Ray)- 60- BOGLE, James- 100-111-
BOGLE, F.C.(Freeling Clay)- 386- BOGLE, George- 292- BOGLE, John- 64-264-508-531- BOGLE, Julia A.S.- 491-
BOGLE, L.D.(Lorenza Dow)- 54-214-236-279-299-311-
BOGLE, Nye- 204-214-216-285- BOGLE, Ralph- 511- BOGLE, W.P.(William Paris)-16-17-28-47-72-136-141-
149-158-176-186-204-208-246-538- BOOTH- E.G.- (Edwin G.)- 20-79-89-110-131-167-211- BOTTOMLY,
James P.- 373-419- BRADHAM- A.H.- 31- BRADHAM, D. J.- 31- BRALLEY, A. (Anslem)- 99-107- BRANDEN, f.m.-
174-177-178-226-229-280-303-313-321-477- BRIDGES, John H.- 383- BRIDGES, S.A.- 326- BRIDGES, William
L.- 286-300- BRITTON, Rufus- 76-91-93-100-107-117-134- BROOKS, William B.- 85-152-170-225- BROWER,
J.M. & Bro.- 231- BROWN, A. B.- 36-139-172-218- BROWN, Charles- 287- BROWN, G. W.- 53-90-112-139-
172-215 -218-241-246- BROWN, J. M.- 342- BROWN, H.P. & Co.- 119- BRUCE, J. H. (J.Henderson) - 72-248-
270-443-588- BRUCE, Joshua- 99-106- BRUCE, Josiah- 528- BUCK, Felix- 65-70-316- BURGESS, Josephine-
-393- BURTON, Henry- 79-130-171- BURTON, J.T.- 280-289- BURTON, Pendleton- 609-

CALDWELL, Andrew- 76- CALDWELL, Lendo- 44-122- CAMERON, J. A. E.- 606- CAMERON, Joseph- 271- CARR,
Jack- 535-554-561- CARROL, ADAMS & NEER- 84-140- CARTER, Russell- 603-606- CASSELL, John M.- 182-576
-581- CECIL, William P.- 19-132- CHANDLER, Ellen- 309-352-362- CHANDLER, George W.- 540- CHANDLER, H.
A.- 60-122-164-214-252-256-268-285-315-331-352- CHANDLER, Hannah- 306-352-362-405-424-445-446-
469-498-511- CHANDLER, Henry- 540- CHAPMAN, A. A. - 18-126- CHAPMAN, E.I.V.- 404-231- CLARK, James-
147-172-178- CLARK, Jacob- 118-125- CLOUD, Armstead- 228-230- COLE, William & Co.- 134- COLLINS,
John- 512-532-562-572-575-599-602-603- COLLINS, Samuel- 567- COLLINS, Thomas- 473- COMPTON, John
R.- 17-18-46-91-92-133-146-150-156-172-203-225-231- COMPTON, J. W.- 64-194-296-224-287-299-
COMPTON-MCGINNIS & CO.- 16-17-22-26-37-43-45-65-66-76-85-92-138-143-146-152-166-170-218-225-
COMPTON, Newton- 35- COMPTON, William E.- 307-316-322-329-335- COOK, Thomas- 154-161- COOK,
Zachariah- 212-283- COOLEY, Joseph T. -130-131-172-211- COOPER, Mary- 172-212- CORDER, Julia A.- 435-
466- CORONER'S JURY- 239- COURT NOTES- 82-239-464-555-448- CRABTREE, John- 161-431- CRABTREE,
Reese- 62-194-207-297-393-444-491-587- CRAWFORD'S ESTATE- 392- CRAWFORD, William- 36-45-54-68-
115-392-399-435-564-574- CRESS, Aron & Son- 52-129-208-237-247- CROCKETT & BLAIR- 67-83-134-153-
321-232- CROCKETT, Calvin G. (C.G.)- 330-339-341-396-435-466-469- CROCKETT, Catherine C.- 339-
CROCKETT, John C.- 15-76-126-148-172-219-243-303-313-315-330-373-381- CROCKETT, John G.- 214-285-
449- CROCKETT, John S.- 292- CROCKETT, Joseph- 184-188-204-208-280-287- CROCKETT, Kate C.- 449-
-471- CROCKETT, Robert- 119-173-212-267- CROCKETT, S. R.- 214-285- CRUMP, S. J.- 20-83- CRUTCHFIELD,
William J.- 457-471-574- CUBINE, Melvina- 174-177-178-226-229-280-303-313-321-477- CUBINE, William-
542-544-546-562-571-597- CUNDIFF, Mary V.- 276-

DAVIDSON, Henry- 18-139- DAVIDSON, Hugh- 42- DAVIDSON, J. C.- 37- DAVIDSON, John A.- 266- DAVIS, Addison- 215- DAVIS, Dow- 382-414-419- DAVIS, E. A.- 586-592-594- DAVIS, H.G.L.- 67- DAVIS, Isaac J.- 204-303-397-595- DAVIS, James W.- 575- DAVIS, J.M.- 155- DAVIS, J. Mosby- 146-172-177-225- DAVIS, John C.- 19- DAVIS, Samuel C.- 155- DAVIS, William P.- 224- DAY, Perry- 490-529-535-562- DEAVER (DEVOR), George W.- 2- DEAVER (DEVOR), John- 44-76-271- DEAVER (DEVOR), James- 78- DEAVER (DEVOR), - William- 141-158-176-186-204-208-246-538- DELINQUENTS, (Taxes)- 300-602- DENNIS, H. G. - 435-436-518- DILLMAN, Andrew- 562- DILLMAN, George- 111- DILLOW, J. A. - 429- DILLOW, Sophia- 211- DILLOW, William - 261-265-293-294-394-405-443-518-607-570- DILLS, P. H.- 109- DILMAN, John D.- 367-602- DODD, B.- 94-102-114-127-128-188-192-198-214-215-234-280-285-289-348-349-360- DODSON (DOTSON), N. B.-22- -132-155-209-210- DOUGHTY, J. H.- 157- DOWLING, Henry- 214-285-288- DOYLE, T. J.- 376- DOYLE, Thomas- 150- DUNN, D. W.- 99-105-106-151-158-176-186-203-204-207-248-268-387-214-285-377- 399- 400-433- EAKIN, William P.- 243- EASLEY, George W.- 303-344-345- ELECTION OF JUDGES- 495-578- ELLIS, Henry- 155- ESTIL, H. B.- 214-285- EWALD, J. & Bro.- 95- EWALD, Joseph- 72-95-

FANNEN, A.- 208-339-477-484- FANNON, Acles- 26-66-178-199- FANNING, George W.- 71-200- FANNING, Hugh C.- 16-37-46-63-136-149-194-297-391-587-579- FANNING, J.M. (James M.)- 114-208-237-247- FANNON, Jasper N.- 374- FANNING, John- 107-361-373-374-381-384-386- FANNON, J. N.- 95-272-294-299- 309-312-315-331-352-374- FANNING, Joseph- 25-33-38-99-107-114-279-287-299- FARMER, Orlenia- 601- FINLEY, J.W. (Jackson Weaver),- 27-36-79-119-151- FINLEY, T. N.- 36-68-114-129-311- FIZER, Allen- 570- FLETCHER, R.   (Rowland)- 128- FOGLESONG, Elias- 64-305-587- FOGLESONG, Henry H.- 582- FOGLESONG, Simon- 418-427- FOSTER, William B.- 176-204-208-243- FOX, Mathias- 67- FRANKLIN, John- 416- FRANKLIN, Thomas- 216-256- FRENCH, Albert- 28-43-120- FRENCH, Austin- 18-94-351-358-590-598- FRENCH, Fulton- 44-124-164-258- FRENCH, G. D.- 87-102- FRENCH, J. H.- 175- FRENCH, Jas. M.- 155-156- 174-180-182-200-209-210- FRENCH, John W.- 123- FRENCH, Rufus- 28-35-39- FRENCH, St. Clair- 18-133- FRENCH, William P.- 30-

GIBBONY, Elizabeth G.- 176-177- GIBBONY- Robert- 177- GIBSON, S. T.- 85-149-171- GILES COUNTY IRON WORKS- 334- GOLLEHORN, I. T.- 432- GOSE, George- 92- GOSE, Stephen- 321-342-435-465-584- GREEN, G. W. K.- 325-333- GREEN, Robert C.- 20-44-85-138-172-211- GRAYSON, A. J.- 79-89-256-381-419-440-523- 538-550- GRAYSON, Cynthia- 17-46- GRAYSON, Franklin- 208-239-234- GRAYSON, James W.- 352-359- GRAYSON, John- 276- GRAYSON, Randolph (R)- 17-46-311-316- GRAYSON, W. W. - 390-452- GREEN, R. E.- 269-271- GREEVER, David B.- 391- GREGORY, Thompson E.- 63-193- GROSECLOSE, Eli F.- 27-51-86-116- 140-141-143-144-145-150-168-176-177-210-220-221-264-266- 294-317-318-321-332-369-400- GROSECLOSE, George W.- 79- GROSECLOSE & HANSHEW- 171- GROSECLOSE, H. C.- 50-51-80-81-96-101-141 147-149-150-163-169-177-179-186-215-217-220-324-591- GROSECLOSE, J. A. L.- 452- GROSECLOSE, Sarah- 491-512-526- GROSECLOSE, William- 86-126-142-171-264-266-278-281-338-414-422-436-522-593- 598- GUGGENHEIMER, CONE & CO.- 144-494-520-553-567-573- GULLIAN, Susan- 439- GUYNN-OGLESBY & CO.- 184-

HAGER, E. R. J.- 30- HAGER, Jacob J.- 96- HALE, William H.- 36- HALLER, William P.- 20-133- HAMILTON, J.M. (James Marion)- 368-384-389-394-444-511- HAMILTON, William T.- 117-181-342-387-498-546-591- HANCOCK, George- 532-560- HANCOCK, James A.- 457- HANSHEW, Andrew- 490-491-504-513- HANSHEW, Samuel - 492-491- HANSHEW, & WILLIAMS- 373-419- HANSHEW, William H.- 556-574-579-587-598- HARMAN, Elias- 20-23-36-49-66-78-88-91-105-115-119-127-151-158-175-176-185-186-204-207-225- HARMAN, F. M.- 225-227-553- HARMAN, Grimes- 28-40- HARMAN, Hezekiah- 54- HARMAN, I. S.- 321-343-472

-484-457-555-585- HARMAN, James H.- 157- HARMAN, J. N.- 95- HARMAN, John W.- 15-348-386- HARMAN, O. C.- 504- HARMAN, Rachel- 528-579- HARMAN, Robert W.- 128- HARMAN, Victoria- 540- HARMAN, Wilburn- 89-268-278- HARMAN, William N.-15-21-33-36-37-38-46-50-68-84-88-89-107-114-115-134-144-145-153- 169-183-207- 208-210-225-237-247-285-289-316-320-323-324-325-329-230-340-382-432-436-453-473- -491-507-511-524 -539-545-554-601- HARNER, J. J. - 145-172- HATCH, John W.- 368-399-531-540-583 -605- HAVENS, John W.- 22-132- HAVENS, N. M.- 505-512-514-515-601- HAWKINS, W. H. - 401- HAWKINS & WOHLFORD- 606- HAYES, P. P. - 452- HEARN, Ella- 113- HEARN, Joseph- 113-532-535-563- HEARN, William- 99-106-370-375-473-491-507-511-524-554- HEDERICK, William- 130-136-176- HELVEY, Baltzar- 101- HELVEY, F. G.- 77-194-298-359-368-390-432- HELVEY, J. B.- 483- HELVEY, John K.- 65- HELVEY, William- 573- HENDERSON, Elizabeth- 432-436-519-533- HENEGER, Thomas- 91- HENSHEW, T. G.- 544- HICKS, John M.- 467- HICKS, J. M. - 68-286-318-331-414-422-436- HICKS, J. M. & CO.- 375 HICKS, Joseph T.- 513-523- HICKS & NEWBERRY- 253-268- HICKS, W. W.- 104- HIGGINBOTHAM, T. J.- 374-443-479-507-522- HOBACK, John S.- 554- HOGE & EWALD- 50-145- HOGE, James H.- 221- HOGE, J. Meek- 59-273- HOGE, John H.- 18- 49- 127-277-508- HOGE, Robt. S.- 18-214-285- HOGE, William E.- 59-75-146- HOLBROOK, G. J. - 591- HOLBROOK & SPENCE - 157- HOLMES, James P.- 20- HONAKER, A. B.- 374- HONAKER, A. J. - 139-177-248- HONAKER, James D. (J.D.)- 196-304-315-532-561-585- HONAKER, P. C.- 22-139-172-197-218-254-349-350- 376-524- HOPKINS, HARDIN & KEMPER - 21- HORNBARGER, W. P. - 583- HOUNSHELL, Henry- 430-470- HOWARD, Thomas S. - 376- HOWE, William H.- 19-79-83-132-232- HUDSON, E. S.- 269- HUDSON, M. J.- 101-241-246- HUDSON, T. G. - 195-295-506-522-529-544-555-556- HUGHES, Reuben- 115-208-237-247- HUTSEL (HUTZELL), R. A.- 113-

JACKSON, Winton- 214-258-272-325-333- JAIL INSPECTORS- 497- JAMES, Paul- 197-386-586- JAMES, R. C. - -36-37-79-91-93-94-96- JAMES, Sarah- 73- JOHNSTON, Catherine- 266- JOHNSTON, Jas. D. - 183- JOHNSTON, John- 166- JOHNSTON, J. Newton- 490- JOHNSTON, John R.- 60-94-96-243- JOHNSTON, John W.- 23-139-177-248- JONES, Ellen- 114-124-165-211-213-229-271-310- JONES, Frances- 284- JONES, James- 355-570- JONES, Sally- 201-114-124-165-211-213-229-271-310- JONES, Wesley- 563-

KEELING, A. J.- 254- KEGLEY, J. G. (James Gordon)- 318-389-462-463-471-476-500-507-513-546- KEGLEY, Isaac- 24-173-174-212-225- KELLEY, R. K.- 96- KIDD, E. S.- 322-343- KIMBERLING, Joseph- 465-484- KIMBERLY & MOREHEAD- 146-170- KINDER, Peter- 131-167-211- KINDRICK, Joseph- 279- KING, David- 130- 166- KING, Millard- 532-563-567- KINSEL- John- 531- KINSER, George W.- 79-198-249-394-520-607- KINSER, Thomas H.- 62-195-295-388-394- KITTS, Ganam- 388- KITTS, H. J.- 209-215-315- KITTS, Harvey- 112- KITTS, Henry- 283- KITTS, H. M.- 455- KITTS, J. W.- 15- KITTS, Jacob- 77- KITTS, Lee A.- 33-156-552- KITTS, Nancy- 464- KITTS, Peter- 37-45-66-77- KITTS, Ray- 22-23- KITTS & STOWERS- 369- KITTS, William- 185- KITTS, W. R. - 592- KYLE, Rebecca- 351-

LAMB, Louisa- 179-230-238- LAMBERT, A. D.- 441-511-520-541-547- LAMBERT, Adam- 439-452-473-492- 496-499-507- LAMBERT, Henry- 28-40- LAMBERT, Isaac P.- 172-212-600- LAMBERT, James- 376- LAMBERT, Polly- 315- LAMBERT, Stephen- 182-587- LAMBERT- Victoria- 129- LEVEL, J. M.- 525-534- LINDAMOOD, George- 24-28- LINDAMOOD, John- 28- LINDAMOOD, John H.- 386- LINDAMOOD, Wilkinson- 43- LINKIOUS, Albert- 418- LINKIOUS, Giles- 532-561- LINKIOUS, W. A. - 550- LITZ, Peter- 76- LOCKE, John F.- -138-149-172-205-221-272-318-386-586- LOVEL, William- 28-46-121- LUDWIG, E. A. - 582-

MARCUS, John- 42-122- MARTIN, Richard- 39- MCCALL- J. M.- 37- MCCORMICK, C. H.- 183- MCCOY HEIRS- 245- MCCULLEY, James- 116-126-176-187- MCDONALD, J. E.- 69-82-143- MCDONALD, Isaac- 143- MCGINNIS, J. W.- 37-45-66-77-305- MCGUIRE, S. P. (Samuel)- 163-606-613- MCHAFFEY, 123- MCNEIL, D. O.- 102-109-118- 158-176-186-203-208-265-539- MCNUTT, John S.- 324-343- MCPHERSON, H. S.- 178- MELVIN, George- 242-246- MILLER, A. F.- 44-302-585- MILLER, A. W. (Abraham Woodson) - 382- MILLER, Charles- 513-524-

MILLER, D. A. (Daniel A.) - 159-525-535-547-551-554-567- MILLER, George W.- 584- MILLER, Jacob- 609-
MILLER, J. B.-21- MILLER, L. J.- 78-388-392-525-535-551- MILLER, Rufus- 451-459-453-462-463-557-567
-568-573-582- MINNIX, George- 473-481-493-497-500- MITCHELL, T. E.- 130-168-592-594- MOORE,
Richard- 613- MORGAN, G. H.- 79-132-134-140-154-224- MORGAN & WRIGHT- 119-140- MOSS, Joseph-
346-359- MUIRHEAD, A. A.- 22- MUIRHEAD, D. F.- 65-374- MUNCY, James H.-59-75-277-305-341-386-564-
-585- MUNCY, Tunis- 477-484- MUNSEY, Hiram- 89-127-149-172-221- MUNSEY, Jacob- 150- MUNSEY,
Samuel- 73-321-342- MUNSEY, T. J.- 187-202-284-434- MUSTARD, Allen- 84-144-169-207-197-290-
MUSTARD, H. R. 15- MUSTARD, James H.(Harvey)- 232- MUSTARD, John- 20-25-372-416-421-513- MUSTARD,
John J.(Jasper)- 374- MUSTARD, W. G. (William Gratton)- 130-168- MUSTARD, William P.- 25-157- MUSTARD,
William S. (Samuel)- 519- MUSTARD, S. P. (Samuel Patterson)- 610- MYERS, James M.C.- 157- MYERS, John-
175-225-.

NEEL, D. M.- 108-118-158- NEEL, John R.- 199- NEEL, Nancy- 352-355-374-413-431- NEIDERMAIER, Ida- 79
-81-83-101-132-144-217-483-494-520-553-567-573- NEWBERRY, H.- 62- NEWBERRY, Harman- 186-210-
238-247-249-257-322-340-348- NEWBERRY, H. C.- 71-108-219-266-298-522- NEWBERRY, Henry- 20-25-
255-311-316- NEWBERRY, R. L. (Robert Lemuel)- 15-89- NEWBERRY, Samuel H.- 20-59-75-131-167-211-
264-286- NEWBERRY, W. C. (Wythe C.)- 383-385- NISWANDER, A.- 388- NISWANDER, Alex.- 387- NISWANDER,
Nancy- 338-380-402-435- NISWANDER, William H. H.- 184- NYE, A. J. - 504-565-

OPENCHAINE(OBENCHAIN)- J. J. - 285- ORY, Stephen- 123- OVERSEERS OF THE POOR- 15-37-72-150-159
-209-215-255-266-280-284-293-307-315-

PAINTER, George- 41- PAINTER, J. C.- 266-455- PAINTER, W. G.- 446- PATTERSON, S. I.(Samuel)- 100-130-
PAULEY, Bower- 255- PAULEY, H.- 457- PAULEY, H. A.- 153-457-553- PAULEY, Paris- 92-122- PAULEY,
Sarah- 532-560- PAULEY, Sebastion- 92-122-173- PEERY, Hiram- 203- PENLEY, B. H.(Braxton H.)- 77-571-
PETRIE, B. F.- 65-69-70- PERRY, Martin L.- 556- POOL, M. S.- 348-358-372-379-391-401-418-429-444-
447-448- POOR HOUSE- 375- PRESTON, James- 16- PRICE, C. B.- 383-385-421-592-594- PRICE, I. K.- 62-
174-180-317-555- PRUETT, Henry M.- 306-340- PRUETT, J. M.- 551- PUBLIC PRIVY- 436- PUBLIC ROADS-
2-8-11-12-384-396-406-413-433-441-477-483-484-505-521-528-559-565-566-571-575- PUBLIC SQUARE-
334-

REEDER, S. S.- 298-394- REGISTRARS- 480- REPASS, Eli- 164-340- REPASS, Elias- 137- REPASS, Emeline-
114-124-125-165-207- REPASS, James A.- 60-67-193-340-389-571-588- REPASS, J. Wharton- 401-405-422-
REPASS, John- 589- REPASS, P. G.- 130-136-176- REPASS, W. S.- 318-325- RICE, P. W.- 586- RICHARDSON,
William J.- 27-140-168-220- RIDER, Charles- 567- RIDER, Fulton- 363-377-380-401-420-422-423-424-
RIDER, G. F.- 430-447-467- RIDER, Hiram- 67-292- RITTER, George S.- 564-576- ROACH- J. P.- 597-
ROBINETT, A. J.- 334- ROBINETT, Daniel- 351-361-437-564- ROBINETT, Elizabeth- 338- ROBINETT, George W.-
392-435-440-523-553-589-605-609- ROBINETT, Hiram- 392-393-472- ROBINETT, James- 20-49-66-89-553-
ROBINETT, James S.- 294- ROBINETT, Jezreal- 264- ROBINETT, M. A.- 382- ROBINETT, Marion- 173-212-
ROBINETT, M. D.- 122-165-270-283-329-330-338- ROBINETT, Prudence- 265- ROBINETT, Robert- 40-
ROBINETT, Sophronia- 503- ROBINETT, Stephen- 527- ROBINETT, Rufus- 348-358-379-437-514- ROLAND,
Miles- 125-159-.

SANDERS, Gordon- 302- SANDERS, Micajah- 36- SEDDON CORP.- 187-515- SCHOOL DISTRICT- 265-521-
SCHARITZ, George B.- 383- SHANNON, Thomas- 172-182- SHEPPARD, E. A.- 263-277-278-281-299-311-
312-322-382-531-539-579-598-605- SHEPPARD HEIRS- 382- SHEPPARD, James- 60-65- SHEWEY, A. W.- 248
-280-283- SHRADER, Isaac N.- 129- SHUMATE, Anderson- 154- SHUFFLEBARGER, W. J.- 147-172-178-
SIMMERMAN & CO.- 100-101- SLADE, William P.- 141-170- SMITH & HARVEY- 145-171- SNAVELY, P. G.- 491-

512-526- SNOW, D. A.- 20-83- SONGER, A. J.- 585- SONGER, James B.- 554-567- SPANGLER, Andrew- 135- SPANGLER, Elizabeth S.- 349-371- SPANGLER, Joel- 101-241-246-399-570- SPENCER, James M.- 532-567- 570- STAFFORD, B. P.- 101-175-432-436- STAFFORD, Catherine- 371- STAPLES & CALDWELL- 130-166- STAPLES, W. R.- 91- ST. CLAIR, James W.-305- STEEL, Eli- 369- STEEL, Samuel- 375- STIMPSON, N. B.- 154- STIMPSON, S. E.- 94- STOCKDALE-SMITH & CO.- 119- STOWERS, Colby- 37-91-97-193-293-306-390-588- STOWERS, George W.- 308-312-320-390-453-576- STOWERS, I. F.- 347-357-358- STOWERS, James M. - 62-197 -295- STOWERS, John C.- 28-48-49-60-299- STOWERS, Rufus- 85- STOWERS, Warden- 79-130-171- STOWERS, William- 37-79-85-91-93-94-149-171- STRAS, James- 87- STRAS, Joseph- 214-285- STUART, Jas. W.- 153- STUART, Sam- 269- STUART, William- 20-44-138-172-211- SUBLETT, 285- SUITER, Alex.- 440- SUITER, A. T.- 19-30-59-75-185-206-287-299-399-574-579-590-607- SUITER, Ellen J.- 156-183- SUITER, F. I. (Franklin Ingram)- 65-187-220-248-288-322-525-534-605- SUITER, G. W. (George W.)- 16-37-133-136-139 -308-312-320- 576- SUITER, John W.- 109-155- SUITER, William- 277- SWINDLE, Isaac- 15-

TAYLOR, James T.- 292- TAX DELINQUENTS - 516-517-518- THOMAS, Giles- 28-43-121- THOMAS, Joseph- 28- 43-121- THOMPSON, A. G.- 372- THOMPSON, Amos- 284-342- THOMPSON, Andrew- 128- THOMPSON, Catherine Y.- 91-93- THOMPSON, C. J.- 67-76-91- THOMPSON, D. F.- (David Fleming)- 263-278-372-375-383- 492-503- THOMPSON, Henry- 24- THOMPSON, H. G.- 116-124-126-142-157-263-264-265-268-278-286- 300-308-313-318-319-320-321-443-479-507-514-522- THOMPSON, J. B.- 245- THOMPSON, J. H.- 196-296 -496- THOMPSON, Josiah- 292- THOMPSON, Marietta E. (Waggoner)- 263-278-375-492-503- THORN, G. C.- 79-132- THORN. Gordon C.- 19-30- THORN, J. D.-284- THORNTON, K. C.- 42-64-217-225-258-284-367- 368-417-446-462-476-497-505-506-513-525-530-535-539-545-552-553-565-572-589-598-601-604-607- THURSTON, Phineas- 104- TIBBS, G. M.- 59-195-296- TICKLE, D. L.- 22- TICKLE, H. C.- 186-210-247- TILSON, Harman- 265-308-313-320- TILSON, H. H.- 469-473-494-574-579- TILSON INFANTS, - 482- TILSON, Widow- 494- TILSON, W. R.- 96-107- TILSON, Mary J.- 482- TOLBERT, James- 124-128-129-164-238-248-269-279 -339-357-368-374-379-393-405-421-431-446- TOLBERT, Julia A.- 430-447-467- TOLBERT, William T.- 209- 210-243-432-482- TOWNSHIP BOARDS- 311-316-

UMBARGER, Alex.- 200- UMBARGER, E. H.- 579- UMBARGER, John F.- 22-270-309-318-325- UMBARGER, Jonas- 605- UMBARGER, Joseph- 319- UMBARGER, Thomas P.- 77- UPDIKE, A. G.- (Albert Gallatin) 116-126-

VEST, Fleming- 334- VEST, William I.- 334-

WADDLE, Charles- 442-448-458-459-460-461- WADDLE, Daniel- 544- WADDLE, gRANVILLE- 22- WAGGONER, A. (Adam)- 58-59-67-75-76 -91-93- WAGGONER, A. C. (Adam Clark)- 18-51-59-75-76-93-100-107-117-134-143- 150-221- WAGGONER, Jacob- 135-141-153-154-266-375- WAGGONER, Marietta E.- 94-99-106-206-278-287 -299-370-375-484-503- WALKER, A. L.- 588- WALKER, John R.- 307-311-338-347-355-356-361- WAMPLER, Ephraim- 597- WEAVER, Z. T.- 143-214-285- WESENDONCK'S ADMR.-145-171- WHEELER, H. P.- 115-176-204 -215-229- WILKINSON, John- 176-204-208-243- WILKINSON, Thomas- 131- WILKINSON, William- 315- WILLIAMS, Rufus M. - 51-147 -150- WILLIAMS, S. W.- 214-283- WILLIAMS, William C.- 119-210-289-316-473 -491 -507-511-524-554- WILSON, Ballard P.- 179-230-238- WILSON, James M. C.- 154- WOHLFORD, Elizabeth- 20-133- WOHLFORD, George- 374-532-561. WOHLFORD, Joseph- 328-329-340. WOHLFORD, Samuel- 153- WOODYARD, Almarine- 532-567- WOODS, Thomas- 114-125-166- WYRICK, J. S. (James)- 347-403-413-415-422- 423-425-428-438-466-468-469 -567.

YOST, Peery- 404- YOST, William L.- 51-63-275-324-328-341-464- YOUNG & HIGGINBOTHAM- 443-479-507 -514- YOUNG, S. W.- 443-479-507-514-

www.ingramcontent.com/pod-product-compliance
Lightning Source LLC
Chambersburg PA
CBHW080614270326
41928CB00016B/3054